THE
MODERN RENAISSANCE
IN AMERICAN ART

BY THE SAME AUTHOR

FIFTY PRINTS OF THE YEAR. *John Day Co., N. Y. 1925.*

HOW TO SEE MODERN PICTURES. *Dial Press, N. Y. 1925.*

EXPERIENCING PICTURES. *Harcourt Brace & Co., N. Y., 1932.*

CRITICAL APPRECIATION COURSE I. *Design Workshop, Nyack, N. Y., 1940.*

THE NEW ART EDUCATION. *Harper & Bros., N. Y., 1941. Revised edition, 1952.*

EXPERIENCING AMERICAN PICTURES. *Harper & Bros., N. Y., 1943.*

CRITICAL APPRECIATION COURSE II.[1] *Design Workshop, Nyack, N. Y., 1951.*

ARTICLES

A MODERN VIEW. *A column running in Art Digest from January, 1945 to August, 1953.*

[1] This Course was the forerunner of the present volume.

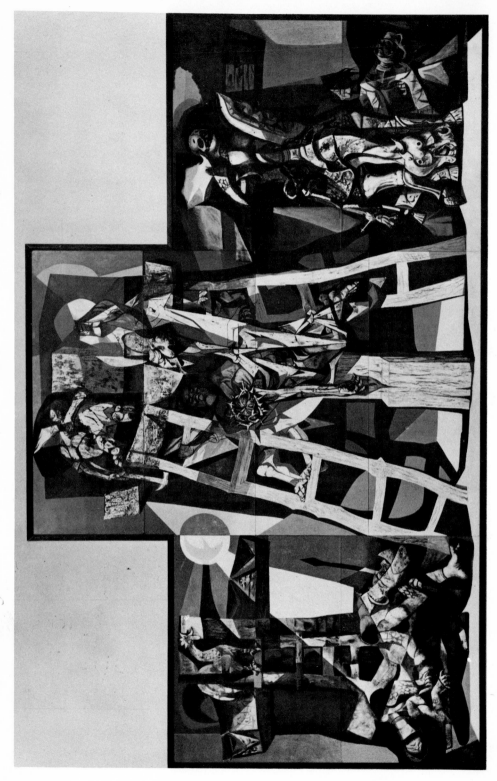

The Crucifixion, by RICO LEBRUN. (Independently produced.) Jaques Seligmann Galleries, N. Y.

THE
MODERN RENAISSANCE
IN AMERICAN ART

Presenting the Work and Philosophy

of 54 Distinguished Artists

RALPH M. PEARSON

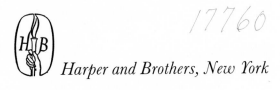

Harper and Brothers, New York

THE MODERN RENAISSANCE IN AMERICAN ART

Library of Congress catalog card number: 53–11856

To all artists who today are carrying on

the Grand Tradition of Creative Art

CONTENTS

PART III - ABSTRACTION   NON-OBJECTIVE

LIST OF ILLUSTRATIONS

xviii   LIST OF ILLUSTRATIONS

PREFACE

This book had to be written.

It had to be written because, in this strange art world of ours, when it comes to appraising or explaining values in contemporary or historical pictures and sculptures, everyone gets a hearing, it seems, except the one central authority whose knowledge is based on experience—the artist who produces the art. For some twenty-five years I have been trying, in what I believe to be the public interest, to help in the important task of correcting this miscarriage of logic in public relations.

Two questions—who is Pearson and why should anyone listen to him? —are pertinent and can be answered briefly. Pearson, an artist academically mistrained, was reorientated by modern philosophy and practice; his present knowledge, therefore, is based on experience. A few high spots in the story are:

An academic training at the Chicago Art Institute; many years as a successful etcher with ample publicity and sales; a shocking out of complacency by the Armory Show of 1913; a migration to New York the following year to find out what "this crazy modern art" was all about; the discovery of a school which was undoubtedly the first in this country to initiate its students into the modern principles—taught by Hugo

Robus in his Washington Square studio; intensive study with Robus that winter to learn form as form and form design for the first time in student and professional life. There followed an amplifying of that knowledge by study of the French moderns, the Aztecs and Mayans, the Mexicans, American Indians, the Primitives of many times and places and the classic arts of history, including the European Renaissance. After some ten years of slow and painful reorientation, came application of the findings to etchings (the first such in this country, I claim), then the old, familiar story—of public misunderstanding, loss of former support and a living wage, the turn to education, triggered by economic necessity but supported by the feeling that it was part of the artist's responsibility to pass on to others his hard-won knowledge.

The educational program has been continuous and fairly heavy and has included:

Inauguration of the art courses in theory and practice at the New School for Social Research in New York (about 1928); lecturing and teaching there for the next ten years; founding of the Design Workshop, an independent school, with summer and winter classes in Painting, Modeling, Drawing, and Critical Appreciation. These classes, planned as condensed courses, gradually evolved into teaching by mail in the same subjects, which has continued to date. There were special outside engagements, including two summer sessions at the Utah State Agricultural College (1940-41), a year as Guest Professor of Art Education at the University of Texas (1948-49), and many lecture trips covering nearly the entire country. There was the writing of six published books and some two hundred and fifty magazine articles. This is the story. And this is the seventh book.

Much of the material here presented in revised and amplified form was first privately printed by the Design Workshop as *Critical Appreciation Course II,* a part of the school's educational program.

I would like to pay tribute to a book published in 1928 that probably did more than any other to focus and clarify the issues posed by modern art in this country following the initial impact of the Armory Show. After a quarter of a century I have again read this book. It's theme can be inadequately condensed to a single sentence: *"The idea of art on which the Modern Movement is based is the idea that the typical function of the architect as artist is the typical function of the sculptor and painter as well."* This theme and its amplification have been proved authentic through the intervening years and are validated by many quotations from artists in these pages. The book is *The Modern Movement in Art* by R. H. Wilenski (New York, Frederick A. Stokes Company).

One other point deserves mention. I have known and shared experiences and discussion with a large number of artists working in this country during the past four decades. I have watched the development of their work and kept records both of it and of the philosophy and goals expressed by them through these years. During the life of The American Artists Congress (1936–40), as a member of the Executive Board (and Chairman of the 1937 National Convention), my association with these artists was especially close and active. Because of this long association, the critical appraisals in these pages have the validity of firsthand knowledge and present a considerable amount of source material which should be of value in arriving at an historical perspective. It is my hope that they will so serve.

RALPH M. PEARSON

Design Workshop,
Nyack, N. Y.

INTRODUCTION
WHAT KIND OF ART CRITICISM AND BY WHOM?

There are several kinds of art criticism. One is all sweetness and light; it finds something good in all works and proceeds to praise in a spirit of good will and generosity. It scatters sunshine wherever it goes, forgetting that too much sunshine over too long a time causes drought —in nature and in matters of the spirit. It is optimistic criticism.

Another kind is more harsh in its approach. It assumes that nature, art, and life are composed of positives and negatives in conflict with each other, that sunshine is normally balanced by storm, that praise will be actually sweeter when fortified by the jagged flashes of adverse comment and the thunderous roll of critical warnings. This kind is not pessimistic, except in so far as it realizes that no man can attain perfection in art or life; it attempts rather to be judicious in its awarding of praise and blame. To be judicious it must have standards and apply them with all possible fairness, but ruthlessly once a decision becomes clear.

Thus and thus only can criticism become a constructive force rather than a palliative. The test of its constructiveness will depend on the validity of the critic's standards; these are what the reader of any criticism must examine carefully. Critics are human and subject to all the usual failings, including temperamental bias, superficial and inadequate knowledge. Standards also are an uncertain element in that they are anything but standardized and so vary endlessly; no one set can be proved adequate for the satisfaction of all observers. Criticism, therefore, becomes a many-sided testing process. It tests the work under consideration. It tests the critic. And it tests the person who reads or listens to the criticism. Such all-around testing is healthy; there is no need to be alarmed by its challenge. It is an awakening experience for all concerned—and life becomes more interesting when one is awake than when he is asleep.

Adequate, well-rounded criticism demands a dual response on the part of the critic: that of intellect and that of visual sensation or sensory awareness of quality. Of the two, the latter is undoubtedly the more important as a means to apprehending the artist's total message.

I respect scholars; in fact I often have tinges of jealousy at their superior erudition. But when scholarly intellect is unaware of the "form" wherein mainly lies the *art* in visual art, erudition alone cannot give a balanced judgment. There is logic in the old saying, "You can know all about art except the thing itself." And when such minds, often brilliant in their historical role, gravitate to positions of authority in the art world (as they increasingly tend to do), the results can be near-catastrophic to the cause of a distinguished living production and valid public understanding. This situation clinches my argument that every art-lover today must equip himself to make his own aesthetic decisions.

These criticisms will not attempt to scatter too much sunshine. Neither will they embrace pessimism. In fact, in the long view, they will be optimistic, for we have much to be proud of in our art of today. The evidence shows without any doubt that we are in a series of productive decades that will go down in history as a renaissance of the creative spirit in art and some other aspects of life, including, obviously, the scientific. But the optimism must be tempered by an awareness of the many negative influences at work on us and in us which cannot be white-washed or ignored. Our collective responsibility is to gather all the evidence, then see that our decisions are carefully weighed.

Artists are the source of contemporary culture in all fields where we make use of their professional equipment. Philosophers, scholars, and critics should, and frequently do, amplify the artist's contribution; but it is they, the artists, one should always remember, who are the source. For this reason, in the criticisms of individual artists herein, I have sought to quote the artist on the philosophy and purpose back of his work whenever possible, and then to bring to bear such opinions as result from my own experience. If one result of this study should be an increased respect for our living leader-artists and an increased use of their products, the task of the writing will have been well worth while.

It is characteristic of the present decade that we do not have several giants who are the Great Leaders making momentous contributions and reaping all the glory. Instead, we have a surprisingly large number of genuine and serious artists whose gifts to the national culture are valid and of great actual and potential usefulness. This tends to diffuse both the contributions and the honors—a fruitful condition. All parts of the country can thus share in the glory of regional achievement. Each can discover, reward, and use its own. Such a situation is far better than the hero-worship which exalts the few and inevitably tends to cause fame to take precedence over quality in the general public regard. If a few towering geniuses do ultimately emerge, nature will be but taking its inevitable course in human affairs, for we do like to worship heroes. But the wide cultural base is infinitely more solid.

There are at least two findings of such a study as this which have profound cultural implications. Many others emerge, of course, but two seem to take precedence. One is the problem faced by the mature creating artist of integrating his inheritance from the European Renaissance of the fourteenth to the sixteenth centuries, especially the masterly rendering of form and a mastery of functional design, with his recent inheritance from the Modern Movement. This is a heavy task for all artists and relatively few, even of our leading talents, have solved it satisfactorily. To examine various individual solutions is one of our critical goals.

The other finding is that a considerable number of our producing artists have become dim reflectors of some one phase of the modern revival, and have carried on year after year within the narrow confines of such partial understanding. They have not explored its full potentialities or even attempted so to do. Curiosity and a spirit of adventure have not prodded them. They have built a fence around one pasture and grazed contentedly therein. They have not learned from their fellow artists or from events transpiring around them. Pierre Bonnard of France, Oskar Kokoschka of Germany, and James Ensor of Belgium,[1] easily come to mind as examples of this self-imposed isolationism. But there are many others both abroad and here. If such cases were few and scattered, the reason could be quickly assigned to the limitations of personality. But when there are scores or even hundreds, as is true today, the problem becomes elusive and pressing. Something appears to be wrong with our cultural climate. What can the matter be?

Confusion rampant is the answer—a confusion that, in extreme cases, has reached the ultimate limit of outright chaos. To clarify this situation is one of the purposes of this book.

The power to experience the excitements of disciplined creation as an amateur or folk-artist, delving into the aesthetic mysteries for keen-edged pleasure, is the minimum requirement for the comprehension of significant art—and for intelligent criticism. This does not mean that every art lover and critic must be an artist. It means that rewards are increased by adequate preparation for these high offices. And, Heaven presumably knows, our entire art world needs the utmost development of its critical faculties to deal intelligently with the mass of confusions that besiege it from all sides. Our renaissance is based on and draws its vitality

---

[1] These three artists, who learned little or nothing from the Modern Movement (except, perhaps, a release of spirit in the cases of Kokoschka and Ensor), have each been featured with large solo exhibitions at the Museum of Modern Art in New York City.

from the Modern Movement. But there is bad modern art in voluminous supply. There are fakes, imitations, blunderings, and stereotypes that are just as academic, just as much within a set pattern, just as external in motivation, as academic naturalism. These works do not enrich history. They clutter it. They confuse issues and befuddle students. They also, unfortunately, befuddle some professional artists and museum directors who serve on juries—as has been shockingly proved during recent years when some of the country's highest awards for contemporary painting and sculpture have gone to various products of the school of confusion and undisciplined emotion.

This situation presents our art world with a dilemma. We have contradictions. We honor irreconcilable opposites. Our art community's left hand, apparently, does not know what its right is doing. We need help to pull ourselves out of a morass of bewilderment. What help can be more effective than *informed* criticism?

EUROPEAN ARTISTS IN AMERICA

In these appraisals we shall deal with the modern renaissance as it has become manifest, mainly during the past decade, in the United States rather than on the international stage. Such segregation is difficult because this movement is truly international in scope with its continuing interpenetration between countries and continents. Since limits are necessary, however, a segment of an international scene can be considered separately. The aim then should be to observe how the universal theme reveals itself in the particular setting.

What happens to the Paris-born revival when it is diffused throughout the U.S.A.? What do American artists contribute to it? What happens when distinguished and famous European artists move their bags, brushes, easels, and paintings to New York, Arizona, or Hollywood? Do established habits maintain their control? Or does our atmosphere at least flavor the new productions? Does it go deeper than flavoring? Do these men bring to bear their mature equipment on an interpretation of our life? If they do, here in operation is a cultural interchange that should have far-reaching values. If not, if they are immune to the shifting of the scene, they at least are bringing to us in tangible form their established expressions of their philosophy of art and life, and that also is valuable.

It is Man and Art that are important, vastly more important than the specific stage on which they play their allotted roles. The emigré artists driven to this country by the tragedies of war are now a part of our national scene, and they earn a welcome. Some of those whose contributions have been most significant will be considered in these pages. The bulk of our attention, however, will go to the genius which, through birth or long residence, is our own.

ARTISTS AS DESIGNERS OF THINGS OF USE

No section of contemporary cultural life needs constructive criticism as desperately as does that which includes the design of objects of use. The mature modern creative artist knows the art of design of color, space, and form more thoroughly than any other professional because he has inherited all the vast accretions to design knowledge bequeathed him by the Modern Movement. At his best, therefore, he is a master-designer of pictures and sculptures (the most complex manifestations of three-dimensional design). He is thereby equipped to deal with any and all design problems as long as he also meets and masters the demands of special techniques and functional needs. The training of *artist-designers,* then, should take this into account and include the *fine art* of design as the foundation on which to build in special fields such as jewelry, textiles, rugs, ceramics, furniture, and the like. In other words, a designer must be first an *artist.* And a leading designer will automatically be a leader-artist. To say this is to state a truism which any informed person will, or should, approve.

But, unfortunately, the informed individual finds himself in a minority on this issue. With a few honorable exceptions, the powerful forces in our society have not yet made the crucial cultural discovery that leader-artists are the supreme authorities on the art of design. They—the powers that be--are understandably jealous of their own authority and have confidence in it because they know what pleases the millions. Design commissions, therefore, tend to go automatically to business people called commercial designers, who profitably supply the market demand. The result can be condensed to a word--commercialization. The American home is being, in fact it already has been, commercialized to the point where it has lost practically all evidence of individual taste and become a spiritually barren assemblage of standard brands.

The same is partly true of community centers such as churches, college buildings, hotels, clubs, even some railroad depots, skyscrapers, and banks; it has been standard practice to fashion these as imitation Greek, Roman, Gothic, and their furnishings as imitations of this or that "period style." The revolt from this confession of impotence, implemented by our leading artist-architects, is well under way, however, and slowly and steadily gaining. The courage to be honestly ourselves and evolve our own designs is infectious once its excitements are tasted. The industrial designer has speeded this process with his easily accepted functional designs of tools, instruments, and machines; everyone likes "modern" design in a bus, train, vacuum cleaner, egg-beater, bathroom, kitchen, typewriter, and furnace. Where utility dominates, good design is practical. In this field our robust industrial machine can function normally. Here we are strong.

In that other great field, where design becomes an art instead of mainly a functional means, where its appeal is primarily aesthetic rather than practical, where decoration is added to function--here we are still afraid to be ourselves in our mass-production wares. We copy. We adapt. We evade. We conform and submit. We are pathetically weak.

We have few if any critics or feature-writers on newspapers and magazines who make it their task to appraise forthrightly the art, or lack of it, in these things of use. Whether the easy explanation that it does not pay to offend an advertiser accounts for this lack or not is a question. It may also be a lack of standards; nobody cares if the shops are filled with aesthetic atrocities, if the hunt for a ring, a brooch, a set of table silver that is a work of art designed by an artist is long and difficult. All too few even know that the hunt is an aesthetic necessity.

We are not here surveying or reporting on the useful arts. But I do wish to emphasize the close relationship between them and the fine arts and the pressing necessity of acknowledging and supporting the leader-artist as the primary source of all contemporary design where aesthetics are involved. One appraisal herein—that of Ruth Reeves— illustrates and must represent this important issue. *Our future antiques must be designed by living artist-designers.* Then and then only can we exercise our logical right of enjoying them today.

THE GRAND TRADITION

This book is not a survey of the fine art, even the modern fine art, of our time. It is not a history, although it deals with events and productions which are making history. It is not a philosophy of aesthetics despite its presentation and discussion of the specific aesthetics on which a philosophy thereof must be built to be authentic. Rather it applies in critical appraisal an interpretation of the basic philosophy of art that has grown out of the Modern Movement, as this artist-critic sees it. The attempt is to find and report on those artists who are carrying on this basic philosophy, or tradition, as it can be called, since it ties into the Grand Tradition of history with its timeless characteristics of creation and design. Many scholars have written and are today writing within this vast field. But their perspective, as observers rather than practitioners, is inevitably limited. Few artists have so written. This presentation of the artist's viewpoint is, I dare assume, the most important characteristic of these pages and the main reason for their publication.

Another reason, and a close second in importance, is the featuring of "form" as among the essential ingredients of enduring art. Many contemporary judgments grant it little, and in extreme cases, no weight. I admit belaboring this issue and shall doubtless be adversely criticized therefor. My excuse for the overemphasis is the fact that "form," or design, cannot be fully grasped by intellect alone, that it demands, as has been said, some degree of participating experience to unlock its full values. Take the following critical comment by the editor of a prominent art magazine as evidence:

> Yet they [certain colors] are much more than incidental spots of color, such as many painters introduce into their pictures *merely for the sake of design.* [Italics are mine.]

This editor does *not* overstress the importance of design.

Perhaps the appraisals of individual artists in these pages will stimulate consideration of the events and values described, to decide if and why they constitute a renaissance. Then comes the decision as to which artists among the thousands at work among us are making a valid, durable, and leading contribution to the rebirth; no simple task, this, for author or reader. As author, I shall select as cannily as my equipment allows. As reader, you will undoubtedly do the same. We both may make mistakes, to be rectified by later appraisals, and possibly again by still later ones—because we are human and fallible. It is comforting thus to share the prospect of fallibility with my prospective readers. Such appraisals as we are making, by the way, should be a continuing process in order to keep pace with the cultural parade.

The works chosen for discussion will be limited mainly, but not rigidly, to those produced in the past decade, one or more earlier pieces by each artist often being shown to illustrate growth or change. We are exploring the field of *contemporary* art.

Artists who have played their constructive roles in the long, hard battle for the survival of the modern ideals, and then passed on, should have their well-earned place in any survey of this wide panorama. They were pioneers. They blazed trails, some of which we now follow with ease, others which we must endlessly blaze over and over again. Their bodies may have come to the end of their individual trails, but not their spirits; these live on in the works they left behind. Among such pioneers, tribute is due to Arthur B. Davies, Alfred Maurer, Emil Ganso, Arthur Dove, Charles Demuth, Marsden Hartley, and John Sloan. I regret that limitation to recent and current work prevents their inclusion herein.

The problem of group classification of artists under a specific title such as realist, abstractionist, expressionist, and so forth, is difficult. Aesthetic compartments are not standard-tight, either in the matter of definition or performance. What is abstract art? What exactly is expressionistic art? Who practices the one and not the other? Because answers can only be approximations, it seems logical to make compartmental assignments also approximate. Artists with similar approaches will be loosely grouped together—as a matter of necessity and convenience. But groupings will be thought of as fluid and subject to change. The sequence of artists has no significance beyond that roughly of time priority, or seniority.

PARTICIPATION

The spectator of the passing art scene, he who goes to exhibitions and follows the art news, once he does prepare himself for informed judgment, can thrill to the great adventure of participating in the national culture. He can so participate in two ways: (1) By deciding which contemporary artists are carrying on and adding to the grand tradition, then giving them his support, he can widen understanding within his segment of the public domain. (2) By purchase of distinguished examples *he can cause more, perhaps history-making works, to be produced.* Cultural construction need have no side lines. Anyone can lend a hand.

PART I - FOUNDATIONS

The Modern Movement is a Renaissance
and It Has Leaders

In our contemporary art arena there is considerable disagreement as to what and who constitute the avant-garde of modern art. Some bestow this important title on those who have recently revolted from the earlier modern revolt and embraced an emotional release into varying degrees of chaos. Others award the title to today's leaders of the original revolt who are carrying on the old, enduring standards of disciplined creation. This book will argue and illustrate the case for opinion belonging in the latter category.

REVOLTS AND PROGRESS

Revolts are constant irritants in human affairs that, as history shows, are frequently valuable and compel progress. Art history has had its full share of mild and strenuous revolts.

Personal revolts, as well as group rebellions and revolutions, all marking conflicts of ideology—the new and different versus the old, familiar, and respectable—line the highway of recent history. As far back as 1826, the National Academy of Design was founded by Samuel F. B. Morse "in rebellion against the older American Academy of Fine Arts." Increasingly, after 1872, when the Metropolitan Museum was founded, a spirit of revolt was in the air—against academic tradition, against prevailing standards of taste, and against the long-time deference to Europe in art matters. There was ferment in Paris, and American artists returning home clamored for attention. In 1875 most of the forward-looking painters were excluded from the annual exhibit of the National Academy and, as a result, two years later, the rebels founded the Society of American Artists which inaugurated The Art Students League. John La Farge, not long thereafter, had the resurrected idea of collaboration between artists and architects; the result was the beginning of mural painting in this country. Albert Ryder was a rebel, daring to paint according to his own lights. William Chase, on his return from Paris, was among the most aggressive leaders of the "progressives"; he delighted in the controversy then continually raging.

Subjects, up to about the dawn of the twentieth century, had been respectable. Romantic human episodes and landscapes, aristocratic portraits, copious still-lifes, were the rule. Then, in violent revolt, came the Ash Can School, the Independents, Alfred Stieglitz and his "291" gallery and finally the Armory Show of 1913—the advance sample of the atom bomb applied to aesthetics. Abstraction displaced the genteel subject in a burst of, not glory, but vituperation. Expressionism, creation, the harmonics of relationships, transgressed academic tradition by transferring "beauty" from a source in nature outside the picture frame to one within the artist to be *created* (not reflected) as an entity inside the frame. This radical shifting of the source of the aesthetic experience was undoubtedly the greatest single contribution of the international modern rebirth to the art of our time. "Beauty" was not discarded, it should be well noted; its fabrication was merely transferred from God to man. The naturalistic school could not then, and still does not, accept this revolutionary concept of the source. It continues to believe that art is a reportorial process to be conducted by skilled craftsmen.

It was the lonely, dogged, personal struggle of Paul Cézanne, starting in the 1880's, that inaugurated this international revolution. For Cézanne and those who followed him discovered foundations underneath the then recognized ones—foundations that dated back to the dawn of recorded human history—of *designed creation,* of symbolic interpretation, of emotional sensitivity, of an escape from the factual to *disciplined* freedom. It was because these discoveries were so revolutionary at the time he made them that the paths of Cézanne and the other innovators were so tortuous and the recognition of values so long delayed.

DADAISM

A revolt within the revolt of the Modern occurred in Europe in 1916 and lasted till 1923—the dada movement. As defined by its advocates, it was "a metaphysical attempt toward the irrational," that "condemned inexorably literature, art, philosophy, ethics and reason, because it believed them ineffective, not only theoretically but also for the pretentiousness of the men who were their high priests and exploiters." . . . "Dada, in one word, was liberty. Every dadaist could sing and say anything he liked without the risk of being hanged." . . . "As yes was equal to no, order and disorder found unity in the momentary expression of the individual." . . . "Dada never preached, having no theory to defend; it showed truths in action and it is as action that what is commonly called art will henceforth have to be considered." As a revolt mainly against the ravages of war, dada parodied war's devastations by a deliberate extravaganza of un-reason and chaos. There was reason, in other words, behind its un-reason. But, and this is exceedingly important to note, *the work of the Dadaists never achieved the rioting the words proclaimed; These men were artists; they could not jettison art.*

Revolt can, however, lose its validity by becoming mere revolt for its own sake—or for that of the attendant publicity; revolt is news.

THE ACTION PAINTERS

Since about 1947 we have been witnessing in this country such a revolt. In obvious imitation of dada, its creed, in the words of one of its spokesmen,[1] includes the following:

[1] From an article by Harold Rosenberg on "The Action Painters" published in *Art News,* December, 1952.

At a certain moment of time the canvas began to appear to one American painter after another as an arena in which to act—rather than as a space in which to reproduce, re-design, analyze or "express" an object, actual or imagined. . . .

The big moment came when it was decided to paint—JUST TO PAINT. The gesture on the canvas was a gesture of liberation, from Value—political, aesthetic, moral. . . .

When a tube of paint is squeezed by the Absolute, the result can only be a success. The painter need keep himself on hand solely to collect the benefits of an endless series of strokes of luck.

In line with this creed of substituting "action" for art, these devotees of revolt publicly and noisily embrace chaos or the early beginnings of the emergence therefrom. Aside from the unrealized creed of Dadaism, there has been no similar regression since the Stone Age cave painters emerged from chaos into their relatively mature discovery of both content and form. Yet some museums and critics call this debacle the avant-garde of modern art.[2]

WHAT ART IS SIGNIFICANT?

A Chinese author of the eleventh century said' "Some painters produce as a rule nothing but colored representations of forms and do not know how to reproduce the spirit and the skeleton."

All pictures and sculptures made by the hand of man can be divided into two main schools. One school believes in transcribing a subject as seen in nature, literally—the naturalistic school. The other bases its philosophy and practice on disciplined creation—the classic or, in our time,

[2] The Museum of Modern Art honored this movement with a major exhibition called "Fifteen Americans" in 1952, has added a number of examples to its permanent collection and characterized one of them (by Tomlin) as "one of the major mid-century paintings produced by an American."

Of four directors of major art museums who were asked why they exhibited the work of these "beginners," three answered, "Because it is in the news and we feel we should show the public current events." The fourth said, "Because I like it." A dealer who is promoting several of them, asked the same question, answered, "Because something may come out of it."

The answer to the directors should be—how about your responsibility for leadership? And, to the dealer—why not wait till "something" does?

the modern school. The former has existed only in a few scattered periods in the long history of art. The latter has constituted the main stream from the Stone Age to now—except for scattered deviations.

Works falling under the modern banner can be subdivided into five main categories—the realistic, the semi-abstract, the abstract or non-objective, the expressionistic, and the surrealistic. In all of these divisions, subject, when there is one, is re-created into a symbol rather than a replica and built into that least common denominator of all the arts—Design. Modern art is designed creation.

Generalizations of this type are not rigid; the ever-diverse personalities of artists see to that. Personality represents change—the change of flavor, stage setting, tempo, and vision with which a recurring theme may be played in a timeless and placeless world theater. Underneath the diversities lies the constants, with which we also must be concerned. Foundations must support all structures.

All significant art is creative art. It is expressive art. It is man's expression of life, of the tangible and intangible forces which play on him and in him. It is dramatization of events, scenes, thoughts, feelings, emotions. It is a transformation of the particular into the universal. It is the building of a new entity under the sun with its own values which are different from, or an amplification of, other values. It is a transmigration of idea into a designed art form. It is controlled sensation to delight the eye as well as the mind. It is a universal language understood under normal conditions both by the unconscious emotions and the conscious thoughts of (almost) all men. It is timeless and placeless at the same time that it is contemporary and local. It is the antithesis of imitation—of other arts and other periods and styles, and of the superficial facts of the observable data of any specific subject or scene. It is expression through dramatized re-creation.

The decline so noticeable in the art of Europe after about the middle of the sixteenth century is measurable in terms of its gradual departure from these timeless or classic qualities. From them, emphasis slowly and unevenly shifted to the particular and the skills necessary to portray its visual facts. The skilled hands and their tools were increasingly honored above the visions of heart and mind. Materialism blossomed; the voice of spirit waned.

Anyone seeing and studying an exhibition which surveys European art from the twelfth to the twentieth centuries will be shocked by this disturbing trend—a trend which has incredible implications difficult to explain. Pictures and sculptures from the twelfth to about the end of the sixteenth centuries show the balanced blending of subject and form into a unity which, according to the teachings of history, is a prerogative of great art.From then to the beginning of our twentieth century there is a general and gradual decline of the art of the form and a corresponding increase, also gradual and with many breaks but accelerating toward the end of the nineteenth century, in the importance of techniques as a means to a masterly rendering of subject. If the art of the picture and sculpture can be divided about equally between the artist's expression of his subject and his mastery of form, this decline in the form can mean only one thing; the art has dwindled radically. When form has faded to a mere remnant, as in the naturalistic copy of literal subject, the art also has declined to a fraction of its normal functioning. The sculptures of Chartres Cathedral, as they date from the twelfth to the end of the sixteenth centuries, run the gamut of this slow decline, in one architectural structure for all to see. The great display of French Tapestries which visited us in 1948 dramatized it—and showed the modern revival. The German collection of masterpieces rescued from Hitler's salt mines and shown at the Metropolitan Museum, again verified the recession. Hans Baldung and Lucas Cranach, who died in 1545 and 1553 respectively, mark the dividing line, in that collection, with a clarity beyond dispute.

To illustrate further this shifting of the art scenery from the balanced unity of content and form to the unbalanced domination of subject and skills, it is only necessary to contrast two pictures of a similar type, such as portraits, one by an early master like Dürer or Botticelli, the other by a later one such as Rembrandt or, in recent history, Sargent. The Dürer will be masterfully designed realism. In the Rembrandt skilled rendering of individual form in actual light and shade, as literally seen, is on its way to obliterating design (but does not yet do so). In the Sargent that process is approximately complete.

The French tapestries showed the decline more dramatically than could any display of paintings because, in the history of painting, the general downward drift is broken by endless deviations from the norm. Techniques and realism gained but so did profundity of concept and statement to an extent which honored and justified the technical dexterity. In the tapestries there was no parallel fluctuation. Up to and through the fifteenth century the humanities and a forthright and fairly simple design achieved works of art that took their rightful place in the Great Tradition. Thereafter technical exhibitionism gradually usurped the stage with masses of ornate and often meaningless decoration and with a proud display of lavishness in costumes and furnishings, matched by a lavishness in weaving craft, that buried deep any more profound significance either in subject or art. The technical extravaganza gained through the sixteenth and seventeenth centuries, reached the height of absurdity in the eighteenth and nineteenth, until it bought the long and honorable tapestry tradition of France to a logical death in the late nineteenth. Only in our time, in the last three decades, has the seed again sprouted into a modern revival with the French painters, among whom Jean Lurçat has been the leader and outstanding master, providing the designs.

To indicate how the moderns have picked up the basic virtues of the Grand Tradition as these came to maturity in the early period of the European Renaissance, and carried them on in their own idiom in the Modern Rebirth, it is sufficient to extend the comparison of the sixteenth-century masters with such modern ones as Cézanne, Van Gogh, Renoir, Braque, and the best of their successors, in whom reality and design again merge into Modern Classicism.

It is not my purpose to attempt the difficult task of explaining this sad story of the decline of a great European art tradition. Undoubtedly the growing interest in science and all knowledge facilitated this dwindling of art and acceleration of concern with tangibles and techniques. For those whose sensory powers balance intellect, no explanation in words is needed; the museum exhibits are sufficient confirmation. For those whose reaction to all art is limited to intellect, an entire book filled with documentation would be insufficient. Many years in art education have shown that creative practice in doing, even crudely as a novice, the things in color, space, form, and symbolic expression which the primitives and old masters did, is the most effective way to develop comprehension. He who himself creates understands creation. He who himself controls and organizes comprehends design. Practice implements observation and analysis. Art needs experiencing to give forth its full values. The returns on such an investment are ample to cover all costs involved.

ORDER VERSUS CHAOS

For those who have experienced the ordering of a picture or sculpture into a unified whole of aesthetic and functional elements, no supporting explanation or evidence in favor of order is necessary. For those who have not, both are imperative. *Order, organization, design,* or *form*—whatever name we give it—is without doubt the least understood of all the contributions to visual art. This author has explained its complex ramifications elsewhere according to his lights;[3] there is no space here for an ample summary. A statement or two, however, may help.

The eleventh-century Chinese author already quoted undoubtedly meant *structure* or *form* by his word "skeleton."

George L. K. Morris, one of our leading abstract painters, states the case against undisciplined emotional "action" in these words:

> Now we come to the source of salvation and disaster. To free one's emotions—that's necessary but not very much in itself. Anyone can find a way for that, but it certainly takes much more to produce life that will endure upon a wall. I've found that in the long run it is a counter-force, the effect of control and the pacification of chaos, that releases character. It's this harnessing of freedom that has endowed great paintings with a poise and

[3] In *Experiencing Pictures* (New York: Harcourt Brace, 1932), and *The New Art Education*, Revised Edition (New York: Harper & Brothers, 1952).

distinction to move us still after centuries. There lies a danger, always threatening, that the artist's sense of freedom will lead to false assumptions —that his own personality, seemingly so precious and unfettered, is more important than the thing he is after. The demands for controlling forces— those that fit the emotional gamut exactly—are all too easily submerged.

An endless number of statements defending *form* in the various arts could easily be assembled. Music, the dance, poetry, the novel, the essay, architecture—all are unthinkable without the *plan* evolved by the genius of an artist. Drama would cease to be drama without controls. In other arts this fact is self-evident and generally acknowledged—except by individuals or cults that may be carrying on similar happy "activity."

In pictures and sculptures, however, we actually do have a situation where the best of Stone Age cave paintings are superior, in meaningful symbolism and an intuitive design sensitivity, to the uncontrolled emotional flounderings of our neo-dadaists—who have achieved their creed. *And in many high places the flounderings not only go unchallenged but are exhibited and honored with prizes and purchases.* Since we have to go back in history considerably more than 25,000 years to find a parallel in formlessness, there would seem to be something out of kilter in the easy bestowal of the "avant-garde" title thereon. Leader-artists really are not fumbling, or even promising, beginners. And never before has chaos been honored as art. (See Figs. 1 and 2.)

It is easy to say, and possible to prove, that unawareness of fundamentals is the root-cause of such a debacle as this. But why the unawareness? With all our means of international, instantaneous communication, with our museums and libraries bursting with originals and reproductions of masterworks, why is it that basic knowledge in a field touching the life of every literate or illiterate human cannot penetrate across a city, a village, a street, or an isle?

What about the future effects of this strange situation on critical values? Will the production and honoring of works which have discarded both content and form continue? Will they die out? My prediction is that they will not die out quickly due to the incredible lack of understanding of *form* on all levels of our society and because of the amazing mass of publicity won by this rear guard masquerade. Young students, artists, and observers are being widely influenced to imitate and applaud the honored chaos, thus insuring a continuing flood of such works. Current exhibitions already amply indicate the wide penetration of the influence. Familiarity may in time breed contempt, but knowledge is the only force that can reestablish a just balance.

Since the qualities which motivate our contemporary renaissance are deeply embedded in man and cannot be eliminated by any degree of neglect, ignorance, or direct attack, they will work themselves through all opposition and emerge in the creations of those more original souls whose basic inspiration comes from their reactions to life rather than data in the raw. And there is the fortunate minority of art students whose internal as well as external resources have been developed and who are thereby equipped to play their part in the actual forefront of the art of our time, each according to his capacity. Between these two types of the survival of he creative spirit, we do now get, and shall continue to harvest, the significant art of today.

The study of aesthetics, when it depends on the medium of words and the ideas they convey, is an intellectual exercise. But intellect is capable of knowing all *about* a work of art and its maker without profound *comprehension* of either. For comprehension demands the sensory amplification of knowing. One must feel, sense, and enjoy a work in addition to other reactions. One must be aware of those qualities which are to be so felt, sensed, and enjoyed as well as those appealing to reason. Since the appeal to conscious mind via subject is the dominant—one can say almost universal—approach to art in our time, and the sensory appeal to emotion an almost forgotten byway, a critic may be forgiven if he overstresses the latter and to a considerable extent neglects the former, in order to reestablish a just balance in the participating art of appreciation. (A contributing response to a work of art can in some measure become a parallel activity to its creation and so become creative in its own right.) Art is the product of spirit, and spirit resides not alone in intellect but in the whole man.

Subject and the artist's relation to and interpretation of subject are

Fig. 1. A Stone Age cave painting which shows that semi-abstract symbolism and a genuine sense of not-so-simple design existed in man 20,000 years ago. This line-space design rings true to our sophisticated eyes today. It is good design.

Fig. 2. Another and more sophisticated painting, from the Caves of Altamira, Spain, about which the same can be said. This is good "modern" design.

the natural province of intellect, and when intellect stays within this province it should serve well. But when it oversteps objective boundaries and attempts appraisal of the emotions, it finds itself on dangerous and largely uncharted ground. But these dangers must be faced and a way through them found, with intellect as our partially trusted guide and words and ideas as our only immediately available means. Study of the subjective response must supplement that of objective facts.

THE MODERN MOVEMENT IN ART: DEFINITION OF TERMS

The Modern Movement in art is a rebirth of the creative spirit in man. It involves a violent break with the skilled naturalism inherited from the nineteenth century and an adventurous espousal of the age-old elements of creation, symbolism, and design. The word "modern" is open to question because of its continuously shifting inclusiveness, but the acquired meanings of the term "modern movement" are definite enough to cover continuing events which are its outgrowth. No other title owns these acquired meanings sufficiently to be adequate. The Modern Movement carries on the Grand Tradition of creative art into Modern Classicism.

Expressionism

A term used by some critics as an alternative to "modern."

Naturalism

Naturalism in art is based on the presumably skilled reporting, or outright copying, of the visible, and thereby external, facts of subject. Composing by means of the rearrangement of the parts, or selection and omission of details, will mitigate the factual record, but not change its essential character.

Realism

The *reality* of a subject implies inner as well as outer truth or facts. The meaning is more profound. To gain inner as well as outer reality an artist must interpret subject into a symbol. A symbol can be designed, whereas a replica cannot.

Surrealism

The meaning of Surrealism may briefly be defined as "beyond the real." This powerful movement, made famous by Dali and copiously written about by André Breton and Sidney Janis, has now come to an end as a movement, but not as a continuing field for exploration by several of its prominent devotees. Characteristics of that field, therefore, will be outlined later in the articles on individual artists.

Abstraction and Semi-Abstraction

Abstraction means taking from some subject certain elements and from them creating a new entity with accented or different meanings. It can use any degree of reference to its source from the slight to the complete elimination of the original facts. As meaning becomes more obscure or is eliminated, the role of design becomes increasingly important until the playing of pure visual music can be the ultimate goal.

Non-Objective

The Term Non-Objective is applied to works without reference to any subject—complete abstraction.

DESIGN

Design, to recapitulate and condense what has been said more fully elsewhere.[4] is organization of all elements in a picture (or any art medium) into a plastic unity that makes the expression of subject more effective and at the same time plays sensory visual harmonics to give keen aesthetic pleasure. The building materials of design are subject, medium, colors, spaces, lines, light-darks, textures, planes, and forms. Design, used in the modern sense, includes "composition" but goes far beyond that word's usual meaning of arranging subject-matter within a frame (which subject can then be copied from nature as observed). It controls *all* elements. Design also includes the so-called "art principles" of rhythm, harmony, dominance, subdominance, balance, transition, and variation, but exceeds their usual functions. For all of these, with the

[4] See the chapter on Design in *The New Art Education.*

possible exception of rhythm, can be applied to the naturalistic picture. *The art in a picture lies as much in the created design as in mood, expression of meaning, or psychological insight.* It is the least common denominator of all the arts. It, like the symbol, is part of man's universal language.

The term "design," as here used, does not imply an "infallible set of rules" or a "period style" or "the formal spirit of an epoch." It implies the organizing sensitivity within man himself regardless of time and place. This inborn sensitivity will be modified by outside pressures in any given setting, as is normal and desirable. We are thinking about and dealing with the primary power itself.

PLASTIC PAINTING AND SCULPTURE

When all parts of a painting perform the double function of portraying a subject or idea and at the same time weaving all colors, spaces, forms, and so forth, used to build meaning into an organization that acknowledges and decorates the surface of the canvas (picture plane) to give visually pleasing sensations, that work becomes, in modern terminology, a plastic painting. A plastic painting is a designed painting. But design only becomes plastic when it covers the full range of its organizing function by controlling all parts. The same applies to all pictures, regardless of medium.

This condition also applies to sculpture, except for the shifting of emphasis to three dimensions.

WHAT IS SCULPTURE?

Recently there has been a trend in sculpture away from solid form into the open work of metal constructions. Gargallo in Italy, who was the first to open up the human figure into semi-abstract designs in metal that still maintained subject character; Moore in England, with his holes into and through solid body forms; and Alexander Calder in this country, with his mobiles, were the innovators undoubtedly responsible for this development. But each of these men kept his aesthetic controls over the solids and their openings as well as over the filaments or flowing

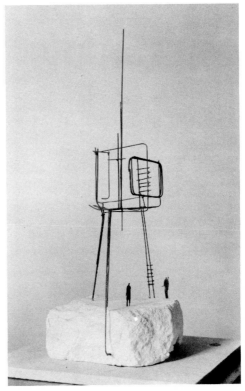

Fig. 3. *The Unknown Political Prisoner,* by REG BUTLER. Winner of the Grand Prize of $12,500 in the International Sculpture Competition of 1953 sponsored by the Institute of Contemporary Arts of London.

bands, *and the spaces between them.* Design, with them, in other words, extended its domain to the spaces between forms.

This new type of work has been exhibited in sculpture shows, has received copious publicity as a new development and attracted an ever-increasing number of honors and devotees. Some of the latter know the disciplines and some, as usual, have not even begun their learning. Results, therefore, have ranged from good through indifferent to the bad of chaos. And—incredible to relate—one of the latter, in March of 1953, won the Grand Prize in the international sculpture competition on the theme, "The Unknown Political Prisoner," sponsored by The Institute of Contemporary Arts of London. (See Fig. 3.)

To test the presence or absence of that basic requirement of the art of sculpture—form design—compare Fig. 3 to the Stone Age drawing of Fig. 1. The latter has a self-contained, recognizable symbolism that anyone, from a cave-dweller to a contemporary college president, can understand. It also owns a sense of rhythmic relationships of every line and space between to which all people can respond. The Grand Prize-winner has neither. It vaguely suggests a caricature of a three-legged chair with a radio antenna attached; the intended symbolism relating to the "unknown political prisoner" has to be explained in captions. There are none of the organized relationships or other fundamentals native to the art in man.

This situation raises three questions. Are "constructions" (or gadgets) sculpture? Or shall such be listed separately as what they actually are—Constructions? And, in open work involving spaces between lines or forms, is formlessness art?

I would answer the first two questions with the suggestion that constructions should be listed and shown separately as such and as a related outgrowth of sculpture. The answer to the third question I shall gladly leave to the reader.

In South Dakota's massive Mount Rushmore Memorial, the heads of five American presidents are carved into the solid rock of a mountain. The artist, working under his nineteenth century inheritance of skilled naturalism, here achieved *content* without *"form."* Today, such gadgeteers as this winner of a grand prize have discarded both. The recent complete art debacle is but the logical companion-piece to the former partial one. Neither "artist" knew the design of form.

SUMMARY

All of these terms and definitions have grown out of, or been amplified by, the Modern Movement. The branch activities or characteristics of pictures which they describe have again come to a focus in that movement. None are really new, that is to say, although some, like Surrealism, plastic quality, and the aesthetics of design, have been exploited more in the past half century than ever before. This exploitation has provided a testing ground for the values involved and the results have been, in the main, an increase in the scope and understanding of these elements of the picture. Pictures have gained in stature and in the variety and richness of their contribution to all observers because of these events. Artists have learned much and so has their public. A contribution has been made in our time to the stream of historic art—a significant event.

Artists today are continuing to test and exploit these increased dimensions of the picture. They are discovering, each for himself and in the aggregate, which are outworn, which can be refurbished, and which have still unguessed potentialities. This is as it should be. Art is a continuing experience. It is our responsibility and pleasure to participate in the grand experiments, at least by an alert and sympathetic observation of events, but better, by the more fruitful sharing of burdens by active support. We are now ready, perhaps, to inspect the work of our own leader-artists to see how they are making use of their valuable inheritance.

A number of artists who are doing distinguished work have been omitted from these pages due to limitation of space. Their omission is keenly regretted and in no way reflects on their standing, in the author's opinion, in the contemporary art community. When and if an injustice has been done in relation to inclusions, time and future tributes to their achievements will, it is hoped, rectify the present inequity.

PART II - THE EXPRESSIONISTS

Realism in varying degree combined with semi-abstraction

Classification of artists is tentative and mainly for convenience.

Priority in arrangement is based roughly on seniority. It does not necessarily imply relative degrees of merit. The final name is so placed because it represents a different medium.

MAX WEBER

Speaking of culture some years ago, Max Weber had this to say:

Culture will come only when every man will know how to address himself to the inanimate, simple things of life. A pot, a cup, a piece of calico, a chair, a mantel, a frame, the binding of a book, the trimming of a dress. Culture will come only when people touch things with love and see them with a penetrating eye.

Elsewhere, some dozen years ago, he put it this way:

The art consciousness is the possessing of the spirit of things, rather than the matter of things.

About the same time he said of Cézanne, whose paintings in a Paris dealer's shop in 1906 he was probably the first American to discover, these words:

The moment you begin to sense the value of Cézanne, he becomes instrumental in leading you away from triviality. He shows the way to true craftsmanship. He is the most concrete way of binding yourself to the fundamentals of art. Since Cézanne, we know better than his predecessors could have known the true meaning of structure, of substance and of subjective plastic eloquence.

During the Great Depression of the 1930's, when Weber had moved down from his ivory tower into the streets of life and when he and many others of us were working hard in the American Artists Congress, he said to the writer:

> I find my geometry in the things I am doing. I'm painting the people who carry the burdens of the world. We can't be remote. I'm tired of painting a woman's breasts in this position and then in that. We must paint as forcefully as the iniquitous forces of the day act their evil influences upon us. . . .
>
> To write on an artist is to ask him what he is. . . .
> Folk art comes from the womb of the people. . . .
> I am trying to bring to my new subject-matter an even greater and stronger plastic quality and I shall never make my art subsidiary to subject-matter."

In 1941, in the foreword to the catalogue of the largest showing of new paintings Weber had had in a number of years—at the Associated American Artists Galleries in New York—the late Donald J. Bear summarized the contribution of this rebel and American pioneer in international modern art about as well as can be done; I quote:

> The art of Max Weber is something that is deeply personal and sacred to him as artist. It admits of no compromise. It is backed by the integrity of a lifetime's conscientious striving to express an impulse that is akin to religious worship or the hard discipline of the ascetic. In his pictures, colors, forms, lines are richly orchestrated into the full expression of an ideal. It springs from the traditions of the monumental and religious arts of the past belonging to all peoples and all times.
>
> A man is as old as his knowledge—as old as his understanding of what greatness has meant and what it can mean. The art of Max Weber is very old indeed. It calls upon the sculptural and fresco arts of Egypt, the arts of the Mesopotamia Valley, the textiles of the Copts, the great mystic arts of China, India and Japan, Persian miniatures, Byzantine painting and mosaic, Gothic glass and sculpture; in short, everything included in the evolution of art has in some way suggested and prompted ways and means to Weber to give his own work more purity of intention.

Fragmentary quotations and comments such as these do not measure an artist adequately, but they serve as a partial index to his philosophy of art and life and the goals for which he works. Each of the above statements could be amplified endlessly, but nuggets of truth are hard to dig out of any profound human life and a few, if thoroughly understood, will lead the way in a search that need never end for others. Nuggets of solid truth are here expressed.

Culture has other requirements, obviously, than seeing simple things with a loving and penetrating eye. Culture requires experiencing, practicing the act of creation, as in a folk art—which becomes an effective means of insight to the sympathetic eye, an aid to comprehension of the mature arts of the day, and all yesterdays and tomorrows. Weber sees all things and all life with sympathetic awareness; he would have others share with him that insight and learn with him the unassailable truth that art consciousness is concerned with spirit rather than matter; an axiomatic truth it is. To say Cézanne has revealed to all who follow him "the true meaning of structure, substance and of subjective plastic eloquence" is to condense the contribution of that master into true and eloquent words. To find his "geometry" (by which Weber means design) in his subject, instead of imposing it arbitrarily on reluctant material, is the functional way of inner necessity which creates authentic form. Yet granting this, and without contradicting it, to insist that the aesthetics of plastic painting shall not be dominated by subject is to maintain the integrity of the artist who has an aesthetic creed and lives up to it with consistent logic.

An authentic art may well be defined as one which is "deeply personal and sacred to the artist," particularly when the personal is buttressed by, and the sacredness drawn from, an identification with "the traditions of the monumental and religious arts of the past belonging to all peoples and all times." The influence on Weber of the Paris moderns, whom he discovered for himself, and of the monumental arts of history, which he also discovered for himself by long, intensive, and happy research, has been obvious enough at various times in his career. But the influence never netted mere imitation; it was the drinking in of the spirit and the striving toward his own form for its expression. Both the drinking and the striving have born rich results. Before the rude awakening of the Depression he was finding his own form; since then both concept and design have assimilated all influences and become eminently his own.

The Young Model, of Fig. 4, done in 1907 while Weber was studying in Paris, shows the artist's assimilation of his academic training (at Pratt Institute where he was influenced by Arthur Dow and his early delvings into two-dimensional design). He obviously "knew how to draw" and to represent the subject's external facts faithfully. The four years in Paris—1905 to 1909—allowed him to unlearn and relearn along with the young French rebels, Les Fauves, who were then applying their findings from Cézanne and the African Negro sculptures. Picasso, it is interesting to remember, first showed the modern influence in his painting in 1901. In 1909 Weber returned to the United States and his exhibit of that year in the Stieglitz Gallery was the first public showing of modern art in this country. By 1911 this artist had achieved his personal revolution; his art was no longer subsidiary to subject (as it was in Fig. 4); he had learned the "true meaning of structure, substance and subjective plastic eloquence."

Fig. 5 demonstrates this learning. Here subject has shifted from a posed model to people, to bodies torn asunder so far as surface facts are concerned and reassembled with the plastic eloquence dominant, with the interplay of forms, colors, spaces, and textures—note the accent on textures—that is the different life of art. This organization of human forms, often in the nude, as in Fig. 6 of 1927, continued to concern him for the next twenty-five years, and still dose; the fact that clothes gradually again covered nude bodies is of slight relative importance.

A direct Picasso and cubist influence is obvious in these grouped figures and other paintings of this period. Because such influence, however, dealt with universals and because it was gradually absorbed into his own expression, it need not be taken too seriously; all artists inherit influences. *Winter Twilight* of 1938 (Fig. 7) demonstrates a full emancipation from all influences; it is a masterpiece of plastic landscape painting. So do the series on musical and Jewish themes mark his independence, his finding of his own way. See *A Family Reunion* of 1944 (Fig. 8).

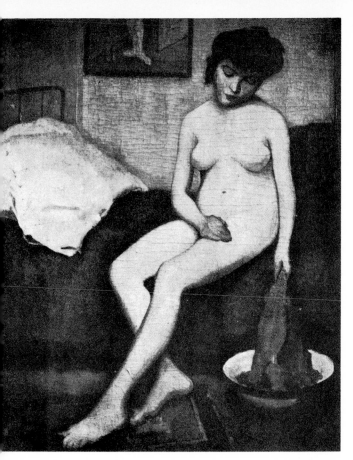

Fig. 4. *The Young Model,*
by MAX WEBER, 1907.

Fig. 5. *Conversation,*
by MAX WEBER, 1919.

Like many other artists of today, Weber has recently turned more to abstraction, to abstracting from the subject its essentials, or the specific essentials with which he is concerned, because the obvious truths do not satisfy. Thus the series on music and musicians, done around 1944 and 1945, are not portraits of people playing instruments; they are an evocation of the spirit of musical creation in which the instrument is accented, but not unduly, and the person subdued to a kind of non-humorous caricature. This realignment of the actual scene allows the attention of the observer, or his imagination, to shift to the main theme—music. And the shift is augmented by the artist's parallel theme of color music—of color and space orchestration—which ties together the two fields of aural and visual sensation, here effectively achieved. A visual artist obviously cannot paint music. He has to paint overtones and undertones of that theme, as Weber has done in this evocative series.

His recent folk-group themes, such as *Discourse, The Toilers, Family Reunion,* and many others, are likewise serious caricatures in different degrees of semi-abstraction with certain desired characteristics extracted and developed, both in theme and design, into mature expressions. (See Fig. 8.)

In answer to a request in the year 1948 to sum up his philosophy to date, Max Weber contributed the following to these pages:

I shall never forget or abandon my craving for and quest of the great and eternal canons of art as against the bizarre, fragmentary, spectacular and fugitive—the fads. My adoration of the great ancients who laid the indestructible, immutable foundations of art for all time shall never dim or tarnish. Their legacy has always been and will always be my spiritual refreshment and renewal. The great ancients worked with God. They interpreted and embodied the glory and wonder of the elements. The moderns work with geometry.

Abstract art, the countless *isms,* have reached an impasse. The greater body of modern art is trailing modern industry, modern dynamics and is servile to them. The art of the ancients stems from the soul; art plus humanity, art social, will always survive and surpass, with no fear whatsoever of even approaching the dangers of an impasse. Servility in art to modern speed, to modern gadgetry and decoration is as inimical as it is for

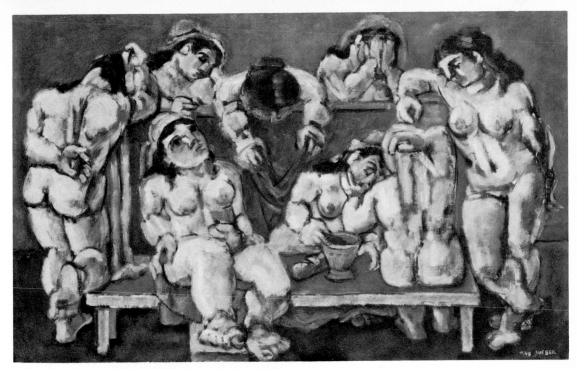

Fig. 6. *Eight Figures,* by MAX WEBER, 1927.

Fig. 7. *Winter Twilight,* by MAX WEBER, 1938.

Fig. 8. *A Family Reunion,*
by MAX WEBER, 1944.

art to concede to fashion, fad and intellectual snobbery—which can become another kind of pot-boiling or academy.

Impregnating the plastics with human passion, pathos, eloquence, spiritual aspiration and vision will put the artist on the path to the infinite, the universal and eternal. The artist who becomes entangled in the intellectual complexities and processes is building a scaffold but not an edifice. Climbing those ladders only, he will inevitable reach doubt and despair.

A profound and thought-provoking statement is this. Its general logic cannot be questioned. Exception can be taken only to the too general claim that "the moderns work with geometry." Such an unqualified, all-inclusive charge is obviously unfair and inaccurate. Some moderns, like the ancients, also work with God, also strive to embody and interpret the glory and wonder of the elements. Some call on geometry (in line with the advice of Plato) to give precision and controlled relationships to the strivings of spirit. Some let geometry dominate and are insensitive to the resulting dilution of spirit into the sterile, externalized formula. Some even imitate the geometry (design) of others and sink into deserved oblivion. To distinguish between these diversities is the critic's task—a task and responsibility that should not be forgotten by the most informed of all critics—the artist.

Exception must also be taken to the claims that abstract art has reached an impasse and that the bulk of modern art is trailing modern industry. It is not abstract art that has reached an impasse; it is the aesthetic capacities of some artists. And modern art, the moment one looks beyond the purely functional logic of the design of machines, has motivated the unwilling and blundering excursions into the outlying regions of a genuine art thus far assayed by industry. Having set down the experience of a quarter of a century in this field and on this theme in a book on the artist-designer of things of use, I will defend the theme with my life-blood, even against Max Weber. With these exceptions the Weber philosophy is, I believe, impregnable.

Max Weber is the pioneer in modern American art, and one of the pioneers in the international modern rebirth, who has held his honored place since 1909 to the present day. He, more than any other American, has become our living old master. But *he* is not old. His art is old, as old as it is new, which fact again establishes the synthesis of living art traditions in which the new carries on the old. In this respect Weber has done his task well. He is a rock of ages in the history of contemporary art.

PAUL BURLIN

Paul Burlin's paintings are motivated by a profound metaphysical attitude toward his life experiences. They need explaining, therefore, to those whose psychological and aesthetic alertness cannot match his own, or run in different, even if parallel, channels. Since no one can explain as effectively as the artist himself, let us listen to Burlin's words. Divorced from his highly sensitive personality and its quickly donned camouflage of caustic humor—which can twist itself at times into an almost brutal aggressiveness for purposes of attack, or of defense covered by attack— the words lose some of their fire-power, but by no means all. There is no floundering in this artist's program; his course is sharply defined.

> These paintings of mine [says Burlin], are a denial of the rationality of realism, which philosophy, as I see it is a false and vicious concept based on bourgeois taste and a lack of spiritual values. My paintings are what the Jungians might call the inherent myth concept of man; they have no root in anecdotes or literary ideas. If some of them are polemic, they do not seek that expression through representational means, but rather through images and a kind of contrapuntal color related to each subject which is its reality. In other words all their subjective ideas, aesthetic or otherwise, arrive at a psychological truth through image, shape, and color.

Is the meaning here obscure? Is this the "aesthetic jargon" that the materialists so enjoy condemning? Or is he telling us quite clearly about deeper objectives and values than the literal? An "image" is a made-to-order symbol. "Contrapuntal color and shape" is another way of saying design. That realism is the only rationality, or that it is rational at all as a means of getting at ultimate realities, is a concept that is obviously open to attack—and should be attacked to shock us, the public, out of our materialistic complacency. To call the rationality of realism a false concept certainly is not difficult to prove and to say it is vicious, if one thinks of the spiritual values it helps to by-pass, is hardly to overstate the case. Enlarging on the significance of the image, Burlin continues:

There is a possibility that these new images will have a magic of their own. They can be propitiatory, they can be aspirational, they can be ironic or blasphemous. But, since the modern artist destroys naturalistic images in order to find aesthetic equivalents, he destroys in order to build. He uses artifice to make reality again.

It was the arts of Guatemala and our Southwest Indians which first awakened Burlin, after a visit to Europe in 1910 had not given him an orientation. Telling of his first meeting with Indian arts, he says:

> In truth the American Southwest was practically the beginning of my interest in painting. My introduction to the art of the Indian stirred up strange conflicts. I was ignorant of the Indian and knew nothing of his work. And since I didn't know him, I feared him, although I wanted to know how he lived and what he did. I travelled to distant places to learn; I heard his chants; I saw strange ceremonial rites in remote parts of New Mexico. I was entranced with his witch doctors and the whole aspect of the metaphysical propitiation of the forces of nature. Mayan architecture and sculpture overpowered me. I wished to understand these configurations that were indigenous to the character of the land. How could I translate them? What ethnic brotherhood brought about these two-dimensional designs on utilitarian objects? Why was a bowl decorated in this abstract fashion? By contrast, all other picture-making seemed like story-telling trivia. These disturbing factors, none of which had anything to do with "representation," were the vague beginnings of an aesthetic credo, though perhaps I should not call it a credo since it did not then find its form.[1]

I quote so much personal ideological history particularly to show that a leading American modern found his initial stimulation and gained the aesthetic bearings which have guided his course from 1913 to now, from the arts of his own soil—but from the "primitives" of that soil, not its present "sophisticated" tenants. He did not get it from the Paris which had also been inspired by the primitives—of Africa. Later, in Paris, Van Gogh and Matisse shocked this American, in 1918, as they had not in 1910; the inspiration of the Indians found its counterpart and carried on into more profound regions.

What happened to me in the eight years after 1928? Building. Destroying. Rebuilding. All in an attempt to translate the metaphysical into the

---

[1] I first met Burlin in 1915 while he was on this quest. He visited my ranch near Taos, New Mexico.

concrete. The daily scrutiny of the artist confronting himself in his work was my chief occupation. Essentially I was trying to destroy visual form in an attempt to build a new reality by the invention of distinctive color shapes. This is man's need to find the inner germination of creation. These shapes dissolve and transmute themselves—you never pin the butterfly. This is no mere technical performance. It's a whole new act of creation. Representation as such limits such invention. Many painters who make nature their eyes, their tongue, reward their model (nature) by subservience. These are the realists. In contrast, I, as an experimental painter, believe that nature affords merely hints for the artist to conjure with, to depart from. Yes, even to lie about and, in turn, reward nature by new images. . . . I think the art of the future must depart from the materialistic concept in order to find its God. And the God idea is a universal one; man is ever in search of his spirit.

This is all personal explanation of an individual creed, but it far transcends the personal. It tells us again that art is in man and that it erupts through the smothering crust of the long-dead ashes of materialism in strange and diverse places—Guatemala, New Mexico, Africa, Paris, New York. The break-through comes easiest with primitive peoples and children (before they are spoiled by adult standards), where the crust is thinnest or has never formed. It is toughest among us "highly civilized" citizens of the modern world who have no time to cultivate spirit. The valiant struggle, therefore, of an artist like Burlin to get back to the deeper realities is something to be watched and sympathetically supported.

The chaos of forces contending for supremacy in contemporary life and his own battle-scarred reactions to that chaos are reflected in the paintings of Paul Burlin. All are tumultuous. Masterful, felt design takes its cue from this tumult and synthesizes it without suppressing the riotous emotions. *The riot is tamed by the design,* in other words, *without being tamed in spirit*—quite an achievement, that (which some rioters are quite unable to effect). Color schemes throb with vitality within Burlinesque limits of muted primaries; grayed reds, blues, yellows, purples, and greens play in lively chords, with blacks and delicately grayed whites in contrast. Subject is always the symbol instead of the replica, and becomes more and more abstruse after 1945 until vague, unreadable hints replace

Fig. 9. *New England Landscape,* by PAUL BURLIN, 1928. This was painted in the period after 1928 and shows the beginnings of his efforts to "build a new reality."

Fig. 10. *Soda Jerker,* by PAUL BURLIN, 1936. Received first prize of $2500 in the second Portrait of America Exhibition sponsored by Pepsi-Cola.

tangible meaning; compare Fig. 12 to the *Soda Jerker* of Fig. 10. Nevertheless, the diverse forces are organized into the seemingly perfect whole. I say "seemingly" because there is no such thing as ultimate perfection. This critic has often been disturbed by the tumult in these paintings but has thereupon had to admit to himself that such disturbance may well be one of their many virtues. For the tumult is always under full control; that is the vital matter. A long study of Fig. 12 in a recent exhibition confirmed these controls; their results felt eminently right.

Burlin for many years now has been compensating for such portraits of external America as *Street Scene* of 1931 and *Soda Jerker* of 1936, by excursions into the metaphysical realities of our time. In 1941 and 1943, *The Omen, Anno Domini,* and *Play in Three Quarters Time* pointed this more profound search. In the next several years the search gained momentum with a veritable flowering of apocalyptic expression of our age of "terror and ecstasy." To assume that the years of war, destruction, and heroism which man has endured can be adequately realized by the picturing of external facts is aesthetically childish. Human tragedy, as revealed to those who have suffered and as glimpsed by those who are not the immediate victims, should demand from our artists deeper understanding and attempts at expression. Burlin has sensed this largely inchoate hunger. He painted the innate tragedy of the human race in such works as *The Eternal Jew* (1943), *The Pity of It* (1944), *Anno Domini* (1943), *News from Home* (1945), and others. Here is inner reality run riot. Here an artist is digging ruthlessly into the minds of man and woman. Here is the tragedy of all war—of thoughts born of war, of a world of men torn, bleeding, devastated, of what war and its destruction does to the mind—not the physical, external details, but the inner destruction. Here is the soul of man stripped of the comfortable camouflage of clothes and masks. Here is the Great God Brown in painting. Here are thoughts gone naked.

Other works of this same period supply the Shakespearean juxtaposition of opposites—tragedy versus laughter, the tears of the race contrasted to hilarious absurdity in *Witness the Whatless* (1945) and *Young Man Alone with His Face* (1945), of Fig. 11.

There is another theme in this artist's repertoire. Men and women

Fig. 11. *Young Man Alone with His Face,* by PAUL BURLIN, 1945.

Fig. 12. *Red Theme,* by PAUL BURLIN, 1950.

exist in the world—the male and female elements. The male owns lust as well as love; the woman seductiveness. The painting *Golden Lore* tells the idyllic side of this eternal drama. In *Oh, the Pity of It* we see the Othelloan tragedy again (about to be) enacted in our day. And *To Have and To Hold* (1942) plays on the age-old theme, so differently in means yet similarly in concept, dramatized by Rubens in his *Rape of the Daughters of Leucippus*.

Burlin believes that pure abstraction dehumanizes the picture, that painting should be dynamic and human. He relies on a "personal magic incantation." "Incantation is magic," he says, "and the magic is the picture." To this observer it seems that his steady march toward more obscure meaning, toward the near-complete abstraction, is a violation of this belief; that he would do well to return to the humanized symbol with its unobliterated meanings.

A friend once handed me the following, asking to whom I thought it referred:

> This stripping is essential to art, to which is also essential a flat distortion in the drawing; it is an art of caricature, a great caricature. It is a caricature which is beautiful and a great humor which is serious; it is a world of poetic imagination; it is somber. There is brutality, a lack of sentiment, a polished surface, a handling of large bold design in brilliant colors.

"This is about Paul Burlin's paintings," I said with quick assurance.

"No, you are wrong. It was written by T. S. Eliot about Ben Jonson, the seventeenth-century dramatist."

Art, it seems, bridges time, space, and medium.

HUGO ROBUS

First, let me take this opportunity to acknowledge a long-standing indebtedness.

In 1914, having been drawn from Chicago to New York by the impact of the Armory Show and the consequent urge to discover what this "crazy modern art" was all about, I found a small school on Washington Square South taught by Hugo Robus, just back from Paris. Under his able direction, during that winter, I first learned to implement that more or less forgotten law of the ages to the effect that sculpture involves the realization of form as form and the art of form design. This pregnant discovery changed the main channel of my life more than any other single event after the Armory Show, thanks to Hugo Robus.

Sculptor Robus (who was also a painter until 1920) has been implementing that law, it thus appears, for over a third of a century—which honorable record makes him one of the hardy pioneers of the modern in this country. For this reason, plus the impact of his evolving work itself, we shall do well to listen closely to any statement of his experienced philosophy. What has this artist-sculptor been practicing and teaching in these 40 years?

First, patience and modesty, I would say.

The artist lives by his hopes [says Robus] rather than for his accomplishments and the most any one of us does create is so little qualitatively that he who realizes this difficult fact can be only modest and quite humble about his efforts.

Art cannot be realized just by the eyes: a work has the possibilities of creative art only when it expresses the reactions of the artist to sensations which pass through the eyes. Human capacity to experience, projected by rhythmic and ordered composition of volumes and voids, is for me the basis of creative art, and quality depends on how complete the experience has been and how well the forms and voids have been chosen and developed toward the expression of that experience.

For this purpose the artist must be a well self-disciplined person in the matter of his profession. We all know that a subject such as Chaos can be expressed as a work of art only by an ordered composition even though the subject-matter is disorder. *In art the uncontrolled emotional and the entirely intellectual are extremes which are incomplete in themselves; man's emotional quality is the motivating force which must be guided by intellect.*

Creative art appeals to the inner man and is not art by formula as academic art is. We have both creative and academic art in all periods. Non-objective work, of course, can be just as sterile as any other.

Free standing sculpture is only true sculpture in the round if it is expressive from every viewpoint. The mere fact that a work has three dimensions does not make it sculpture in the round. Here I am stating an ideal —which I try for but never achieve—and it is probably safe to say that no one else does either.

The human form when used in sculpture should be architectural rather

Fig. 13. *Girl Reading,* by HUGO ROBUS, 1935.

Fig. 14. *One Who Danced,*
by HUGO ROBUS, 1940.

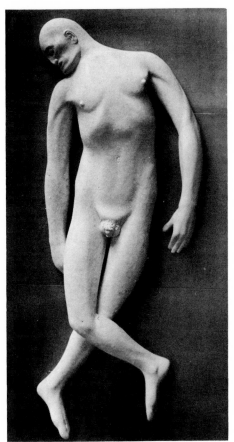

Fig. 15. *First Born,* by HUGO ROBUS, 1950.

Fig. 16. *Cellist,* by HUGO ROBUS, 1950.

than surgical in anatomy and should convey the idea of structure in a visual sense rather than from an engineering point of view. Though I believe a piece of sculpture must have a vitality of its own and need not be based on animal form, I find that for my own desires the human form is eternal as a source of aesthetic form and mood. I modify this source material toward more complete expression within the design pattern I have chosen for the work. Modification of form is not arbitrary and so no one form can be changed without a compensating adjustment of all forms within the framework of the whole structure.

Craftsmanship is important only to the extent that it facilitates the projection of the inner content of a work. That which has nothing to say remains sterile regardless of the quality of workmanship displayed.

A number of these statements of the Robus philosophy need to be underscored and taken to heart. The modesty of the man, for instance, deserves honoring if only for its rarity. The rhythmic ordering of volumes and voids, the emphasis on expression of experience, the necessity of disciplining the emotions, the architectural treatment of human form without abandoning it as a source of aesthetic form and mood—all of these are matters of basic importance which must never be forgotten. Perhaps the artist condensed all of them into a single sentence when he said recently, "All I am trying to do is *to express some of the essences of our living world as I see and feel them.* So easy to say and so difficult to do."

Robus does achieve his ideal of sculpture in the round which expresses living essences much more adequately than his modesty allows him to claim. Each work here shown demonstrates this. In the 1930's he was extracting the essentials of feminine form, as in Fig. 13, and building them into "rhythmic and ordered compositions of volumes and voids." Fig. 14 I would call a near-perfect blending of the architectural and surgical (or animal) treatments of human form plus strong characterization and an unusual design. Fig. 15, of 1950, goes more abstract in its summarized statement of general truths of body form, as in the necks and heads; here rhythmic movement impinges on the domain of truth, but without actually sacrificing essential character; this *is* the great triumvirate of human life. Another masterwork (and it is that) of 1950 swings back to a more subtle and mellow merging of the rhythmic and the real, thereby, for this critic, paying richer satisfaction dividends. (See Fig. 16.) The same trend has continued through 1953.

The sculptures of Hugo Robus are well within the Grand Tradition, yet have a unique personal flavor. They are distinguished works.

JOHN MARIN

John Marin learned his modern art the slow, hard way. He learned it by an inner-driven searching of his own soul, and nature's soul, that persisted through a quarter of a century of flounderings, discovery, despair, realization of partial but growing achievement, and final fulfillment of his goal. That goal was to extract essential meanings from nature and hammer them on the anvil of his inviolate personality into keenly sensed harmonic relationships on the flat surface of his *created* picture. He has held to that goal through his entire professional life, thus escaping the distractions of successive periods or styles through which many artists pass. His art lifeline, plotted into a statistical diagram, would emerge remarkably straight—perhaps the most undeflected of any recent important American artist.

Born in 1870 in Rutherford, New Jersey, Marin, by the decade from 1888 to 1898, was sketching in pencil and watercolor whenever he could escape from school or other imposed duties. In those early days he seemed to realize that there have to be symbols in a picture, that a sketch only stands for nature's forms; it cannot duplicate them. He began even then to compose his own time-saving symbols, to invent his own idiom, to search for his own means of expression, and to arrive at the philosophy which said art must show action. "A man paints a boat so it looks like a boat," he said, "but what has he got? The boat doesn't *do anything*. It doesn't move in the water. It is blown by no tempest. That copy-boat might sell boats but it cannot be art. Art must show what goes on in the world." Thus developed the individualist during the years of his scattered and fragmentary training, which was more self-training than school-training; the Academy with its copying of posed models was not for him.

Marin deserves considerable credit for working out his main orientation before 1905, when he first went to Paris. It took many of us who were formally educated at the turn of the century longer than that; it needed, in fact, the shock of the Armory Show of 1913 to crystalize vague doubts into concrete revolt and the search for the new values. With many the search was external—to find out what the Paris pioneers were doing. With Marin it was dominantly internal, based on his own reactions to nature. Throughout his entire career he seems to have learned little from others. Cézanne was blazing his new trails while Marin was growing up in the 1880's, but this American artist never discovered him until 1911. Picasso had revolted and solved many of the new problems from 1901 to 1905—problems which Marin only partially resolved many years later. But the point is that he did work out by trial and error over the years a creed which paralleled the modern in basic values, thereby indicating that the creative revival is in man and works out in many ways in many individuals who provide the right soil to nourish it. Let the artist explain his goals and growth in his own words. The following quotes are taken from the book *John Marin,* by MacKinley Helm,[2] which tells the life story of the artist with sympathetic insight and a remarkably complete documentation:

[1912]—Shall we consider the life of a great city as confined simply to the people and animals on its streets and in its buildings? Are the buildings themselves dead? We have been told somewhere that a work of art is a thing alive. Therefore if these buildings move me they too must have life. Thus the whole city is alive; the buildings, people, are all alive; and the more they move me the more I feel them to be alive.

It is this moving of me that I try to express, so that I may recall the spell I have been under and behold the expression of the different emotions that have been called into being. How am I to express what I feel so that its expression will bring me back under the spell? Shall I copy facts photographically?

I see great forces at work; great movements; the large buildings and the small buildings; the warring of the great and the small; influences of one mass on a greater or smaller mass. Feelings are aroused which give me the desire to express the reaction of these 'pull forces,' those influences which

[2] New York: Pellegrini & Cudahy, 1948.

play with one another; great masses pulling smaller masses, each subject in some degree to the other's power.

While these powers are at work pushing, pulling, sideways, downward, upwards, I can hear the sound of their strife and there is great music being played.

And so I try to express graphically what a great city is doing. Within the frames there must be a balance, a controlling of these warring, pushing, pulling forces. This is what I am trying to realize. But we are all human.

In the entire Helm biography I cannot remember a quotation in which Marin uses the word "design." But this control of warring forces here so aptly described is exactly what many modern leaders mean by that potent word.

[1916]—Painting is like golf. The fewer strokes I can take, the better the picture. I want a full, mellow ring to each stroke.

In the same year, 1916, Marin wrote of "floundering along *new lines.*" Helm explains this in speaking of a certain painting of a full panorama in the colors of autumn thus:

It is a simplification of the motif, a "made" picture, with abstract forms overlaid to cause purely plastic excitement. In Marin's opinion this is one of the most significant pictures of his entire career. It was the first time, he modestly felt, that he had "played" with a subject and come richly out with something that was clearly the expression of painterly intellect rather than an impression of his feeling for nature. His purpose was plainly to indicate the architectural structure of nature under the surface appearance, under the fleeting impression. He was not afraid then, as he has not been since, of showing subjective feeling in pictures, but he liked to make sure that the analytic and objective matter was primarily present.

Here Helm, interpreting Marin, is saying that it was not till 1916 that the artist "floundered" into the discovery of designed semi-abstract creation as a subjective contribution over and above (or under) the contribution of subject. Helm calls this an expression of "painterly intellect"—an opinion open to objection; but he gives it an important place—which significant fact testifies to Marin's belated identification with the Modern Movement. He could have made this great discovery at any time after

1901—if he had been more alert to the events transpiring around him both in Paris and America.

Marin often thought of his art in terms of music. In 1927 he was saying,

There are all sorts of rhythms; rhythms in beats, say, of one-two-three, two-two-three, three-one-one. These beats are seen and expressed in color: for color is life, the sun of life reveals all things in the colors of light.

But never did Marin take the easy next step into complete abstraction and the playing of pure visual music. Consistently he held on to the subject motivation. In 1946 he repeated the basic creed of the years:

The most important thing about a river is that it runs downhill. Simple, isn't it? Art is produced by the wedding of art and nature. Go look at the bird's flight, the man's walk, the sea's movement. They have a way to keep their motion. Nature's laws of motion have to be obeyed and you have to follow along. The good picture embraces these laws—the best of the old did —that's what gives them life.

Mr. Helm uses the word "plastic" several times in reference to the Marin paintings, but nowhere do I remember a quotation in which the artist has employed this key word to define the art of design in painting whereby symbols extracted from deep space are hand-wrought into the flat plane of the picture surface. Marin defends the process and justifies it by an elaborate reference to nature in which "earth and sea are ideally (and pictorially) flat." He cannot also justify it, apparently, for its subjective sensory value as a means to realizing the visual music he approves.

The two paintings shown herewith, covering as they do the time span from 1922 to 1950, illustrate the straight, but not too narrow, path Marin has followed for more than a third of a century. All fit snugly into the creed so eloquently expressed in 1912 as quoted above. The scene shifts from city to ocean forms but there is the same deep emotional response to the warring influences of the great and the small forces, the same awareness of "great music being played." The fact that this artist seems to give too much credit to nature and too little to the man-creator for the apprehension and tangible realization in the picture of the "warring influences" and the "great music," can probably be credited to modesty.

Fig. 17. *The Old Salt,* by JOHN MARIN, 1922.

Fig. 18. *From Weehawken Heights,* by JOHN MARIN, 1950.

He must know that he himself is pictorially creating both the warring influences and the great music.

Just how great is the Marin pictorial music? If an impressive success story involving almost fabulous fame and sales, considering that the artist has just died in October 1953 at 80 years of age, is a fair criterion, the music must be great. The obvious fact that it is authentic music, product of a highly sensitized personality, speaks well for the aesthetic awareness of a wide public. That other, not unrelated, fact that Marin enjoyed and profited by the uncannily shrewd promotion of his long-time friend Stieglitz, who dared to ask (and got) from $3000 to $6000 for single water-colors from the middle period of his career onwards, certainly greatly stimulated the success, but need not be taken too seriously, since solid values were involved. It was, however, preferential competition with other artists and therefore unfair to them when used as a measure of relative merit. To say that John Marin is the "greatest living American artist" is to forfeit perspective and the weighing of art values. Many other American artists are equally sincere. Many have dug more deeply into the rich veins of aesthetic experience we call modern art. A considerable number have expressed equally authentic reactions to life and nature in more diverse and complex ways. To say that Marin has validated and honored the subjective emotional approach, and that it has returned the compliment, should be sufficient.

Incidentally, it is amusing to note that Marin has been practicing for nearly half a century the "emotional or psychological release" which our international devotees of confusion have only discovered in the past five to seven years. Only he has owned intuitively the disciplines which they lack.

GEORGE GROSZ

GROSZ'S ART IS A STORM

George Grosz has recorded the great phenomenon of our century—the collapse of human reason. He has recorded it as an artist—aloofly, stingingly and sometimes even humorously. In his thousand and one drawings of war and war-makers, the rage and futility of a floundering species grimaces mazingly. The technique with which Grosz has drawn our world is unique in modern art. It is the swift and powerful technique of Daumier, Dürer and Rembrandt. His color speaks rather than stares. It lends always a wild tongue to his life. There are many lyric passages in the art of Grosz; sun and trees, clouds, water and lovely textures smile occasionally from his canvases. But essentially, Grosz's art is a storm. It is a storm of derision and protest. Alone, among modern painters, Grosz has recorded the spiritual descent into hell.

BEN HECHT

In the *Art Digest* of April 15, 1948, Alonzo Lansford summarized the career of George Grosz so briefly and effectively, in reviewing his exhibit of the "Stick Men" at the Associated American Artists Galleries, that I quote his article in full:

YES, WE HAVE NO MANANAS

For one's peace of mind (if one can afford that luxury, these days), it would be well to try to forget George Grosz's record of prophetic accuracy while visiting his current exhibition.

In 1914, as an infantryman in the Kaiser's army, he painted a picture foreseeing its defeat. In 1919 he painted the *White General,* a swastika-helmeted maniac trying to conquer the world. In 1934, having fled Germany for the United States, he anticipated the Spanish Civil War with *Street Fight, Madrid.* Three years before World War II, he depicted himself sitting among the wreckage of a world still smoking. Now he is presenting a series of water colors portraying the "Stick Men," a race of humanesque creatures who inhabit a gray world of desolated ruins, who are called by numbers instead of names, who follow banners that are empty and meaningless, men who wear slave collars no longer chained to anything and perhaps are a little proud of them. In these paintings Grosz is more interested in *what* he says than in how he says it. This is far from being a pretty world he pictures, but that is how he means it to be. Grosz paints because he violently dislikes our world.

After the first World War, Grosz became the bitterest of the social satirists. Later, in the U.S., he calmed down, became preoccupied with tranquil still-lifes and lush nudes. Now he has again risen in wrath, with wormwood in his mouth and the eloquence of Jeremiah in his brush. But this time it is different. During the '20's Grosz struck out at the German militarists, the profiteers, the Nazis; this time he is mad at the whole human species for being fool enough to destroy itself.

But let the artist speak for himself. He is the unimpeachable authority on his own work and its meanings. Others may speculate and interpret—a healthy enough and necessary process—but he knows. The following comments were written in 1946. They were printed in the catalogue of his exhibition of that year.

A PIECE OF MY WORLD IS A WORLD WITHOUT PEACE

I don't know how much my pictures have to do with a dubious "reality" —as a matter of fact it interests me very little. My pictures are the witnesses of my inner world, of a world that is difficult to photograph, so that my pictures do not compete with the camera or the newsreels.

Thus I create my own frightful fairy-tale world, full of ruins and populated with ugly dwarfs, terrifying supermen and evil magicians. A piece of teutonic heritage seems to be embodied in this—in this desire to symbolize and to meditate—in this yearning for fairy-tale.

But, in contrast to the "expressionists," I try to recreate my world as realistically as possible. Over and over again I say to myself: Be more exact—more exact—because the more of a nightmare it is, the more I must recreate it in an understandable way. So I go on studying again and again the manifold forms of nature. The result is evidenced in my paintings, in the love I have for details. I am trying to paint "finished" pictures like certain medieval painters to whom I feel much more related than to the modern experimenters.

When I paint and when I look at pictures I prefer to think of a maxim of Aristoteles, "the pleasure of recognition," rather than of the abstract speculations of Plato. However, there is not only this one side to my paintings. I am not only and forever a specialist in horror and death. Here and there I have within me regions without fear, death and war. Here and there are sensuous landscapes where nymphs live. I admire the artist's gift to invoke an innocent, bucolic-arcadian world. I admire Renoir who never had the vision to depict one of his beautifully painted nudes as disfigured, raped or mutilated. I have little of this wondrous gift within me. My world is usually a gloomy and haunted one.

My pictures can be "explained." Often, like parables, they are open to multiple definitions. If there remain here and there "unexplainable" parts, then it means that these "unexplainable" or "fluid" pieces have been painted this way quite deliberately, to present a certain single exactness and description more accurately. . . . In the fairy-tale world, contrasts exist beside one another just as they do in the world of reality. Here are a few notes on the "meaning" of my pictures.

In *The Survivor* [Fig. 22], we see a picture of a humanity aged too early.

Fig. 19. *Model in the Studio,*
by GEORGE GROSZ, 1937.

Fig. 20. *A Piece of My World No. 1,*
by GEORGE GROSZ, 1939. "Half mad
mankind, tattered and old, advancing
for a cause they cannot comprehend, to
fight an enemy they cannot overcome."

Fig. 21. *I Woke Up One Night and Saw a Burning House*, by GEORGE GROSZ, 1942.

The composition is interesting; a close look will show the form of a swastika. This design of lines and directions was, incredible as it may seem, completely unconscious. I was surprised myself when I discovered it later on.

The ghost-like man there in the bloody pond has become insane with fear. In his "world" he is perhaps the only survivor, and yet he is afraid of those "others" who are no more. (Fear and terror live the longest.) On an old rifle butt he has a rusty table fork. (This insane world is not free from the grotesque.) The fork is a symbol of his terrible hunger. What will he hunt? Rats—those symbols of uncritical craving which reappear so often in my pictures? Or are these rats only "hallucinations"? In reality are they thoughts living under the bloody earth which have changed into rats and are climbing up to the earth? In the world of fairy-tales there are multiple explanations.

Fig. 22. *The Survivor,*
by GEORGE GROSZ, 1945.

Fig. 23. *The Painter of the Hole,*
by GEORGE GROSZ, 1948.

This explicatory example, and the pictures themselves, give spectators plenty to think about, to dream about, in the long winter nights of our "one world" travail. They shock. They clarify. We do live under the man-imposed double standard of the divine and the beastly, in us and in our world. We must remember this hard fact. Artists should remember it and take it into account in their overall production. It is logical to be aware of and interpret both. Renoir is incomplete when he gives us only the lush beauties of nude bodies and shimmering sunlit scenes. Bonnard is naïve in his absorption in literal surface color charms. All naturalistic art is feeble and escapist in this sense, in its failure to see and express the hidden meanings. We need artists who recognize this double standard and use the awareness thereof to ameliorate both departments of their expression. Art is as wide as the total horizon of man—all men of all time.

Grosz says he feels more closely related to certain medieval painters than to the "modern experimenters" of today. One reason for this is undoubtedly the greater universality of medieval art on two main counts—symbolism and design. Medieval artists did not paint the immediate and particular; their realities were broad, their meanings and applications profound. Kinship, therefore, with moderns of similar breadth of vision is obvious. Grosz is not the only contemporary who earns this kinship. Many today carry on the great tradition. To them also Grosz is related.

Grosz's desire to paint his world "as realistically as possible," to appeal to the pleasure of recognition rather than abstract speculation, is logical because he has a message and wants it to reach the widest possible audience. But he does use *realism* to gain this end, be it well noted; never does he descend to mere naturalism. His marvelous details and textures, as in Fig. 21, are masterfully designed.

Grosz presents a profound challenge both to the artists and public of his day. To the artists he demonstrates how the burning convictions of a deeply felt "message" automatically transmit their fire. To the public he proves forcefully that artists have something to say to their fellow citizens which may be of importance—and uncannily prophetic. The conclusion should be obvious. When artists speak out from deep conviction the world should listen. The message will be worth the hearing.

RUSSELL COWLES

The history of Russell Cowles illustrates, perhaps as well as that of any artist working in this country today, the dilemma of contemporary art and its professional creators. To get the full impact of his participation in this dilemma and the significance thereof one must know his thoughts as well as see his paintings. Both are self-revealing and period-revealing. The work has wandered through the maze of influences our age and its artists are heir to; the thoughts express the matrix of this inheritance as it affects one individual. These thoughts were written into the record in an article, *What the Artist Is After,* published in *Magazine of Art* for September, 1941, and will stand as a frank and authentic mirror of our contemporary confusion, at least for the decade of the 1940's. Rarely does an artist set down so clearly and sensitively his personal reaction to his inheritance.

In this article we find all the influences of the day measured against a questioning and searching mind. There was the influence of the academic art training of the early years of the century and a healthy rebellion against it. There was the impact of the 1913 Armory Show which "intrigued" but could not capture allegiance without understanding. There were five "wonderful years" in Rome as winner of the Prix de Rome and an absorption in the work of the Italian masters. Back in America, there were paintings reflecting this classical tradition which won prizes—and were later destroyed as a logical step in a mentally distressing period of reorientation and as a necessary gesture of liberation. There was a year in the Orient—in China, Japan, and Bali—which gave a better perspective on our "Occidental jumble of Classic, Romantic, Classicistic, Academic and Modernistic." There were experiments with abstraction in answer to the seeds lying dormant from the Armory Show—which proved to be not what this artist was after. There was an eight-year chapter in Santa Fe which swept away many cobwebs and brought a better understanding of the Modern. Then, back in New York, came the reflections on these varied influences, their meaning and value.

From the vast catholicity of art in the long perspective, emerged the realization that historical knowledge is not enough. The changes in spirit from age to age are crucially important. They invalidate artifice and make-believe, the fancy dress of bygone days "speaking the lisping tongue of infancy," or anything done merely to attract a jaded public sick of the present and wanting to be transported to the past. Art, in other words, should not flout the laws of reason and naure to end as a shameless exhibitionist and sensation-monger. Today's technical discipline is important, Cowles came to believe, and American artists, because they tend to have a puritanical resistance to letting themselves go emotionally, frequently seek compensation in technical mastery. But over-indulgence in any sort of pyrotechnical trickery of handling or effect seems an adolescent trait that our virtuosi shed as they become artistically mature; it has little to do with art. Sound craftsmanship, in its proper place, and when it leads into the larger discipline, is a basis for a healthy, sane, and great art for this country. "The good painter must be concerned with good painting, and good painting means discipline as well as eager enthusiasm. It is not a stunt."

In the discipline of "good painting" Cowles includes the art of design. Painting is color-shape on a flat surface and how these color-shapes relate to the world of reality, and what effect they have because of their particular pattern on the eye and mind of the beholder—this is the whole problem in a nutshell.

> Space is the matrix of reality [he says]. The control, the manipulation, the organization of space in relation to the picture surface lies at the heart of the art of painting. This I must assert categorically. Should a painter deny it he would thereby class himself as either a decorator or an illustrator, the former thinking only of the picture plane, the latter forgetting its existence. This discipline of space underlies all great painting, from the Chinese masters of T'ang and Sung, to Giotto, to El Greco, to Cézanne. It does not endeavor to realize on the canvas the three-dimensional or "deep" space of the physical world. Imitative painting, where the frame is like an open window onto the world outside, eats away the picture surface. The aim

Fig. 25. *Prodigal Son,* by RUSSELL COWLES, 1948.

Fig. 24. *Parade,* by RUSSELL COWLES, 1940.

Fig. 26. *Forest Boundary,*
by RUSSELL COWLES, 1952.

should be quite the contrary, to preserve this surface. Art is all a matter of relationships, and in this instance it is the relation of the canvas surface to "deep space." It is a paradox. In my opinion Cézanne devoted his life to the solution of this problem.

I quote Cowles at length on this matter because his words clearly show that a long and complex experience has brought him to the heart of the modern revival. "Art is an affair of the spirit," he says in summing up his experience. "Spirit and discipline—another paradox, in fact one of the oldest." And under "spirit" he includes feeling as well as rationalization —the two to be in balanced relationship. He has no fear that spirit and its emotional powers will be injured by a just admixture of deliberate reasoning. The resulting art, he thinks, can take it.

In his paintings Cowles has implemented his mental and psychological adjustment to the art of his day to a remarkable degree. In works like *Parade* of 1940 (Fig. 24) the classical influence of the European Renaissance has been absorbed and mastered and emerges in a designed realism that is timeless. Characterization is masterful, form organization is right; design unifies all parts.

The experiments with abstraction, for its own virtues and as a means to a deeper mysticism, which began in the mid 1940's, have born rich fruit. The *Prodigal Son* of 1948 (Fig. 25) brings to a focus the long striving for a synthesis of the abstract and the real. Note the simplified mastery of characterization of the "swine," the unusual portrayal of the Son, the subtle textures and spaces. Colors again are fanciful, with softened pinks, purples, and blues ascendant. In all the work of this period, symbols hold their reference to reality and so, unlike much modern symbolism, can be easily read. Fig. 26 of 1952 shows the continuation of the same quest.

"I learned nothing from my schooling," says Russell Cowles, "beyond the merest academic representation. My own development has been slow, and any enlightenment has only come in recent years, along with a certain blessed freedom of spirit, an inner freedom, which seems perhaps the most valuable thing of all."

Inner freedom buttressed as it here is with plastic maturity has gained a distinguished goal.

MAX BECKMANN

The death of Max Beckmann on December 27, 1950, was a heavy loss to the Western art world. It is a loss because Beckmann was an artist-commentator on life who had, and still has, many messages for his fellow men to which they will do extremely well to listen. The artist speaks through his pictures and the occasional words which amplify them, in a sense, for all artists. The messages are addressed to people—all people— not solely to the art world, and if they fail to get through, with our vast means of mass communication immediately available, that is one of the ironic cultural paradoxes of our time. Why indeed should messages like these be limited to books and articles which reach only the intelligent, curious minority?

I must look for wisdom with my eyes. I repeat, with my eyes. For nothing could be more ridiculous or irrelevant than a "philosophical conception" painted purely intellectually without the terrible fury of the senses grasping each visible form of beauty and ugliness. If from those forms which I have found in the visible, literary subjects result—such as portraits, landscapes and recognizable compositions—they have all originated from the senses, in this case from the eyes, and each intellectual subject has been transformed again into form, color and space. . . .

What I want to show in my work is the idea which hides itself behind so-called reality. I am seeking for the bridge which leads from the visible to the invisible, like the famous cabalist who once said, "If you wish to get hold of the invisible you must penetrate as deeply as possible into the visible. . .

One of my problems is to find the Ego, which has only one form and is immortal—to find it in animals and men, in the heaven and in the hell which together form the world in which we live. . . .

Art is creative for the sake of realization, not for amusement; for transfiguration, not for the sake of play. It is the quest of our Ego that drives us along the eternal and never-ending journey we must all make. . . .

In principle any alteration of the subject is allowed which has a sufficiently strong creative power behind it. Whether such alteration causes excitement or boredom in the spectator is for you to decide. . . .

MAX BECKMANN   67

Fig. 27. *The Street,* by MAX BECKMANN, 1913.

If the canvas is filled only with a two-dimensional conception of space, we shall have applied-art or ornament. Certainly this may give us pleasure, though I myself find it boring as it does not give me enough visual sensation. To transform three into two dimensions is for me an experience full of magic in which I glimpse for a moment that fourth dimension which my whole being is seeking. . . .

Color, as the strange and magnificent expression of the inscrutable spectrum of Eternity, is beautiful and important to me as a painter; I use it to enrich the canvas and to probe more deeply into the subject. Color also decided, to a certain extent, my spiritual outlook, but it is subordinated to life and, above all, to the treatment of form. Too much emphasis on color at the expense of form and space would make a double manifestation of itself on the canvas, and this would verge on craft work. Pure color and broken tones must be used together, because they are the complements of each other. . . .

These words, however, are all theories, and words are too insignificant to define the problems of art. My first unformed impression, and what I would like to achieve, I can perhaps only realize when I am impelled as in a vision.

Profound thoughts, these, that are far from insignificant. Primarily they define the purpose of one artist but, allowing for differences of emphasis and personal interpretation of essentials, they can stand as a creed for the International Modern Movement.

As a German artist who won the honor of being branded by Hitler a "degenerate," Beckmann escaped to Holland in 1937 and worked there through the Occupation and until his migration to this country in 1947. The fact that his modernism is international, that it paralleled the developments in Paris, is highly significant and demonstrates the universality of the movement. Unlike Bonnard and his fellow-countryman Kokoschka, both of whom immunized themselves from the revolutionary events happening around them, he, like Kirchner, Nolde, Marc, Schmidt-Rottluff, Lehmbruck, Dix, Hofer, Klee, and Grosz, did learn from, add to, and carry on the great rebirth. We sometimes forget Germany's vast contribution because the focus on Paris has been so widespread and continuous. Beckmann is an important member of the honorable band whose works demand a rectification of that injustice. That we can claim him as a recent citizen is an honor to us.

The Germans, more than the French, indulged the "fury of the senses" as a means to their expressionism. It is characteristic of German art and literature to express their themes in subjective and emotionally profound terms, to search inner lives for inner meanings, to dramatize soul conflicts. Some Germans, unlike the French, forgot formal organization in this search and its appeal to the senses. But not Beckmann. For him "each intellectual subject had to be transformed again into form, color and space." He demanded "visual sensation." Compressing three-dimensional forms from life into the two-dimensional picture plane "is an experience full of magic." This is plastic painting validated. Many artists agree with this preference for the greater profundity of form—but without necessarily relegating flat pattern to the minor role of applied art. The lighter touch, play, and amusement also have their place. The search for the Ego is logical and inevitable; Beckmann acknowledges it openly. As for

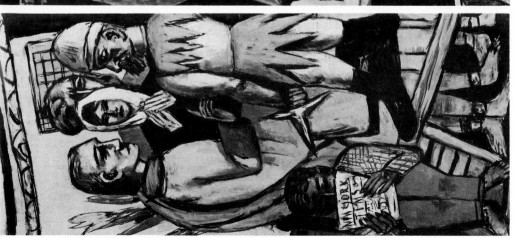

Fig. 28. The Actors, by MAX BECKMANN, 1941–1942.

Fig. 29. *Self-Portrait,*
by MAX BECKMANN, 1950.
One of his last paintings.

the quest for the idea behind reality via the bridge from the visible to the invisible, we can join that search wholeheartedly.

The paintings of this artist amply demonstrate his words. *The Street* of Fig. 27, done in 1913, illustrates his inheritance of the literal impression from the actual scene bequeathed him by nineteenth-century art. In later works, as he gradually overcame this crippling handicap and learned to "find the idea which hides itself behind so-called reality," he increasingly applied the principle that "any alteration of the subject is allowed which has a sufficiently strong creative power behind it."

His characters, whether they perform in the many triptychs of dramatized pageantry or in a solo role, always exist in deep space as they do in life. But he packs them into a condensed section of this space which becomes his picture; here they act their parts lustily with concentrated meanings pervading the concentrated forms. In a triptych such as *The Actors* of Fig. 28, he does this by assembling figures symbolizing the actors on the stage and behind the scenes, as well as orchestra, property-man, and audience, into a compressed picture of events transpiring at a single moment of time.

It is interesting to note that Beckmann achieved this transformation between the years 1913 (Fig. 27) and 1920. This was a dozen or more years after similar developments in Paris, later than the explorings of our Max Weber, and about parallel with the effects on us of the 1913 Armory Show. Dates, however, are relatively unimportant; much more significant is the fact that such a revolution can take place well within a six-year period. Which raises the question: why, some forty years after the Armory Show, are so many epochal cultural discoveries of Beckmann and other pioneers still widely unknown or misunderstood?

The outstanding contributions of Max Beckmann are his search for and finding of reality—the invisible behind the visible—his belief in and disciplined control of the senses, his mastery of designed realism and the plastique of painting, his giving priority to form over color and his deep, far-reaching humanism. In his brief residence among us he greatly enriched American art.

PEPPINO MANGRAVITE

In 1933 Peppino Mangravite was painting masterful realistic portraits. In 1950 and 1951 he has been painting semi-abstractions of saints, demons, virtues, and sins which beset man today as they did in medieval times, with the abstract rendering of the symbols steadily gaining the ascendancy. This swing from the reality of the eye to the reality of the known is a trend of the times, as we have amply seen in these pages, but the trend is prompted, in the case of each genuine artist, by an inner necessity, not by any need for conformity to a style. Leader-artists normally are non-conformists; they dare to be themselves. When, therefore, a number of them move in the same general direction, there must be compelling reasons. The old masters were, in the main, realists. When modern masters add to the old tradition by seeming to abandon realism, reasons become important and must be understood.

> Some of my old academic friends [says Mangravite], tell me, in effect, that I have changed, as if changing were a sin, by turning to subjective painting.
>
> In answer I tell them I have not changed; times have changed, and I have always been contemporaneous with times. When one has attained competence and honors in a certain period in his work, it is the thing in him that is glorified, not himself. The creative individual is a dynamic, imperishable self that grows within a frame of his own design. My belief on the subject of growth is not unlike that of the Roman poet Ovid: "All things are changing; nothing dies. The spirit wanders, comes now here, now there, and occupies whatever frame it pleases. . . . For that which once existed is no more, and that which was not has come to be; and so the whole round of motion is gone through again."

Italian-born Peppino came to New York from his native Italy with his family in 1912. He then, while still in his teens, returned to Europe to continue his academic studies in Italy and France. Back in New York in 1914, he painted by himself for six months, then studied at Cooper Union and in 1917 with Robert Henri at the Art Student's League. His basic training, it thus appears, was academic but tempered with the human insight and fresh viewpoint typical of Henri.

Where and how did this mercurial Italian temperament learn the additions to academic skills which constituted his inheritance from the moderns? I did not ask the question during a recent two-hour renewal of old ties, because I knew the answer from having myself gone through a parallel experience. He learned from many sources, including his own internal ones. To abandon copying of posed models for re-creation, he could have learned from the old masters. Design can be, and was in his case, intuitive as well as conscious. In all of his work since the early 1920's, the two have blended into the integrated whole. Fig. 30 is riotously designed in harmony with its subject, *Ecstasy;* organization in Fig. 31 is classical; all its parts are under full control. Here is an artist who

Fig. 30. *Ecstasy,*
by PEPPINO MANGRAVITE, 1928.

Fig. 31. *Passions and Feverishness,*
by PEPPINO MANGRAVITE, 1943.

Fig. 32. *Mountain Bouquet,*
by PEPPINO MANGRAVITE, 1947.

Fig. 33. *Of Sin and Error,*
by PEPPINO MANGRAVITE, 1950.

Fig. 34. *Succubus,* by PEPPINO MANGRAVITE, 1949.

knows the functional design of the old masters. He has learned much from the more sensory adventurings of the moderns. He should be prepared to integrate the two.

Through the two decades of the 1930's and 1940's Mangravite was painting the drama of life as he saw it, not still-lifes and scenes. His subjects were actors in that drama. They loved, they dreamed, they celebrated and sinned; they lived. In the former decade each work was complete in itself; in the latter, it was a series that emerged—the "Song of the Poet" series and, in the past few years, "Demons and a Secular Saint," a series dealing with man's guilt and fear arising from within himself. Man lives in terror of fears he cannot explain, thinks the artist, and delves into these fears with an Oedipus-like fascination that threatens to consume him. In *Of Sin and Error* (Fig. 33), man is frozen in terror while a huge, evil bird pounces on a defeated angel. In his words:

> I have often been called a poet-painter or a philosopher-painter. It would be more true if it were said I am a sententious painter. I like to paint in sentences full of axioms or maxims. And I endeavor to paint sentences in a striking or memorable style.
>
> In the series known as "The Song of the Poet," which I executed seven years ago, my sententious statements were conveyed objectively; I looked at man's universe and sang about its perennial aspects.
>
> And now I seem to be deeply preoccupied with the universe within man, and I find I can express that best with a pictorial context contemporaneous in style and subjective in direction. I call this latest series "Demons and a Secular Saint" because through these paintings I wish to communicate a sympathetic understanding of man's theistic fears.

These words are self-explanatory and give the reason for the change from the objective to the subjective. The universe within man can hardly be expressed otherwise than by mood and symbol. Meanings may become increasingly obscure as the symbol grows more abstract, but there are compensations for the observer in the ideological challenge and the added sensory pleasure from a more purified design. *Succubus,* of Fig. 34, will illustrate. "The legendary female devil inspires pleasure through the creamy whiteness of her body and the poetic dream she brings to man, while fear and guilt reign in the awesome abstract forms and in violent reds that suggest death." Somewhat terrific symbolism, this. In contrast, the quiet external beauty of Fig. 35 is certainly free of mental strain. But *Succubus,* with its subtle color and delicate traceries plus elusive meaning, is, to this critic, by far the most rewarding. Does it not combine adequately the virtues of the old and modern creeds?

In 1953 the exploration of the mysteries of the "universe within man" was continuing, and significant results were emerging on canvas. *Succubus,* the artist agrees, remains adequately representative of that quest.

ADOLF DEHN

If ever an artist dramatized the life of his time, Adolf Dehn earns that description. And the drama is vivified, as it was with Shakespeare, not only by a keen insight into the individual and group virtues and vices of human nature, but by a never-failing sense of humor and a compensating response to the tragic. When these humanities are balanced by a basic, indigenous concern for organizational controls, as they are in his case, we have the stuff out of which enduring art is made. The Dehn paintings, watercolors, and lithographs, as I see it, will honorably represent the art of our time for many decades to come.

Born in Waterville, Minnesota, in 1895, Dehn progressed through a healthy outdoor and farm life to studying at the Minneapolis Art Institute, then, on a scholarship, to New York's Art Students League and to years abroad.

With the early ambition (so common in youthful breasts) of being a cartoonist, the young artist worked naturally in black and white in drawing and prints. While still studying in Minneapolis, he found the old *Masses* with its drawings by Sloane, Bellows, Henri, and Boardman Robinson; the latter's work and personality as a man influenced him most profoundly. In 1917 he sent a batch of drawings to the *Masses* and one was accepted—a great event. Later, going to New York, he met this group and, in 1921, exhibited his first lithographs in a show invited by Robinson. As a result, Carl Zigrosser invited him to the Weyhe Gallery, where, shortly thereafter, a first drawing was sold, to Arthur B. Davies.

Fig. 35. *Sunday Painters*, ADOLF DEHN, 1945.

Fig. 36. *Jungle in Venezuela*, by ADOLF DEHN, 1946.

Then abroad for two years, home for his first one-man show (at the Weyhe Gallery in 1923), abroad again for three years. The total time in Europe was seven years in the 1920's. Thus, while never losing touch with his native soil, he reaped the cream of a life of civilized leisure in Paris, Vienna, and Berlin.

Drawings and prints were selling—to magazines and collectors—all in black and white. But the law of diminishing returns in print sales had set in and by 1936, after another summer and fall abroad, he was painting watercolors, with the first show thereof in 1938. Since then production has been lusty in both media and, during the past few years, after a three-month sojourn in Haiti, heavy color, in oils and casein, has been discovered and canvases are flowing from his tireless brush with amazing and sustained vitality. "For the first time in my life," says Dehn, "I am really letting myself go. I have always tended to the use of restrained color, then suddenly let go. Now restraints are gone."

There have been two main directions in this artist's work—lyrical, romantic landscapes (of which Fig. 36 is typical), and human figures acting out their life drama. Not all the former, however, have been romantic; some exploit the vastness of western plains or the rugged, interlocking masses of mountain forms; see Fig. 37—a truly great dramatic landscape.

The dramatizations of human life have grown steadily through the years—from the humorous but often hasty take-offs of human foibles of "upper class" gossips or socialites, Negro night clubs, and the like, to the more mature Sunday Painters of Fig. 35, and the recent series on life in Haiti. Here the black bodies of Negro women, balancing huge loaded baskets on their sturdy heads, interlace with each other in patterned gestures that intrigue the seeing eye at the same time they dramatize their folk story. "I like to play with gestures," says Dehn. And the play has been eminently successful in a canvas like Fig. 38, where the gestures become interlocking rhythms of visual sensation. "I am getting a new excitement," he adds, "from experimenting with the semi-abstract, with more design, more interplay. Too much abstract is not for me, but to experiment—that is the excitement of painting."

This series on Haiti, shown at the Associated American Artists Gal-

Fig. 37. *The Garden of the Gods,* by ADOLF DEHN, 1948.

Fig. 38. *The Dark Night,* by ADOLF DEHN, 1951.

leries in New York in November, 1951, represents, I believe, the richest maturity of this artist to date. "Form" here comes nearer to balancing, with its own merits, "content" than it has in any previous works. Colors, spaces, textures, dark-lights, movements—all play together into exquisitely sensitive harmonies; these pictures sing.

I have never asked Dehn where he met and absorbed the modern. No need to. The answer is obvious. Creation was born in him; in art school he rebelled from copying casts. Design has been assimilated gradually from many sources, internal and external, and has been gaining momentum recently. Both, in other words, have "just growed." The modern, in Dehn's case, has proved its validity without undue fanfare.

Asked to contribute a statement to these pages, Dehn promised one by Tuesday. It came as promised. I quote:

> Sunday midnite. I avoided attempting this serious job until tonite. And, as a result, good came of the avoidance for I painted hard and furiously and it seems to me the two paintings started promise to be among my best.
>
> The statement I've been sweating over for the past two hours is like one of my too-ambitious pictures and I must scrap it. No subject should be more interesting than oneself, one's painting and ideas about painting. But this writing should be a masterpiece and when it comes to writing, I'm a primitive. So, I beg you, let's have you do all the writing. And, believe me, I've tried.

All right, Adolf, you go on and paint more pictures like these last ones. And I'll do my best with the writing.

EMIL BISTTRAM

In each of the two major national painting exhibitions of 1951 in New York City, one at the Metropolitan Museum and the other at the Whitney, was included an outstanding work by Emil Bisttram of Taos, New Mexico. Both were semi-abstractions of marine subjects, evidently dear to the heart of their author because, or in spite, of the distance of his exciting, semi-arid home state from the sea. Both are important for two main reasons. They are mature, adult, complex, and highly finished works. And the obvious emotional drive behind their creation—and they

Fig. 39. *Koshares,* by EMIL BISTTRAM, 1933. "New Mexico Indian Dance" series.

Fig. 40. *Bulldogging,* by EMIL BISTTRAM, 1939.

certainly are inspired creations—was tempered by the discipline of a masterly knowledge of design.

Bisttram knows Dynamic Symmetry, probably as thoroughly as any artist living today. He is a former student and disciple of Jay Hambidge, the discoverer and developer thereof for art purposes. He knows all about its root rectangles and their complex diagonals and whirling squares. But he uses these controls of line and shape freely, not meticulously. He combines root shapes when, where, and how he wishes. Hambidge, before he died, endorsed this free method as being the only way an artist could use the mathematical controls without being frustrated. Bisttram has carried on where Hambidge stopped. But let him explain his creed:

I believe with Aristotle [says Mr. Bisttram], that we must not imitate Nature, we must follow her in her laws and principles; only by so doing may we hope to create works comparable to hers.

I believe all truly creative expressions are the result of inner and outer experiences; that is why I must paint, an irresistible force drives me to be constantly working on problems in space, in color, and in design in conjunction with ideas that crowd for expression.

I believe that all great works of art contain the universals that attest to their greatness. It is these universals that I seek to incorporate in my own works.

I believe that Dynamic Symmetry is a Law of Space division of immeasurable use in the solution of space problems. I do not consider it a formula that ties me down to specific limitations, i.e., root rectangles; nor do I consider it mechanical or inhibiting. I find it releases the imaginative powers, liberating the creative forces toward a final unquestionable order. It is possible to arrive at similar space-problem solutions thru taste and/or intuition but these are accidental in most instances and, if constant and controlled, they become an attribute of genius.

Dynamic Symmetery should be studied by the beginner as well as the professional. But it must be considered as an instrument in relation to space problems to be used as a tool and not as the Ultimate or the Absolute. It is important to study the root rectangles in order to understand the underlying principles and the basic philosophy. Once these are understood the artist works freely, released from the need to adhere to exact root shapes. My own method at this period of my career, and one that I have achieved thru the years, is to make many sketches and drawings freely as ideas occupy my thinking; the next step toward a final painting is concern

Fig. 41. *Marine Patterns,* by EMIL BISTTRAM, 1950.

Fig. 42. *The Fleet,* by EMIL BISTTRAM, 1950.

with the space analysis and reorganization of my freely conceived composition.

In art teaching, I am convinced that the art student must master certain fundamental principles of color and design, of technics, research, and experimentation, learning the importance of discipline and control of his mediums of expression in the process. Free creative expression is the next and logical step, but it must go hand in hand with discipline.

I believe that in order to be an artist one must remain the student, must never think in terms of "arriving," of "picture-making." The search for knowledge, not only of one's craft but of one's self and of the world around, is necessary to his growth and to the maturity of his art.

I believe the artist must be a philosopher, a psychologist, a student thru his entire life; only then can his creative imagination bring forth works that will inspire others and stimulate his own aspirations to greater achievement.

Yes, I always use Dynamic Symmetry in everything I do, though I think it is pretty well hidden in most cases.

The paintings shown herewith illustrate this creed. The *Indian Dance* merges symbols and design on equal terms. *Bulldogging,* of Fig. 40, is a masterpiece of abstract design.

Figs. 41 and 42 are the two paintings referred to above as having been exhibited in 1951. Both illustrate the Bisttram philosophy. I have a transparent paper diagram to lay over Fig. 41, which shows the diagonals of two root 5 rectangles and how these marine elements in their space-design are built in relation thereto. The resulting precision, comparable to the precision of musical chords, gives, I believe (and I also have studied and used Dynamic Symmetry), a design refinement obtainable in no other way. Are refinement, precision, finesse in the arts, when motivated by the fire of spirit, an asset? Or can they be a liability? If we grant their validity in music and poetry it seems logical to do the same with the interplay of lines, spaces, and colors in visual art. I grant such validity and have long urged that we need more of it in the arts of painting, sculpture, and the print. And, I thoroughly believe we would have that more, if the values involved were as widely comprehended in the visual, as in other, fields.

Both of these paintings stood out as unique in the two large exhibits but were granted no awards or special attention. Colors were restrained in each; grays, grayed blues, and off-whites, as I remember, were dominant. But more assertive than the color was the power of the form and the symbol in Fig. 41, and the complex relationships of the spaces in Fig. 42. Color enriched these other qualities with quiet authority and sensation, rather than shouting its own merits as supreme—as so often happens. Had this critic been on either award jury, he would have voted for high honors to each work.

The fact that finesse in visual art is sadly underrated today because of lack of awareness makes it exceedingly important to give all possible prominence and honors to works of refined maturity such as these by Bisttram. They win attention on merit. In honoring them we likewise honor ourselves.

KUNIYOSHI

In early 1948 the Whitney Museum in New York gave Yasuo Kuniyoshi a retrospective exhibition. It was a comprehensive showing covering his entire span as artist. Like all retrospectives, it was important in that it gave that wider perspective so necessary for a just appraisal of a man's total production, and because it revealed trends, both of the artist and his time, with profound implications. Both the paintings and these implications deserve and in fact demand careful consideration.

The personal story of Kuniyoshi and his development as artist was admirably told by Lloyd Goodrich in the catalogue of the exhibit and was thoroughly documented with data and photographs. But the implications I refer to were not touched on; the spectator was left to draw his own conclusions.

The paintings showed three definite phases or periods. The earliest, from 1922 to 1928, was "based on dreams," as the artist put it, "without being modified by what I learned in this country during the first ten years." The work of this phase is authentic because honestly based on his oriental influences, which were strong enough to resist the devitalizing impact of our academic training, to which he was exposed soon after his arrival from Japan. These paintings tie to primitive art because their subjects were treated more as universal symbols—of cows, children,

Fig. 43. *Island of Happiness,*
by YASUO KUNIYOSHI, 1924.

Fig. 44. *The Mirror,*
by YASUO KUNIYOSHI, 1933.

women, plants than as specific individual records. Also because they were liberated from the portrayal of actual scenes to dramatized creations, and because design, often held to the simple two-dimensional picture plane, was in full control. This control was maintained as subjects developed greater volume, both as forms and in their placing, yet kept their plastic integrity. These works, therefore, belong to the vigorous early manifestations of the Grand Tradition. Fig. 43 perfectly illustrates these values.

Kuniyoshi's second period, dating roughly from his return from Paris, in 1929, to 1938, shows a shift of emphasis to reality; the individual woman (rather than all women), and groups of objects on sofas and tables, became the dominant themes. Here the artist was confronted with the tougher problems of expressing and designing real subjects—problems which he solved admirably in many notable works, of which *The Mirror* of 1933 (Fig. 44) is typical of the best. These are mature creations. They portray specific character and build functional design into that character; the organization is absorbed but is still in control for those to see who will.

It is amusing, and perhaps instructive, to compare this change from the universal to the particular, from the idea to the fact, in two such canvases of womanhood as *Island of Happiness* and *The Mirror*. The former is the pictured concept of the female of the species. The latter is one specific seductive female with whom, in the here and now, a date might be made for spooning in the park. "During this period," said the artist, "I was attracted to the visual object because of its shape, color, design, or even associative quality. That was *one* of the motivating factors in painting it, but gradually the inner meaning became more important and the thoughts it evoked became my object in painting. Pigmentation and handling of the medium were other factors I was very much aware of and interested in developing."

In so far as this change was to the concrete, particular subject and related technical problems, it paralleled the direction of art in Europe from the early to the late Renaissance—which we now call a decline, in spite of vast technical enhancements. In general this growth, or decline, can

Fig. 45. *Room 110*, by YASUO KUNIYOSHI, 1944.
Awarded First Prize, "Painting in the United States,"
1944, Carnegie Institute.

be summarized as an increasing absorption in subject and a corresponding relegation of design to its functional aspect of clarifying meaning rather than its sensory one of enjoyment.

Kuniyoshi explained this second period by saying he "forgot the idea." He was forcing himself to understand reality, trying to combine it with imagination and experience of life. Gradually he realized he was going too far, that this goal was wrong for him. He must combine thought (the idea) with reality. He must use the object to start, then discard it sufficiently to paint the superimposed idea.

The third period, from 1939 to the Whitney Retrospective Exhibition in 1948, was a battleground between these opposed ideologies—reporting the facts of life as seen or imagined in the concrete subject, or painting the "idea" as it relates to ever-changing life experiences. The works of this era are strewn with battle scars. There are banners of victory in many brilliant passages; there is the debris of organizational defeat in increasing quantity and at an accelerating pace. Conflicts were too profound to be adequately dispelled. In 1947 and 1948 confusion seemed to be the net by-product of conflict.

At the time of the Retrospective, this confusion in the then recent works appeared to mark the down-curve of a parabolic movement which had risen quickly in the early period, held a high level for a long time, and was then descending toward vacuity and, in some places, near-chaos. Meaning, for this critic, was obscured by this preponderant plastic melée. In an *Art Digest* review I called these conflict-scarred paintings a record of the Battle of Kuniyoshi. *Revelation* of Fig. 46 illustrates this confusion.

Since the battle seemed to be continuing after 1948, a long projected talk with the artist was finally arranged (in December, 1950), during which I asked him to explain his recent trend. This he did willingly, effectively, and with ample documentation. After a two hour session in his Fourteenth-street studio, I understood much better the Kuniyoshi goal and the change to different and compensating values.

One point which emerged from the explanation was that this artist was not asleep at the switch of success and fame. He was awake. He was healthily alive. He was not drifting; he had reasons. He was seething inside with the issues of his never-ending quest for his own right way. It was a battle. Life is change. And he quoted the Japanese Zen Principle as his own philosophy:

> Walk on! For we can only understand life by keeping pace with it, by a complete affirmation and acceptance of its magic-like transformations and unending changes. By this acceptance, the Zen disciple is filled with a great sense of wonder, for everything is perpetually becoming new. The beginning of the universe is now, for all things are at this moment being created, and the end of the universe is now, for all things are at this moment passing away.
>
> ——From *The Spirit of Zen,* by ALAN W. WATTS

Man grows with time [said Kuniyoshi] and is concerned with time. His art is an expression of his experience of life. Even fantasy and mysticism derive

Fig. 46. *Revelation,*
by YASUO KUNIYOSHI, 1948.

Fig. 47. *Forbidden Fruit,* by YASUO KUNIYOSHI, 1950.

from life. How skillfully art is manifested is only a small portion of its importance.

Statement is created from contact with reality. If we face our experiences honestly and do not run for cover, if we do not defile our innermost convictions, we help to develop principles by so doing. That to me is essential in any creative expression. Without it, you may achieve timeliness, clarity, structural perfection, and so forth, but such remain a hollow intellectualization of the real.

He who thinks he has finally found himself is a fool. Creation revolves with circumstance and time. For as time goes on we grow; from one day to another there is change. If you try to grasp those things you think are your own and attempt to capture them forever, it is impossible. One has to face reality and move on. I don't mean to join the bandwagon or swim with the current. Once you arrive at a formula it is stagnation. Then again, you cannot tie a branch to a tree and expect it to adapt itself. There has to be a root from which it can spring and some ground from which it can be nourished.

Kuniyoshi was living up to this his philosophy of change and growth in his later works. The obvious, tangible realities of subject are gone, but not a profound subject motivation. His new subjects, far more intangible in their reaching for spirit rather than matter, root deeply in his belief in the humanities, in his feeling for human tragedy and awareness of the comedy that masks tragedy. He had not changed basic principles, he said; he still believed in the universal statement and the organized structure of design. But his design had become more compact and subtle, almost like a bas-relief. Where he formerly used fourteen colors, he now used fifty. Reds predominate in many paintings but so complex and varied are the multitudinous red notes, that the total chord eludes all but the keenest eye. It is these subtle variations that pack close together the receding planes.

The year 1947 marked the early stage of the break with obvious, and search for the deeper, realities by means of intangibles. In *Revelation* of Fig. 46, the tragedy of humanity is implied by the motifs of the dummy with a mask, the atmosphere of make-believe, the hints of the tragic beginnings of fabricated man, the confused anatomical chart, the general feeling of destruction or near-chaos.

Fig. 47, a repeat of an earlier theme, returns to a more subtle, both in color and other means, expression of tangibles.

Kuniyoshi was "walking on."

At the International Biennale Exhibition at Venice, Italy in the summer of 1952, Kuniyoshi was one of four American artists chosen by a committee of leading museum curators and art historians to represent the United States. This was a deserved honor. The other artists were Calder, Davis, and Hopper.

The death of Kuniyoshi in May of 1953 is a severe loss to American art. Throughout a long and difficult career he was true to his convictions and achieved notably within them.

ABRAHAM RATTNER

Abraham Rattner belongs in the advance guard of modern art. He has won that position, after having overcome all the proverbial obstacles, on the merits of a profound philosophy of life and art, on a terrific drive to dramatize the issues his brush discusses, and because he has had the strength to keep under adequate control all the forces that drive has unleashed.

Born in Poughkeepsie, N.Y., in 1895, Rattner survived a conventional art training, always under the financial handicap of having to combine study with the odd jobs that earned a living. "These jobs were numerous and widely varied," he says, "and the struggle I made to keep going I still think of as a poor boy's advantage in life. An education has to be paid for in money, in time or out of one's hide. My art education was paid for in all three. . . . I was interested in creative work ever since I can remember, and I decided to make it a career when I was old enough to think about such things. I never really thought of it as a career, however; I thought of it as something I had to do."

After the first World War, in which he was a G.I., the artist lived and worked in France—to get his bearings in relation to our parent culture —until forced back home by the rumblings of the Hitlerian tragedy. He then roamed this country to get his bearings in relation to it and its different philosophy. Where the pioneers, said Rattner,

Fig. 48. *Still Life with Mirror,* by **ABRAHAM RATTNER**, 1943.

had to meet violence with violence, crudeness with crudeness, savagery with a new courage and primitive cunning. Culture was a handicap rather than a help. Therefore, for a long period in our history, men had to be men first. Later they were ready again to become gentlemen.

I was impressed by the homogeneity of American society. The insistent demarcations of individualism of the French were not apparent here except in a few localities forced by the resistance of natural barriers to standardization. The oneness of purposes, the hopes and beliefs, the conformity of various elements to a pattern of similarity, impressed me. Esthetic and intellectual divergencies were not taken easily. However, there was less similarity of aspiration represented in the art produced all over the country.

. . . We haven't yet reached the imperative need to love art. Yet art is created out of love. Art creation is a manifestation of the mind, heart and spirit and cannot develop out of a tendency to obliterate the variations of individual expression. . . . Our capacity to invest all our hopes in science blinds us to the needs of a simple human being who has but a few years in which to live. Then he dies. What did he have during those few years that gave him some real joy of living? Some token of consciousness that he was a human being and not a guinea pig for this machine world? With all our efficiency at machine-pulsed living, are we ourselves becoming more like machines, enslaved by the machine instead of making it our slave?

. . . I believe a new era is already here, that an awakening has already taken place, that a new age will be marked by the imposition of the spirit on the materialism of tomorrow. . . . The new meanings for which the United States as a people is searching are also reflected in art; a struggle vibrates in it—not the "social-conscious" struggle, but that more profound and significant one that belongs to the *plastic* nature of painting itself. It is seeking that form in which it may most expressively organize the time-space-feeling elements.

When the artist finds himself in the arena—the spectator as well as the gladiator—before a frightening spectacle, at once terrifying and magnificent, how can he help the manifestation of his terror, wonder, anguish, stupefaction and suffering? And now these interpenetrate, one with another. It is then that the great impact must be transposed into a created vision—ennobled, solemnized, ordered, and impregnated by the qualities of his sensibilities into color related to color, to light, to line, and all of it directed towards some majestic form, a symphonic structure, the metaphoric transfiguration of it all.

Such is the profound philosophy of Abraham Rattner as man and artist, ably revealed even by these extracts from more complete and documented statements. Little need be added except to say that the artist amply implements the philosophy in his work. The terror, wonder, anguish, the magnificence, are all there and all are ennobled by symphonic structure. The religious subjects represent man, not the church; they are the story of the suffering of man. He dares to take liberties with the religious ideals—to introduce into them his own concepts. His order, form, design emanates from the emotional drive inherent in the concepts. "The design," he says, "is an integral part of the expression, having the same relation thereto as a bridge crossing a river." It ties together, unifies all elements. The plastic quality is the sum-total of feeling made into an

Fig. 49. *Fisherman,*
by ABRAHAM RATTNER, 1943.

Fig. 50. *Farm Composition #1,*
by ABRAHAM RATTNER, 1950.

objective thing—the painting. Subject is not dominant; it is this totality that dominates all. Color is the life-blood of his painting. On it he depends mainly for the drama. He exploits color—to get the luminous quality in the color itself, its fire, its glow. He deliberately violates the tradition of good taste with the violence of his color in order to express the fullest possible intensity of his emotional reaction to subject, or the ideal or purpose. It is the integration of these deep purposes that places Rattner in the forefront of the art of our day.

Fig. 48 is more than a "still life." It is a "seeking for that form which may most expressively organize the time-space-feeling elements." "Here I was more concerned with the purely aesthetic," says the artist. About the *Fisherman* of Fig. 49, he said, "I painted this after a visit to Martha's Vinyard, but it is also a fisherman of Galilee, caught in the struggle of the load he carries, which itself also suggests wings and redemption through suffering. The colors are blues, greens, and whites." *Farm Composition #1* of Fig. 50 is back again to aesthetics and the symbol and "the plastic nature of painting itself." Rattner achieves his philosophic and plastic goals.

JULIO DE DIEGO

To put it mildly, Julio de Diego is also a hard man to write about. Perhaps this is because he is a "genial, fierce-looking Spaniard" with a fiery Latin temperament which compels an insatiable versatility in his reactions to life and in the art growing out of them. It is not mercurial, this versatility; each phase of it develops over a period of several years. It is epochal and inevitable like the events, so many of them tragic, which succeed each other on the international stage with the regularity of acts in a play. He responds to these acts—the horrors of war, the futilities and defeats of the peace, the mastery of the atom, the neo-atomic war, man versus the machine—they enter into him; they boil and seethe and emerge in the art of color on canvas, unforgettable creations.

When I first knew de Diego in Chicago—it was some years before 1941 —he was painting realism, often with an ironic twist. There was the imaginary war scene, for instance, where one of the opposing armies had posed a nude woman in front of its lines, and was taking advantage of the resulting and effective distraction by sweeping around the flanks to victory. Fig. 51, with its solid forms and expression of a mental dilemma, is typical of this stage. Note the use and control of form symbols in deep space—the most complex of design problems, here effectively solved.

Then in 1941, in Mexico, he suddenly discarded realism. "I was painting with my hands," he said, "not my heart. I wanted to paint with my heart. I was fed up with content and no feeling. So I stopped."

The war then absorbed him. He felt the war deeply. In his own words:

Goya painted the war he saw and said, *"Lo he visto."* I didn't see the horrors of World War II, except through the news in the papers, the communiques and the movies. Goya called his creations *"Desastres de la Guerra."* I called mine *"Desastres del Alma* (soul)." I worked in the solitude of my studio thinking of man converted into a machine to destroy, and, through camouflage, this machine of destruction was more and more identified with nature. The more man looked like nature, the better possibilities he had to kill.

It was in 1943 and 1944 that the brutalities of war were writing their messages into his sensitized pictures. Fig. 52 is an early example of this series on war.

In 1944 and 1945 it was the machinations of reconstruction that absorbed him:

The machine became humanized with remarkable precision—palpitating, breathing, moving rhythmically to begin the reconstruction of that which man had destroyed. Behind and in front of this machinery in the elegant rooms of the chanceries all over the world, the planners of the blue-prints of the future worked feverishly. What were they planning?

And as feverishly, elusive Greek temples were born, in front of nebulous cities, with red, green, and black machines weaving, with wires and unfunctional wheels, strange instruments with teeth in them; these loomed large in the foreground of the pictures. In one, the blue-print was the central theme with hands reaching over it as they emerged from gold-embroidered red gowns of state; here the ruined temple and the machines were far in the distance. Symbolism rampant. Were these sermons in paint? No, I think not. The artist was not preaching at man in order to reform him. He was writing essays in designed color and form

ig. 51. *The Perplexity of What to Do,*
by JULIO DE DIEGO, c. 1930.

Fig. 52. *What Are They Going to Do Next?,*
by JULIO DE DIEGO, 1943.
"Disasters of the Soul" series.

to reveal to man his own actions. He was interpreting the events of his time so that all who looked might see, exactly as did certain artists at Altamira, Spain, 20,000 years ago. And exactly as did before him the masters of the earlier European Renaissance. He was but carrying on.

Ruminating on these portentous events from the jungle-depths of his New York studio, the philosophical mind of de Diego could hardly help but see man and his actions in relation to animals and their actions.

> While man was trying to look like nature, and machinery like living creatures, to destroy each other, I thought of the eternal fight for survival in the animal kingdom—a fight to survive, a killing to satisfy the categoric imperative of existence. Animals, birds, insects kill each other when they are hungry. Somehow, I thought, there is a certain nobility in this attitude.

These reflections poured onto canvas in copious quantity during the years 1945 and 1946. *Unexpected Encounter*, the *Brave Lion*, *Guilty Cats*, and *Flying Feathers* were some of the titles explaining these deadly combats. One called *Forced Against Violent Attack* showed fleets of plane-like insects zooming against each other in battle formation, with fiery, explosive bursts (borrowed from man; insects and animals can kill more economically without fire) marking their collisions. And the ground was evenly covered with the dead, surrounding a rock-like head of man surmounting a low knoll. The moral was clear in these paintings. But, as works of art, they went thin and almost two-dimensional; to this critic they seemed a marked let-down from what had gone before.

Next in this dynamic chronology came a series of paintings, in 1946 and 1947, that certainly are among the most original, let me call them pungent, pictorial creations of our time. In them at last we have a long overdue exploitation of a theme that has pleaded for the attention of artists ever since man took to the air in planes—the panorama of designed colors, shapes, and textures and vast spaces which the good earth becomes to the eye of the mile-high traveler. Every layman air tourist must have noted and marveled in some degree at the incredible richness of the complex pattern—of straight roads versus the massed and changing curves of contour plowing, the meandering single curves of brooks and rivers, the angular groups of buildings, the soft texture of tree masses, the colors that change with each hour, week, and month, the broken, roundish shapes that are lakes. Nature spreads this marvel below us—this "bird's-eye view"—in her master-design as ready-made material for her rival, the man-designer. But he has been unbelievedly slow in accepting the challenge of bending this wealth of material to his will and aesthetic needs.

So, along comes Julio de Diego. He flies to Mexico, back and forth. He responds electrically to these stimuli. He makes his many notes. He recreates nature's designs into the terms of his picture plane. Titles are *Altitude 1000, Altitude 2000, Altitude 8000, Altitude 9000.* As plastic designs, as our familiar earth, seen and interpreted from a new dimension, as original works of art, these paintings are unique and highly significant. They give forth waves of keen, participating enjoyment as the observer allows himself to enter into their rhythmic vibrations. This is abstract art, yes, but nature is the dynamo generating its power. Man the artist is the receiver of nature's power, who transforms it into "the realism of painting" and preserves it for all to see and use. These creations, by the way, are realism as well as abstract design; with this kind of source material the two can be combined. Fig. 53, *Altitude 9000,* is one of the best of this panoramic series.

In 1947 de Diego's friend and dealer, Nierendorf, died and he stopped painting. Then came the next stage—the Atom.

> While I was painting the earth, scientists were working secretly in the development of formidable powers taken from the mysterious depths of the earth—powers to destroy and make useless this same earth.
>
> I was painting, and then—THE EXPLOSION. And another. And another. And we entered the Atomic Age and from then the Neo-Atomic War begins.
>
> I read the descriptions of the power and its results. Explosions fell and man kept on fighting. And when man discovered he could fight without flesh, a new army of bone-structured soldiers was born; new heroes were born; and the old legends were reenacted, by these armies, of this our remarkable Neo-Atomic War.

And so, in 1948 and 1949, the artist painted the Neo-Atomic War, with men without flesh and bone-structured soldiers as the heroes. Fig.

54 is the fantastic interpretation of this weighty theme. Perhaps it is well to let fantasy and irony appear to lighten the devastating impact of that theme. By inverse action they may in fact increase its weight.

In 1950 it was from New Mexico and the life of the Mexican-Americans that this alert artist extracted more and different source material. In the art, it was a return to reality to which he was driven—to the life of people and the symbolic expression thereof. Again he was moved by the drama in that life but this time it was the drama of individual humans rather than epochal man. How did these transplanted Mexicans with their inherited Spanish culture live?

Then, in 1951, it was the realities of Gloucester—its fishing boats and store windows—that attracted his brush. Not one particular boat, but all the fishing fleet of that busy port. Not the single window for its specific reflection of American life, but the one transmuting the cheap trash of all into a creation of extraordinary beauty. In 1952 it was a trip to Spain, his homeland, to see family and relatives that stirred the depths again and found expression in a "Classical" series, of which Fig. 55 is typical.

Any attempt to appraise the de Diego opus as a whole must take into account its diverse motivations, always strained through a philosophical mind, and note how these have been built into the universals. Design? Yes, all pervading. Color has always been orchestrated—with an almost brutal simplicity in the work prior to 1942, as shown in the series of historical-medical subjects done for Abbott Laboratories, with gaining subtlety and responsiveness to subject in the periods above outlined. Color notes played into chords—with dramatic contrasts of slightly softened primaries pulling main objects forward, against grayed neutrals—invariably achieved sensitive harmonies. These were scattered and thin at times, especially in the "Animal Conflict" series, where space and form organization tended to evaporate. But the rounded sensitivity was back in the saddle again in the "Altitude" series and powerful contrasts vitalized the Atom War in its deadly implications. Mainly this artist's controls have been authentic because they are rooted in deep emotion.

Julio de Diego, like many other artists of the ages, is aware of the events

Fig. 53. *Altitude 9000,*
by JULIO DE DIEGO, 1945.
"Altitude" series.

Fig. 54. *Birth of the Atom Form,*
by JULIO DE DIEGO, 1948.
"Atomic" series.

Fig. 55. *Heroic Figures,*
by JULIO DE DIEGO, 1952.

of his day and, with sufficient consistency, has expressed his reactions thereto in tensely dramatic pictorial form.

SAUL BAIZERMAN

Saul Baizerman has worked out for himself a philosophy of the art of sculpture so refined, so sensitive in its felt purposes, and so adequately realized in his serenely moving works that it seems important to write that philosophy into the record, with ample illustrations. That delicate task I shall now attempt, by direct quotations combined with a paraphrasing of a long and serious conversation.

A sculptor is born; [says Baizerman], he only has to discover and learn his language. He must discover for himself the form that will express his own sensations of life; he cannot express such sensations in another man's rhythm. In observing life we see before us the actual—the actual event, or the actual form of, let us say, moving bodies. The sculptor's task is not to capture the actual, as if he were taking a cast of a body in an action pose—this would be static form—but to create an illusion, an illusion of mood, movement, life.

One's work must be basically sculpture, not a fact of life; metal or stone cannot breathe or walk. But they can be made to give an illusion, as though they were breathing, walking or even thinking. That is the problem that has concerned me during the past two decades.

"How can this be done?" you ask.

By rearranging actuality in a certain manner, by combining the parts in a certain kind of rhythm that gives the illusion of speed, slowness, force, or pain. Take movement, for instance, as in the case of a dynamo. Its whirring form moves so fast it cannot be seen. It appears static. But it is not static; it is alive with movement. The analogy, in a sense, carries over to the new sculpture. In expressing the dynamo's life we try to give the illusion of the vibratory that appears static.

A number of times during our talk, Mr. Baizerman would catch me up on my use of the word "design." I used it to cover all the organizations of parts of which he frequently spoke. He objected. "Organization," he would say, "is the bigger word. My object has long been to eliminate design of form because such design has been on the borderline of becom-

Fig. 56. *Serenity,*
by SAUL BAIZERMAN, 1937.

Fig. 57. *Exuberance,*
by SAUL BAIZERMAN, 1938.

ing static. I have wanted to eliminate the stops or edges of the form and suggest continuing motion, because the borderline was the element that registered the stops and thereby created the static state. Design is formalization of form."

His meaning is clear. He is trying in his work to avoid the static, to put the life of the illusion of movement into his forms. And one of his means is the blurring of edges to bespeak moving forms. This goal, it seems, this artist has achieved. There are other necessary values, of course, but the illusion of vibratory movement takes priority with him.

The two works here shown illustrate this vital point. They have the illusion of the movements of life. Actuality is reorganized. The parts are combined in a certain kind of rhythm. The elimination of the stops of the borderline is achieved. "This new principle of sculpture," said the artist, "opens a road of many variations for other sculptors to discover."

In Fig. 56, the quiet body movements of *Serenity* are powerfully realized. And in Fig. 57, a rhythmic interweaving of body forms is beaten out of, or into, the copper sheet with a subtle expressiveness and organizational flow which makes this work outstanding in the history of sculptural art. There is a double achievement here, of distinction on both counts. Actuality is rearranged in each body by "combining the parts in a certain kind of rhythm" and the interweaving of the group of forms is masterfully realized with high aesthetic rewards.

Baizerman has been absorbed by the field of sculpture since the age of thirteen in his native Russia. Coming here as a young man, he studied at the National Academy and Beaux Arts schools from 1911 to 1920. This was academic training which by some miracle failed to engulf him with its literal actuality. He found his own creed by the early 1920's and has been true to it ever since as he hammered his ideals into copper sheets and solid bronze. His works, the offspring of these thirty years, are unique, and imbued with highly sensitized power grown out of deep convictions.

SAMUEL ADLER

The Samuel Adler story reads like one which just doesn't happen except in fiction, and it would not happen there either for the simple reason that no popular novelist would pick this type of artist as leading man in a success drama. Possibly some unpopular author might understand these Adlerian events and dramatize them. Yes, this might occur, come the cultural millenium, when the public and some writing intellectuals learn what happens in the mind and heart of an artist who feels and thinks out his own trail through our cultural jungle.

The story is simple enough. An artist works alone for thirty years, has his first one-man show in New York City in the hectic year 1950. At this exhibit the crowd is so great on opening night that there is a line out onto the sidewalk; all paintings are sold and the dealer beseiges him for more canvases for weeks thereafter. A typical success story. Only it isn't typical; that's the point. The man isn't typical, nor are his pictures. Why then did it take thirty years to arrive at the formula for the paintings? And why did many people buy them?

It was not fame which, when sufficiently cumulative, will sell anything. Adler was not famous. His story was known only to the relative few. It was not the long, solitary research; such is not necessarily interest-compelling. It must then have been the quality of the work. But the paintings are semi-abstract and meanings are often obscure—the very type that is not understood.

> During those thirty years [says Adler] I was beating my brains out trying to consummate the marriage of the forces which contribute to the realization of form, the art, the wholeness of the whole. What we are looking for is cosmic order. It is elusive. But when one gains order, one knows peace. In spite of the dynamic virility of pictures, one is always at peace—when he finds the dynamic integration. For me the dynamic quality lies in structure, including the dynamics of color. Structure is another kind of power. But the statement must grow out of feeling; it is more important than anything. I paint, not what I see, but what I feel; not what I think, but rather what I am, since art, as I reason it, is the articulation of man's intellectual, spiritual, emotional and esthetic impulses in relation to life as experience. It is not for art to hold a mirror up to nature—to freeze a moment out of time —but rather to capture an impulse and sustain it, to capture the moment and protract it into all eternity.

When Adler says that for him the dynamic quality in painting lies in structure, including therein the dynamics of color, he is casting another

Fig. 58. *The Offering,* by SAMUEL ADLER, 1949.

vote for the basic modern creed. Adler's knowing is tempered with passion. Line to him is a favorite means to structure. "I do not use line as
decoration," he says, "nor as a mere delineation of space; I use it as an
integral part of the formal realization itself. I can say anything with a
line; it can be anything—from a breath to a thunderbolt." Sometimes
his line functions on its own and becomes caligraphy. Sometimes, as in
Fig. 58, it merges with all other elements. Always, along with them, it
expresses mood—super-sensitive mood. It is this sensitivity, doubtless,
which authenticates, for the artist, repeats of similar figures in similar
situations; like a great composer, he would play endless variations on a
single or related theme.

108   SAMUEL ADLER

In Fig. 58 the mood seems religious, consecrated. The smooth-flowing rhythms merge with, support, and control that mood. This painting shows what this artist means by dynamic integration." He has articulated man's intellectual, spiritual, emotional, and aesthetic impulses in relation to life as experience.

RICO LEBRUN

Rico Lebrun is an apprentice to the future, [wrote Donald Bear in 1942] inasmuch as he has so thoroughly examined the past and made of this experience a release for fresh creative energy. . . . One feels, when reviewing page after page of his drawings of clowns, street musicians and beggars, fleeing into mysterious, unexploited space that here is an artist who has the power to express definitely, graphically and at the same time abstractly, in a new idiom, these great, constant emotions of our time—fear and pain. . . . His line sings, turns, swells, rises and falls, breaks into garlands of accentuation and, withall, divulges character with startling mobility.

Summing up his own work in that same year, Lebrun had this to say:

I did not descend *en touriste* among the people I depict. I was born among them and am of them still. Wherever I go their friendship always follows me.

On the sidewalks of a Mediterranean town I have seen a woman with child. She seemed the calm Venus of Athens, raked by hunger and love, and her flesh was of dense and eroded substance, of a color that seemed to permeate to the very bone. And I have felt that if I, as a painter, could some day master this, everything else belonging to my feeling of nature and art would follow. The cloud would be obedient and repeat the fierce mass of her tangled hair. The bay and the rock would be the answer to her pelvis and flank. If this organic law were followed, there would not be possible any theatricism, or mirage or collage, but the plastic drama moving and concluding in perfectly adequate space.

This is the plastic writing I would like to learn. With a slowness that I am not too anxious to overcome, I have occupied myself with this kind of task, searching obstinately into a few gestures, hoping to make them fewer and simpler as I learn. They are the gestures of the ritual of today—running, watching the sky for death—and of tomorrow—dances, feasts and droll games.

Having always wanted to say those things, I could not be too crushed by the advent of Vorticism and what followed. I would lament a life spent in ripping apart for analysis that great organ of painting upon which I can play only two or three chords at most. Back from Montparnasse, I willingly carried in my pocket the little parcels of food that I had hoped would benefit my old creed with fresh stimulation. But when I opened them in the Chapel of Masaccio they withered like toys in a furnace.

I have no discoveries. I only know this—that I am a corner of the plastic world where humans can retain dignity and *vis comica,* and where they do not lose all identity and significance at the service of the monster unity of design. A newborn baby is a unit of design, but nature does not bash it into a pill to facilitate birth. Rather the mother shall die.

I have learned what I could from Masaccio, Raphael, Daumier, Picasso and many others. It is not necessary for me to tell. The debts are evident. They too in their greatness had debts to the great. But the heart will ultimately establish the difference between the museum pantomime and the meaningful individual adventure. It is my right to hope that my heart will be equal to this task of love.

These were the world-searching and self-searching words of Rico Lebrun in 1942. In 1949, for these pages, he supplemented them thus:

As you know, I was self-trained in the "classical tradition," with all its connotations of taken-for-granted majesty and also its useful knowledge. From that, I went through a period which has, much against my will, allied me to the so-called "Neo-Romantic Movement"; namely, when I started depicting a more agitated, bewildered and altered human mold—or tried to. The fact that people in rags and bandages—blown into frantic farewells by precision bombing—should appear as "romantic" props to the gentry, was not insignificant in itself. I imagine they recalled the Pirates of Bagdad and the mob scenes of Hal Roach Studios to the citizens of the Bronx and Sunset Drive. To me they were real people of my own land; there was nothing "neo" about their awful role of helplessness; contrariwise, something discouragingly ancient.

Well, that period also went. It called, in its eagerness to retell a story true to me, for immediate graphic recording, and I began to feel that the care of forms was suffering a loss. So I turned to abstraction, was commiserated and bemoaned for being dead or lost to the world of "beautiful drawing and painting," had a twilight full of fighting propositions and solved some of them, and am now at work on a cycle of the Passion of Christ.

To accept the premise of a worn-out, or at least age-old, theme is of paramount importance to me; for there is then no compromise on the validity of the first step. Too many of us, fugitives from the obvious and tangible, were writing the obscure diary of a twisted nerve center or a dislike for fresh air, and creating recondite chirrupings, and expecting miracles of recognition from the indifferent, illiterate, but not abject, layman. The unusual became a very tired item. To the essentially trite motto of Lautremont: that something was as beautiful as the meeting of the umbrella and the sewing machine on an operating table, today we answer that the expected surgical instruments on such a table are even more potent, as an image, and more beautiful.

The reason for my being so completely absorbed by this theme of the Golgotha, could, by an outsider, easily be mistaken for a devotional return, or a refuge into Biblical Wisdom. Yet nothing could be further from my mind. The true task here is that the forms themselves should carry meaning of terror and pity. I am a spectator too. I want more connotations of universality. That is where abstraction, after having helped, fails us now, and that is where my purpose to reforge the human mold so it will be at once an ancient and contemporary machine for joy and pain, finds its motivation. We need to be understood. We must write clearly (not ignominiously, at the expense of plastic force, but to the increase of it), to be clearly understood. Drawing is a formidable tool for this, also color. I do not mean tools for "fine art": that for my mind has gone forever. The fact it was "fine" I interpret more as a suspicious connotation. *If we are to be anything, we shall only survive as spokesmen, never any more as entertainers.*

Here is the creed of an artist, a Neopolitan by birth in 1900, who grew up with and profoundly studied his inheritance from the Italian masters, absorbed what Paris had to offer him from its modern renaissance, came to the United States in 1924, worked and taught in its East and West, and now makes Los Angeles his home. It is a weighty creed. And the voluminous work which implements the creed has vision, depth, range, and weight.

As these comments show, Lebrun has drawn his sustenance from history, the European moderns, from life in the raw, and from himself. This is as it should be. All these sources are authentic. That he should see the tragedies and ironies of life rather than its comedies, that he should be driven to reforge the "worn-out or age-old theme" of the Passion of Christ into both ancient and contemporary terms, is due to the chemistry of his nature and also is as it should be. When to him the Italian woman with child became the Venus of Athens, raked by hunger and love, and when the clouds and mountains ordered themselves in relation to her, in his mind, this was the all-seeing vision of the artist penetrating the depths and bringing forth the stuff to be reforged into art. This is the organic process, he says—this extracting from life of its essentials—and because it is organic, theatricism (but not drama) is impossible. And the ordering of the parts—the design—is also organic because of its primary source in life rather than in a mirage or man-made collage. This statement, however, needs the amplification of a reminder that design is always artist-manufactured, even when its source-material is taken from life, and that its authenticity depends on the integrity of both. Or on the integrity of the artist alone if the source is only in his sensitivities, as in the abstract picture. Note well Lebrun's use of the term "plastic writing." By this he must mean design; it is an excellent substitute for that overworked word.

In view of this so-far unimpeachable meaning and terminology, it is difficult to explain (and forgive) the artist's next strange statement about the "little parcel of food gained from Montparnasse withering in the furnace of the Chapel of Masaccio." By Montparnasse he presumably means the Paris Modern Movement. But this movement also drew its sustenance from the great arts of history and the fertile sensitivities of genuine artists; it exactly paralleled his experience. He admits his debt to Picasso and other artists, then discredits the parallel. In so doing, by inference, he discredits himself. This critic denies both discreditings. Does Lebrun know what *plastic writing* means? Does he not recognize it wherever he sees it? Does he deny authority to all his contemporaries except Picasso and a few others? No, he says "many others." It is a confusing paradox.

Genuine modern art does not wither when paired with Masaccio and other masters; it establishes a timeless harmony. And design is not a "monster unity" in the service of which artists lose their identity and significance—unless they become external imitators of design clichés. In such a case the loss comes from the act of imitation; it is the copyist who is at fault, not the great matrix of all arts—design. Finally, the arts in the museums are not all "pantomime" as Lebrun implies; a great many of them are also "meaningful individual adventures."

112   RICO LEBRUN

This artist, as he reveals himself in these remarks, seems to have allowed the trees discovered in his inward searchings to obscure the woods of which his personal trees are a part. This is unfortunate. Let us hope that time and the perspective gained by still more searchings will mend such opinions.

On his relations to the human drama Lebrun is on firmer ground. Expressing a "more agitated, bewildered and altered human mold" is certainly not "neo-romanticism," and the victims of precision bombing are anything but "romantic props." All honor to the attempt to make these victims "real people"; such an important enterprise commands respect and demands support. And, as he says, the attempt must be stated clearly, "not ignominiously at the expense of plastic force, but to the increase of it." Here, if plastic writing is defined as design, and plastic force as plastic writing, he is approving the *monster unity of design* which he previously castigated. However, that last saying—"If we [artists] are to be anything, we shall only survive as spokesmen, never any more as entertainers"—is eminently right. Unless, perchance, one wishes to revise it to say the artist can also be an entertainer; there is a place for the lighter fare.

When we turn to the Lebrun paintings to observe how a profound vision has been converted into plastic writing, we find a wealth of material all of which commands respect for one or another reason. Also it challenges us to try to "understand clearly" some meanings which are anything but obvious—even at the cost of that "lamentable" activity of "ripping apart for analysis" the works he has played on the great organ of painting.

To describe his early drawings I would not use the lush language of Mr. Bear; but line does flow pliantly and expressively and character does emerge effectively with echoes of Ainge and the older masters. His paintings, prior to 1944, can be summarized, perhaps, in the over-simplified statement that they express the deepest emotions of man with graphic power, a highly personal technique and simplified symbols of his own creation.

Fig. 59. *Vertical Composition*, by RICO LEBRUN, 1946. This was the first choice of the jury of the 1947 Exhibition of American Painting and Sculpture at the Art Institute of Chicago. It did not receive first prize due to a technicality. It was awarded the Norman Wait Harris Silver Medal and $500.

Fig. 60. *Centurion's Horse*, by RICO LEBRUN, 1948 One of the series on "The Passion of Christ."

The *Vertical Composition* of 1946 (Fig. 59) was a justified first choice in a nation-wide exhibition. I saw this painting in its Chicago setting. The symbolism and dramatic power of the rendering of the battered tool of man extracted from the dump-heap of discards which had served their term of usefulness is overwhelming in its direct and indirect implications. The color scheme is a grayed harmony with all colors, spaces, and textures working as part of the design. Forms also integrate. This is plastic writing at its best.

In the series of paintings on the "Passion of Christ," culminating in the *Crucifixion* completed in 1950 (see frontispiece), Lebrun presents observers with a profound and deliberate challenge. His objective of reforging the human mold is convincing in its terminology, but not so convincing, at first sight at least, in its plastic realization. The treatment of *The Magdalene* of Fig. 61 is typical of that of all the actors in this great drama—to get the "awesomeness and the terror into the forms themselves." The brutalizing of the soldiers to gain this end is understandable. But what is gained by a like reforging of the Mother of Christ into an earth-bound Amazon? Why feature her ragged costume as next most important to her coarsened head, as he does? Content is obviously more important than form in this series on the theme of the Golgotha; but the content disturbs violently. The fact that we spectators are disturbed and challenged does not, of course, prove the artist wrong in his conception. A man of the integrity of Rico Lebrun may be "writing" over our tradition-tethered head. We have the right, however, to question. But the questioning must be two-edged. We must question ourselves as well as him.

Asked to answer such questionings, Lebrun replied:

As for the need of brutalizing and distorting the countenances of the figures in the Crucifixion series, you should note that an image related to a bestial slaughter can very well be defaced and unbearable, and will refuse to be tamed by the conditionals of our protective delicacy. . . . Whenever the plastic pomp and convention have strutted to destroy meaning (think of all the Reni and Barocci after the lesson of Giotto and Orcagna), a violent gesture *in the real tradition* has reestablished meaning; and has temporarily horrified the spectator.

It is necessary, therefore, to go as far as we dare, so as to give the symbol as much pertinence as *we need*. If, while doing this, we blunder and stutter and fail, we are still better off than the entertainer who uses the usual and has no conflicts on his hands. (It is he whom I called an entertainer, not the great artists who have adopted truly frivolous and elegant and humorous themes with proper design.)

In the *Centurian's Horse* (Fig. 60), a preliminary study for the Crucifixion Triptych, no questions are possible. Here is animal power, semi-stripped to the bone; the universal is released from the particular and dramatized with uncanny effectiveness. This work illustrates with distinction a solution of that pressing problem of today's artists to resolve their two great inheritances—from the European Renaissance and the Modern Movement—into plastic unity. Lebrun is one of the relatively few artists who is achieving that goal.

The paintings shown in New York at the Jacques Seligmann Galleries in 1950 included the immense abstracted and fragmented *Caterpillar*, suggesting without defining a huge war machine, the incredible symbolism, all in reds, of the *Executioners* and the *Armored Creature*, showing Nature's armor-plated animal with its ironic parallel to warring man. All are profound works profoundly organized with great complexity in deep space.

The final and climactic work—the *Crucifixion*, which is actually a Descent from the Cross rather than the Crucifixion, and which measures 26 x 16 feet, is, without doubt, one of the major, if not the major, paintings produced in recent history. It rivals Picasso's *Guernica* in incisive power, if not as yet in recognition and influence. With its forthrightness and eloquence both in content and form there can be no quibbling. Here is the old, old story told again in modern terms, as valid ancient stories should find continuing renewal. Here history does not merely carry on, but replenishes itself, as history should. A work of this type puts life-blood into the bromidic statement that "all things change; art alone endures." The art endures, in other words, through the act of its replenishing. Life and art *are* growth and change. (See frontispiece.)

This entire series on the "Passion of Christ" has absorbed three years of the artist's time and energy in its execution, plus many years of exploring preparation. It was produced without a commission. Asked whether

Fig. 61. *The Magdalene,*
by RICO LEBRUN, 1948. One of
the series on "The Passion of Christ."

he had any particular place in mind as a final location for the series or
the huge triptych of the Crucifixion itself, Lebrun replied, "No, unless,
perhaps, in some community church, probably nowhere. Maybe there is
no place for it. But it is needed in people's minds."

BEN SHAHN

"I am incapable of separating the art from my feeling of what's going
on in the world," said Ben Shahn recently. "Take the ads in the subway,
for instance. I sit in the rush hour train—and all the ads grin. In the

seats and aisles, nobody grins. I refuse to contribute my two cents to the huge myth of the American grin. . . . Is there nothing to weep about in this world any more? Is all our pity and anger to be reduced to a few tastefully arranged straight lines?"

There you have it. The Shahn philosophy concentrated into half a dozen terse sentences. He refuses to contribute to the perpetuation of the myth of the American grin. There are still things in life to weep about and he sees through the masks, not only the artificial grins in the ads but also those which people—the people he is continually watching—don in self-defense or to fool themselves or others. He sees through, or tries to see through, all masks. Of course there are things to weep about today, as there have always been. The artist's job is to know this fact and do something about it. The additional fact that there are things to laugh about—that inspire gaiety, the song, the dance—he knows this and admits the integrity of that theme also for artists, including himself, to work with, if and when there is the compulsion of the inner drive. But it is the tragic drama which most compels him to do what he has done in his art during the two past tragedy-packed decades.

Shahn's "social consciousness" started, in pictures, with the series done on the tragedy of the Sacco-Vanzetti case in 1931 and 1932. In this series, the *Passion of Sacco and Vanzetti* was outstanding in its pictorial drama, its humorless caricature. There is complete control—of all the actors, the victims of "justice" in their coffins, the judges, the temple of justice, the portrait of the judge taking the oath, the irony of it all. The symbols, and these are symbols extracted from real forms, are compacted into a cross between two and three dimensions (a device which the artist still uses twenty years later) and an adequate design. (See Fig. 62.)

Thereafter it was the "Mooney" series, Prohibition, murals for the Government Arts Projects of 1933 to 1935, and many easel paintings. One of the murals was on the theme of prisons to hang on the walls of Riker's Island Penitentiary, contrasting old prison methods, with their punishment of floggings, to the new ones of prison trade schools. After these had been approved by the Commissioner of Correction and Mayor

Fig. 63. *Italian Landscape II,* by BEN SHAHN, 1944.

Fig. 64. *Hunger,* by BEN SHAHN, 1946.

Fig. 62. *The Passion of Sacco and Vanzetti,* by BEN SHAHN, 1931--1932.

La Guardia, they were rejected by the Municipal Art Commission "because their pictured realities might arouse discontent in the minds of the prisoners; they were psychologically unfit and anti-social." Official masks were the order of that day—among some officials, but not all.

Posters have frequently been used by Shahn as ideological ammunition. In 1946, for the State Department, he did *Hunger,* of Fig. 64, one of the most powerful single documentary posters produced in this country, in our time. Note the sheer power in the distortion for emphasis and in the three dimensions of the important head and hand fading into two dimensions for the less important body.

In 1947, Ben Shahn was given a comprehensive retrospective exhibition at New York's Museum of Modern Art. Of all the paintings there shown, the one which, in this critic's opinion, blended content and form into the most adequate synthesis was *Italian Landscape II* of 1944, one of the many works compelled by war. Here is Europe and its rubble from man-made war. Part of Europe's house still stands. A woman climbs over the destruction and waste to the inevitable beginning over again. All is clarified and powerfully expressed in concrete forms. And the designed "form" is adequate; this is mature three-dimensional design playing its role on a par with meaning. The rocks, in delicate but vibrant colors, build into controlled relationships that delight the eye and provide the perfect foil, as color, form, and subject, to the sturdy ruins of the house. Here Shahn proves that he can blend on equal terms the two forces wherein lies the art of the centuries. (See Fig. 63.)

Like other realists with a profound message to get across to his fellow citizens, this artist, as he puts it, has followed his "instinct for story-telling and social commentary and rejected a conception of art based on aesthetic sensation." He has never granted importance "to a few tastefully arranged straight lines." Design for him is a functional means, not an end.

The great majority of the Shahn paintings over the years implement this attitude. The social commentary, it seems, has to find its own means. And the means are arbitrary, often crude; there are mussy colors, large areas of flat monotony, forms reduced to a thin veil of color and hasty,

Fig. 65. Ave, by BEN SHAHN, 1950.

Fig. 66. *Labyrinth, Detail #2*,
by BEN SHAHN, 1952.

careless outlines, mixtures of flat and three-dimensional forms in the same picture, the unreal symbol mixed with the real, "bad" color combinations, such as brown and blue, pasty near-whites for skin color, and at times naturalism combined with the arbitrary symbol. All of these are things that just are not done in works of mature art. Yet somehow this man gets away with them. The commentary does find its own and adequate means to express the imperial demands of the theme. There is something quite mysterious about this bland dissolution of impossibles. Character and drama emerge along with story.

Charged with these sins of omission and commission, Mr. Shahn was quite unperturbed—and quite ready with his answer.

> When I am working, I do not think of these things. I work in a fever. It is an agony for everyone, including myself. The criteria are inevitable; I want to get the emotional impact. The esthetics are but tools to express the human drama. The work goes on for from three weeks to two months, but I try to make the painting look as if it were done in two days. When I get to a point where added work would not fulfill the original concept, but weaken it, there I stop—even if not finished; I feel I can no longer go on. As to "crudeness" and "raw colors" and the like, I believe that at times the crude areas of a painting have a positive quality—and I use them, consciously approving what feeling demanded. I like all manner of opposites—the large versus the small, the crude against the finished, the amorphous against the concrete. And when a girder behind people on a bridge is faded out to a "film of color or careless lines," the reason is to throw the accent on the humans, to make them the important actors in the scene.

With such convictions welling up from the depths, what can a mere critic do but let the artist win the argument? The "emotional impact," the "fever," is imperious. And when it is supported and documented by strong convictions, it has a validity of its own which we must recognize and may as well consciously approve.

In the *Ave* of Fig. 65, the only "opposites," in techniques at least, are the formless, textured table contrasted to the concrete, if sometimes flattened, forms of all other elements; here Shahn's love of the paradox is indulged. Among the other elements, note the clean reality of the form in the portrait poster, and the rich diversity in the repeats along that poster row—in spacing, size, tone-values, and especially movements. Here is the foil to the sometimes employed crudeness (absent in this work). Note also the eloquent character-expression in the near-flat figures with their typical differentials. All such variations are emphasized, no doubt, by contrast with the monotonous table. As to meaning, I have no news-release from the artist; each of us may interpret as we please.

In a Shahn exhibition of 1952, a quick, surveying glance spotted a wall-panel which flashed the thought, "Ah, Shahn has gone abstract. I see color-space pattern dominant." It must have been wishful thinking; closer inspection again revealed the theme—*almost* in full control. But not quite. The theme was slipping. The aesthetics gained a few yards. Not that I want Shahn to reverse his due process; we all want him to be himself. Nevertheless a mean streak in me rejoices when aesthetics steals a march, even a little one, on social consciousness. Who knows what will happen now? (See Fig. 66.)

It is a good guess to assume that the Shahn highway will continue its well established direction. The human drama will not lose its motivating power; design will continue to be the largely unconscious means. Many an old master, traveling the same road, has found ample nourishment for brush and mind. So will humanist-artist Ben Shahn.

XAVIER GONZALEZ

"I do not read about painting," says Xavier Gonzalez, "but I sometimes write. To read about painting, or art, is unbearable to me." A statement like this can come logically from a dynamo busily engaged in its allotted task of generating current; quite naturally it has no time to pause and absorb competing or even supplementary currents. Gonzalez, the evidence indicates, is such a dynamo. Let us then listen. I quote:

When a painter paints he repeats continuous acts of humility; it is like writing about our own incompetence since we feel we can think more than we can do. . . . The struggle to give form to emotions and our efforts to crystallize an idea are never realized. We must be content with something else, something that appears instead.

Picasso has said the same in different words:

A picture is not thought out and settled beforehand. While it is being done it changes as one's thoughts change. And when it is finished it still goes on changing, according to the state of mind of whoever is looking at it. A picture lives a life like a living creature, undergoing the changes imposed from day to day. This is natural enough, as the picture lives only through the man who is looking at it.

But back to Gonzalez:

Painting is the geometry of feeling. I have to approach painting indirectly, slowly, because a painting like a flower can die by too much handling. The over-statement of a truth kills it.

Sometimes the basis of our work is a landscape, a figure or a gesture, and we know beforehand that the final product will be unrelated to the original idea; we shall end with another thing, another emotion. If we drain our work of that mental struggle, the result will be sterile geometry, or, at its best, mirrors that reflect only one dimension.

Often, at the beginning of a painting, our graphic concepts are so amorphous that we start our work as a purely physical performance, adjusting our efforts to the innate understanding we have acquired of the rhythms of nature and conscious only of forms, textures and colors. Gradually these forms, textures and colors will become alive, and by eliminating the superfluous elements, the scaffolding or framework, the painting is realized; at least we think it is realized, when we get it to the saturation point.

We have seen and experienced a drop of ink, a hanging rope, the movement of a whip in the air, centrifugal force, the sharpness of a knife, the tearing of paper, walking through traffic, sawing wood, mechanical movements, the flight of birds. When we use these forms or forces we create an equivalent or symbol, often using the same motive power that we find in the reality of experience.

A drop of liquid paint on a vertical paper behaves like rain, but assumes another reality; the reality of painting. With this equipment the painter evolves his works making a delicate balance between two fields of behavior, nature as a motor and the painting as a finality in which everything begins and ends on the surface of the painting.

Our understanding of the significance of such experiences, and the intensity of our reactions to the emotions of form and action, color and volume, will be a key to the realization of our aims.

The naturalism of form will be transformed into the realism of painting, even if our newly acquired realism has no apparent likeness to our preconceived concept of nature.

I italicize that last statement because it seems to condense into a single sentence all that has gone before. Also it puts into another artist's words a basic theme of these critiques. Naturalism, it says, will be transformed into a reality created by the artist, which reality may be different from that familiar to us in nature. Creation as against reporting. The symbol versus the replica.

The current of Gonzalez's thought flows rich and full. The listening has been highly rewarding. He again proves that leader-artists know what they are about and can on occasion put their knowledge into words as well as stone or paint.

The Gonzalez career can readily be called checkered if not hectic. Born in 1898 in Spain, where his childhood was spent, the scene shifted to Mexico with his family, then to Chicago, then back to Mexico, then to San Antonio, Texas, where he studied with his mother's brother, José Arpa. Previous art study had been in Mexico and at night classes in the Chicago Art Institute. Art teaching began in Mexico in his own commercial art school and in the public schools, continued in San Antonio and Alpine, Texas, shifted to Newcomb College of Tulane University in New Orleans for fifteen years, was interrupted by the last World War, continued at the Brooklyn Museum Art School. "Association with youth," he says, "their challenging inquiries, their refusal to take things for granted, and my attempts to answer them, constitute a decidedly stimulating situation." As a professional artist, he could never devote all his time to painting, the necessities of life being such that economic pressure was always present.

The production record of Gonzalez, the painter, has been long and significant. He explains:

> During the summer months, I study nature, giving special attention to the humble things or less obvious expressions of physical appearances. My painting then becomes more emotional. I feel that in front of nature I am nothing but a tool and that my brain, eyes and hand do the painting with a sort of automatism. In other words I try to act nature rather than copy or imitate it. During the winter, my work becomes more severe and calculating—like an interest in a kind of non-Euclidian mathematics. I aim toward certain orders and relationships in form and color.

This explanation reveals the balance between the objective and subjective motivations which must inform great art. The naturalist is only the automaton. The abstractionist can rely preponderantly on his inner resources, but the insistence of most abstract painters on their search for realities testifies to their concern for objective, even if invisible, truth. Gonzalez holds to the semi-abstraction which draws from visible reality but manipulates it to conform to his needs. *The Ram's Head* of Fig. 68 is an excellent example of this blending of tangibles and intangibles.

One of his summer watercolors, and he is a master of that medium, will glow with intuitive improvisation and emotional design of color, space, movement, and textures as he interprets, rather than reports, the facts of water, earth, grass, and boats. The summer oils, usually developed in the winter studio, will delve deeper into the realities. The serious winter paintings run the gamut from the tangible realism of the *Portrait of an Artist* (Fig. 67) to the galaxy of symbolic interpretations of *The Ram's Head.* The former shows that he can paint the real with ample mastery of all his means. The latter announces that his true love lies in extracting symbolic meanings from life and beating them into the rhythms of form, texture, color which his sensitivities demand. The mental and emotional struggle of gaining that end has not been drained from this work; there is no "sterile geometry" here or any "mirroring" that reflects only one dimension.

Asked to explain *The Ram's Head,* Gonzalez obliged by saying he began with the skull of the ram with its symbolic implications of the tragedy of death and then carried the tragic motif of eyesocket and teeth throughout the rest of the picture. Beyond this he would not go.

Nor does he explain in words any significance in *The Offering* of Fig. 69, other than we who observe can read into its folk-religion episode. Every segment of this impressive painting, obviously, is packed with meaning, and the meaning integrates with the form. Pictorial drama, human drama, and a complex unity of the whole, all combined with a technical mastery adequate to the task at hand. Some of the works of the past several years depart much more from the real toward the abstract.

The creations of Xavier Gonzalez are solid structures on every count of concept and realization. They attain the plastique of painting. They

Fig. 67. *Portrait of an Artist,* by XAVIER GONZALEZ, 1948.

Fig. 68. *The Ram's Head,* by XAVIER GONZALEZ, 1948.

Fig. 69. *The Offering,* by XAVIER GONZALEZ, 1952.

are well within the Grand Tradition. They are rich in promise of future significant production.

PETER BLUME

Peter Blume is one of that small and distinguished group of contemporary painters who have courageously assayed the tough problem of integrating the old and new concepts of both content and form. His content goes far beyond obvious reality in its allegorical philosophizing about the life of today; his form presents an extremely difficult problem to himself as artist and to the observer who attempts to appraise it objectively. His two masterworks, *The Eternal City* and *The Rock,* products of some eleven years of intense concentration, study, and experiment, testify to this difficulty. In comparison to it, the task of reading meanings into the allegory in each case is fairly easy. Intellect, that is to say, can roam at will through these paintings and find ample food for speculative thought and opportunity for admiration of technical mastery. So abundant, in fact, are these rewards that the alert mind may well wonder if they are not being over-indulged. Does form balance content? Do the two merge into the perfect whole? Is there an appeal to spirit here to amplify the obvious appeal to conscious mind?

Blume's early paintings, it will be remembered, such as *Parade,* of 1930, and *South of Scranton,* of 1931, used much more abstract symbols which were expressed as arbitrarily real forms set in a real landscape. Meaning was obscure. *Parade* had no figures, except the head and hands of one man carrying a cluster of more or less abstract forms before a wall topped with extracts from industrial buildings. In *South of Scranton* (Fig. 70), dancing men floated in air around a ship's mast set on a platform among fantastic buildings with a master of ceremonies apparently directing the dance. What did these pictures mean? Without asking the artist, we can read into them the visual comments of a questing mind on an industrialized society. In the two more recent masterworks, the comments are still philosophizing about society—the one about Mussolini's Fascist state, the other about building anew from the ruins of man's previous creations, or, as Blume describes it, "the continual process of man's rebuilding

Fig. 70. *South of Scranton*, by PETER BLUME, 1931.

Fig. 71. *The Eternal City*, by PETER BLUME, 1937. Completed after three years of work.

out of a devastated world." The symbolism in both these paintings is tangible. The abstract has grown, or regressed, into the concrete. Whether such a change is growth or recession is one of the deep questions the artist, perhaps unconsciously, asks us to answer. Evidently he considers the change as growth. I am not so sure.

In the prophetic portrayal of Mussolini's approaching doom, painted from 1934 to 1937, meanings, at least in some parts of the picture, are more elusive, thus marking it as a logical step in the evolution from the abstract to the created real. The green head of the jack-in-the-box Dictator dramatically holds the center of the stage in its position and garish color, clashing with the otherwise lyric scene as stridently as its prototype clashed with the classics of Italian history. The fragments of previous Roman grandeur quickly tell their story as do the underground galleries of the Catacombs, with people circulating through them toward the sunlit Forum in "underground" defiance. The Christ at the left, bedecked with jewels, swords, and military epaulets, takes some thought but is not too difficult to decipher. The troops in the distant Forum in the act of breaking ranks do need to be interpreted as in the act of defection. The buildings, the scattered columns, the seven distant hills, provide the historical setting for the Fascist drama. This painting is no "fragment of an actual scene." It is an epochal interpretation of history and life.

In *The Rock,* the shattered blood-red rock represents the world today, surrounded by symbols of destruction—skeletons, blasted trees, burning debris, and the crumbling edifices of man. But there are symbols of hope among the destruction. A scarlet fungus springs full-grown out of a dead and rotten stump. People dig and shovel and grub in the ruins, rescuing and reshaping blocks for the new structure rising in skeleton at the left. Lichen grows on the old surface of the blasted rock. Colors can be enjoyed; they do form unconscious chords. Planes build into the design with satisfying control.

Design, like the ideological concepts, is cerebral. It is cold-blooded and calculating. Passion, if it ever had any place in the drive which keeps this artist at his easel over a period of seven years on one painting, has been filtered by intellect. The design thereby becomes functional. It serves

Fig. 72. *The Rock,* by PETER BLUME, 1948. Completed after seven years of work.

Fig. 73. *Shrine,* by PETER BLUME, 1950.

subject, becomes a means to increase its effectiveness. Feeling, however, must have had its place in these aesthetic matters; perhaps I should amend my brazen charge of cerebralism to one which says merely that intellect dominates feeling, that it has strained out nearly all of the sensory reactions to subject and so denied them to the observer. Emotion mellows the art of painting and endows it with a lifeblood that comes from the spirit of man. Intellect, because it is limited to what the mind knows, to tangibles rather than intangibles, is hard and sharp in style and precise in its boundaries. *The Rock* in this sense is hard, sharp, and precise.

The rendering of form in these two important paintings is realistic in the full meaning in that word. It creates its own reality in precise and calculated terms and controls it effectively in every manifestation, by means of color, texture, dark-light contrasts, and planes. Pictured objects are pulled forward or pressed backward to their right position on the stage, by the intensities of color and tone and the clarity or softening of forms. There is little distortion, but that which does appear is concentrated, strangely enough, in the overlarge hands, heads, and feet of some of the figures, especially the central woman and hammering man—explain this as best you can; Blume does know how to draw correctly.

It is interesting to note that *The Rock,* completed after years of research and planning in 1948, won the popularity poll at the Carnegie International Exhibition of 1950—an incredible event, considering the safety and sanity of such previous polls; times, this indicates, do change. The painting is owned by Edgar Kaufman, Jr., of the Museum of Modern Art, who purchased it before it was completed. The skeleton building at the left side of the picture, by the way, is a section of the famous "Fallingwater," the Kaufman home at Bear Run designed by Frank Lloyd Wright.

The *Shrine,* of 1950 (Fig. 73) is a strange painting. The obvious symbolism of the Crucifixion is all there, with the Christ metamorphosed into a Mexican Indian with all pertinent details again exploited to the full—in cross, thorns, rope, coarse cloth, and suspended gadgets or charms. The emaciated body, by the way, is less fully realized than these trimmings—which partly accounts for the feeling of strangeness in this Blume painting. Another work, of 1951, based on this one, extracts the charms and the coarse cloth, changes and rearranges them for presentation in minute detail in their own right.

Peter Blume is a master technician. He is an inheritor of the skills of the old masters and of their concern with the universal theme with symbolic meaning. He is carrying on that inheritance, modifying it to meet the needs of his day. He is building pictorial dramas which explain the mysteries of life to his public as did the religious painters of the middle ages to their public. He is, therefore, carrying on the Grand Tradition into our modern renaissance, which also has provided for him an inheritance. Has he made full use of and integrated both inheritances? The question is too profound for one critic to answer adequately.

DAVID ARONSON

David Aronson has blossomed into a mature style and execution in the past seven years. He has reached this maturity as a young artist; his age was twenty-nine years in 1953 at the time of his third group exhibition in New York (at the Downtown Gallery).

As a boy, Aronson was a religious scholar. When, in his teens, he turned from his religious studies to painting, he carried with him his interest in Biblical motifs. He has written that he believes the situations and incidents of the New Testament are fundamental themes—so basic that they have inspired artists through two thousand years, allowing an enormous range of interpretation and personal comment.

Through the transitions in his painting style, Aronson has continued this preoccupation while developing his interpretations of these symbolic ideas. Originally influenced by Byzantine and Early Christian art, his 1946 sojourn in Italy evoked an excitement about Venetian painting. Since then the artist has integrated both influences. Also, judging by the recent works, he has been influenced by Max Beckmann, as is evident in the crowded stage drama of his *Marriage at Cana* of Fig. 74. But, aside from the stage management of the compressed scene, his rich characterization is his own. This is life as he conceives it to have been lived in Biblical times, transposed into the universal expression. Are the costumes

Fig. 74. *Marriage at Cana,* by DAVID ARONSON, 1952.

and properties of his human drama authentic? The question is beside the point; one does not care about such details. These are humans playing their parts on the stage of life as such dramas have been played through the two thousand years. This is deeply felt, imaginative, well-ordered expression. It is rich in promise of continuing growth.

OLIVER O'CONNOR BARRETT

Born in London in 1908, this self-trained sculptor came to the United States and, driven by an inner compulsion, has been hard at work among us for many years. But let him explain:

> My deepest desire is to express a new affirmation of life—with the accent on human life—as direct and simple as I feel it. I could not avoid, even if I wished to, a basically religious attitude to life. By this I do not mean a set creed or even any particular form of religion, though I am enormously interested in the teachings of Christ.
>
> Nature is my most direct source of inspiration, including human nature. When I perceive deeply the least or the greatest living thing, then I am possessed by a sense of wonder as intense, as pure, as that which I knew as

Fig. 75. *Don Quixote,*
by OLIVER O'CONNOR BARRETT, 1949.

Fig. 76. *The Angry Carpenter,*
by OLIVER O'CONNOR BARRETT, 1949.

a child. A sense of wonder and worship—this is my dominant passion. But how to express it? How to give thanks enough? How to find adequate form for this full-hearted affirmation? This is my main task as an artist.

We live in curious times—in some ways very amusing times. Worship as a passion is such a naked and vulnerable thing; it is almost impossible to speak of it without embarrassment. To create works of art for the glory of God and the love of man! How can one speak in such terms? Yet for me that is the inmost reality and the reason that I should go on creating sculpture even if I knew I should never sell a piece for the rest of my days.

One of the most moving scenes in Chaplin's *Limelight* is when, having slapped the hysterical young dancer back to her senses and sent her back onto the stage, the old clown drops on his knees and cries aloud, "Whoever you are—Whatever it is—keep her going! Just keep her going—that's all." The way Chaplin does it, it is a prayer of the most passionate sincerity, going far beyond its immediate content, as the whole film does. It is the prayer of a great and mature man for the new generation. And then, so typically and wonderfully, a stage hand blunders into the middle of that intense moment and the old clown jumps to his feet and pretends he had lost a button. Most human and most marvelous!

But this is the situation in our age. The modern man of feeling, probing through deep skepticism to a deeper and more personal faith and unable to accept the protective cloak of formal religion, is often forced to pray behind the scenes and, if discovered, to pretend he is searching for a lost button. It is a situation genuinely and wonderfully funny and at the same time intensely serious. I feel that I have perhaps gotten something of this quality into my Don Quixote's deathbed.

The two works here shown implement the creed of this genuine artist.

BEN-ZION

Ben-Zion, in his paintings, has the authentic power of a primitive artist to whom art is necessary and a largely subconscious language. In this art he talks to the members of his tribe, and all tribes, making concrete for them his idea of certain matters of common knowledge and belief. He has painted because the drive was in him to protest Hitler's extermination of six million Jews or to symbolize *Man Consulting the Stars* in his eternal search for truth, or to satirize Wall Street. Since the Tribe no longer directs him as artist to speak for it in weighty matters, he speaks alone because he must so speak and he hopes people will see and understand. In him deep sincerity and strong convictions find an outlet and challenge everyone who sees his work. It will be well for us, individually and collectively, to examine the challenge and accept it. In fact no alert mind meeting these paintings can possibly ignore them. They demand attention.

In the series of paintings under the general title "De Profundis" which symbolize the suffering and extinction of the Jews of Europe, the symbolism is concentrated into bodiless patriarchal heads grouped in subjectively jumbled, but orderly designed, positions. The heads have a monumental dignity of resigned suffering. The symbolic power is multiplied by the repetition and the disorganized positions—telling of the wide reach of the persecution and its resulting chaos. In actual life, suffering is concentrated in the mind. Why clutter its pictorial expression with data about the less important physical body? This was drama, pure, instinctive drama, that Ben-Zion played in these picturings of human agony. (See Fig. 77.)

The same use of the symbol—it is really exploitation of the symbol—together with a powerful autonomous design, hold in the bulk of this artist's work. Both are strongest in the profound subjects and usually weakest in easy picturings, as of a flower still-life; in one such, *Field Flowers in Window,* the color drama expends itself on the vase; the flowers fade out clumsily both as subject and design. In the universal subjects, on the other hand, where Man and his destiny are the artist's concern, the symbol asserts itself with full authority and the design usually, but not always, echoes its rugged power. In all there is the concentrated force of a single theme with no distractions, overtones, or subdominant amplifications. Such brutal simplicity borrows from, but is not limited to, the primitive. An honest folk-art, it can be called.

Color in the Ben-Zion paintings is in keeping with the concentration of theme and the direct expressive design. It also is brutally simple and forceful, often with pure or slightly modified primaries, and using black as a constant element. But there is always, or nearly always, a rugged harmony; the color plays into simple harmonic chords.

Fig. 77. *De Profundis*, by BEN-ZION, 1944.

Fig. 78. *The Poet and the Saint,*
by BEN-ZION, 1946.

Fig. 79. *Symbols of Our Time*, by BEN-ZION, 1949.

The design, considered separately, is built into the paintings as it must be in all enduring work; the emphasis is on function rather than sensory excitement—at least I assume this because of the artist's absorption in his subject. "I let things grow," he says. "They emerge by themselves. I am never conscious of what is happening. Everything is in the canvas to be found and drawn out, as in sculpture everything is in the stone. I never force any line or color. I can't work in cold blood."

Ben-Zion comes about as near as any artist can to being self-taught. Born in Russia's Ukraine, he came to this country in 1920 at the age of twenty-two. He began painting in 1932 with no schooling of any kind. Asked to explain in what way the Modern Movement influenced him, he replied that, in Paris, Van Gogh had first inspired him and that later, as he began to paint over here, the movement gave him courage. History also played its part—mainly in the persons of Rembrandt and Michaelangelo; they were the spiritual influence that helped him find himself. Never did he imitate these sources of influence; it was direction and guidance he received. And certainly he has not imitated his contemporaries, Rouault and Chagall, to whom he is closely related. Imitation is a cerebral thing. The authentic drive of spirit needs no crutch of imitation. It is not dependent on established idioms. It must assert itself and its own idiom, as nearly oblivious to externals as man can be.

In *The Poet and the Saint* the symbolic exploitation is brutal in telling impact. The Saint, with closed eyes and crown of thorns, is invulnerable to the barbed darts of ignorance, superstition, malice, while the Poet, with eyes wide open and withered olive-wreath crown, feels and suffers under the cruel impact of an adverse world. Again there is the concentrated force of the one theme with no distractions. (See Fig. 78.)

The net result of this artist's philosophy and method is pictorial drama of a high order. But Ben-Zion, when this point was stressed, denied he was dramatizing his pictures. Vehemently contradicted, he amended the denial by saying the drama came out by itself. The amendment is accepted. Authentic drama cannot be suppressed by the brush or chisel of a genuine, creating artist driven by the inner compulsions of deep emotional convictions. Ben-Zion speaks eloquently in his forthright paintings because of these compulsions.

In May, 1952, a series of Biblical paintings produced from 1948 to 1952 was exhibited at the Jewish Museum in New York.

KARL ZERBE

Karl Zerbe is a difficult artist to appraise. He is difficult because he does not fit neatly into any one classification. He is not an out-and-out Realist. He is not an Abstractionist. He is not, of course, a Naturalist; there are no replicas of nature in his paintings. He is a modern and has been a leader of that school in Massachusetts, with an ever-widening national influence, since 1937. Add to these the general facts that Zerbe is a sturdy personality, that he has a wide perspective on life, which roots in the Nazi Germany from which he escaped in the early 1930's, that this personality and its wide experiences make him see the life about him in ways which surprise and often shock more placid visions, and that he has the gift of a dramatized expression which ranges from the exaggerated real through the cartoon to the bizarre, and you have the matrix from which the Zerbe paintings emerge.

Zerbe has a style which is certainly his own. He has learned from Picasso and the other Paris moderns, but he has not imported their wares. His style takes its character from his visions and dreams of subject more than it does directly from subject itself. Subject is metamorphosed, that is to say, into something new under the sun, i.e., into what the artist *sees or imagines in it and extracts from it* for his own purposes. Because the Zerbe imagination can run riotously before the winds of its own doctrine—with, however, an anchor to windward which usually catches in the solid matter of reality, but is not restrained too rigidly from slipping—the Zerbe paintings challenge. They challenged the Hearst press, for instance, at the time it was attacking the State Department's European Exhibit of our Modern Art so viciously (in November, 1946), to put the following caption under the Zerbe painting in that exhibit: "Sheer Loveliness. Is there anything more beautiful than a dead fish? Of course there is: Two

Fig. 80. *At Night,*
by KARL ZERBE, 1945.

Fig. 81. *Good Friday,*
by KARL ZERBE, 1947.

dead fish. Or three or five. That is what makes this painting, 'Around the Lighthouse,' by Karl Zerbe, so wonderful. You get five dead fish. And so did the State Department."

Hearst was not really worried by the fish in this work being "dead"; dead fish are an attraction rather than a blemish in many an icebox or popular scene or picture. He hated the painting. He hated it because it was not anchored to reality in its familiar aspect. The artist took liberties with his fish and his lighthouse. He dramatized them. And drama in pictures, for some people, is taboo.

Of the five qualities which give character to modern painting—the creative vision, adventure, symbolism, creation, and design—Zerbe features symbolism above all others. He extracts the symbolic from life and dramatizes it. To do this he creates, adventures daringly, and penetrates surface to essentials. Also he designs. But the design seems to be the least conscious of his tools. It emanates from subject, supplements it, supports the symbolism; unobtrusively it marshals the chaos of conglomerate subject into order and effectiveness—as in that perfectly organized group of symbols in *At Night* (Fig. 80). Here the letters TOKI become the focal point of the design, with their concentrated space-color pattern playing against the more open and diffused forms.

This symbolic dissertation on life, obviously a first cousin to *The Ram's Head* by Xavier Gonzalez of Fig. 68, is another modern masterpiece. Read its symbols as you will—woman, midnight oil, dagger, villain, death's head, wine, moon, ruins; the point is that an artist is giving us adult pictorial drama. The comics are popular with children of all ages because they do this on the adolescent plane—also telling their story in symbols. This painting takes the logical step of using the one valuable ingredient of the comics—the episodic story in symbols—in a mature and complex visual language for grown-up minds. Thus the experience it offers is refreshing. It challenges. We need more pictures of this type for adult enjoyment.

In *Good Friday* (Fig. 81), that gray-white pattern of the distant building with its delicately distorted archway-windows actually takes precedence as a kind of architectural lace-work over the mere structural facts. These

Fig. 82. *Felix Adler*, by KARL ZERBE, 1947.

Fig. 83. *Rome-St. Augustine*, by KARL ZERBE, 1951.

facts exist, not for themselves, but as material for design—and here the design emerges triumphant; it preempts the center of the stage. Which means that design, once in the blood of man—where it belongs—cannot be downed. It will have its way, at times, and shift roles—from flunky to master—and not even its master, the artist, can say it nay. In some cases he may not know what is happening but it happens just the same. Zerbe undoubtedly understands when design-sensitivity defiantly seizes his brush; I see no evidence of brutal repression. But symbolism is his first love; design performs its important tasks mostly from behind the scenes.

It is in his series of portraits of clowns that Zerbe's symbolism concentrates his philosophy of life into its keenest satire. The clown is an outcast from the conventional life; his job is to amuse a sensation-hungry public, to distract it from its own tragedies and boredom by the outlandish absurdities of costume, bulbous nose, erratic and unexpected actions. To laugh at the absurd is better than to weep. Or it is a necessary corollary; it balances to some extent the effects of tragedy. Our somewhat crazy world with its jumble of positive and negative forces playing mercilessly on man needs to be laughed at now and again and the clown performs for us that valuable function. The sad faces of clowns, and of Zerbe's clowns, highlight the dual role.

In his clowns, Zerbe is painting a portrait of himself as artist, and of all artists who would symbolize the tragi-comedy of life. The genuine artist, like the clown, is an outsider, a non-conformist, an individual in an institutionalized age. Because of his "strange conduct" he too is easily laughed at as a "crazy" outcast. Thus his kinship to the clown is established for him by society; this particular artist has merely recognized and expressed in painting that kinship. And in so doing he has freed himself to play the part of the privileged jester whose barbed darts can be laughed at by those who fear to take them seriously, or are too blind to see their biting truths. Karl Zerze plays his role exceeding well.

The *Daily Worker* once printed a review of his work which said, "There is too much of death in all his painting, too much yellow, too much dry-rot, too many symbols of living without a suspicion of life. His people have no blood." Considering the various pronouncements of the Moscow line in art, this critique merely says that the surface truths in Zerbe's paintings are not palatable to the Police State; it fails to see or respond to his deeper symbolism. Or is afraid of it. We need artists who explain life from the vantage point of the profound personal vision and with its natural language of the symbol.

In *Rome—St. Augustine* of Fig. 83, the artist extracts color-space-pattern from the façade of an old building and plays his findings into plastic design of the flat surface of his picture plane. Since he can do the same with the much greater complexities of three-dimensional subject, this may be taken as a lighter theme exploited for sensory enjoyment.

Zerbe paints in encaustic, the method used during the classical period of antiquity, wherein refined beeswax is mixed with pigment and heat applied so that the mixture is baked into the canvas and becomes indestructible. The enduring mummy portraits of ancient Egypt were done in encaustic.

In a recent three-year period, fourteen museums purchased Karl Zerbe paintings—a record in that field for a contemporary American artist—and an example of a welcome, much needed, and compensating good judgment on the part of those museums.

KOREN DER HAROOTIAN

To understand the Armenian-American artist Koren Der Harootian, it is necessary to know something of his background. Born in Ashodavan, Armenia, in 1909, six years before his priest father was murdered by the Turks, his early recollections are of escape with his mother into Russia, whence, not long afterward, he was forced to flee again from the Russian Revolution. After temporary sanctuary in Constantinople he made his way through Greece to the United States, where he landed at the age of twelve. His childhood was thus lived against a stage-setting of turmoil, terror, fear, and flight from the cruelty of man toward man. The outcome was foreordained and is evidenced by such titles of his major adult works as *Man of Sorrows, Suffering Mankind, Death to Evil,* and *Famine.* These themes were not mere words or romantic concepts to this man. They were beaten into his subconscious. He had lived through them. He knew their meanings. And so he has compassion for all suffering. He combats persecution and evil wherever he finds them—on his terms—with his chosen weapons, the art of carved wood and stone.

With such a background it is but natural that the compulsion which drives Der Harootian is toward the idea, the concept and its expression in universal terms and universalized form. He is not interested in posing nudes for their individual charm. His nudes—and he strips clothes from nearly all his subjects to help gain elemental truth—are human beings, all humans; they are symbols of human drama. He knows the symbol is the one and only means to the expression of the universalized idea. Also he knows that such expression to be authentic must be motivated by feeling as well as intellect; spirit and its concerns cannot be stated in concrete terms.

Says Der Harootian:

Sculpture is a combination of the physical, the intellectual and the spiritual. I think of stone and wood in terms of their own growth—as something living and fluid. To be timeless, art must have spiritual quality. Today we tend to be too clever or too gutterish. We forget that even sex can be controlled and ennobled as it is in the great voluptuous East Indian sculptures. Only when the intellect dominates the emotions will the two work together for spiritual quality.

When asked why he uses so many religious subjects, his reply was:

Because in religion are to be found the most significant, gripping and noble themes, which stir the imagination and carry a universal message. "Job" is a symbol of patience and suffering. His life became a tragedy. Still he was faithful to his God and his beliefs. People who have the qualities of Job live again in our time.

When Koren, the boy of twelve, arrived in this country it was Worcester, Mass., that became his home. There at the Art Museum he first realized emotional release through creative self-expression. Largely self-taught he began to draw and paint. Later he moved for several years to a mountain-top studio in Jamaica, where he started the first art movement among the island's native Negro population. Painting had been his medium up to this time. But here, by 1938, an innate urge to form found its opportunity for satisfaction in the many marvelous hard woods avail-

Fig. 84. *Hermaphrodite,* by KOREN DER HAROOTIAN, 1938. The male and female elements combined. This was the artist's first work in sculpture.

Fig. 85. *The Sacrifice,* by KOREN DER HAROOTIAN, 1951. Direct carving in Botticini marble.

Fig. 86. *Descent From the Cross,* by KOREN DER HAROOTIAN, 1952. Direct carving in Georgia marble.

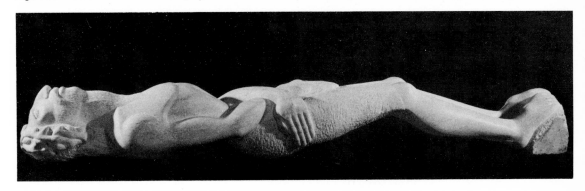

able for the asking, and the chisel became his tool. It has remained his chosen tool to date. Through it, carving in wood and stone, he has developed the thoughts and feelings rooted in his past and re-echoed in the chaos attending and following World War II, which overtook him during a pilgrimage to England. Later, back in New York, he went through all the trials and tribulations that a leader-artist, and especially a sculptor, is heir to in a society that does not quite know how to use its cultural assets.

In England, as a relief from the tragic theme, Koren had turned to sculpting animals, with his source of inspiration in the London Zoo. But back in the United States, the pull of human drama has again asserted itself and a steady procession of mature works have emerged from this sculptor's studio—mostly in stone. The studio, by the way, has now shifted to a seven-acre "estate" in Sparkill, N.Y. Here, as one of the six sculptors chosen by the Fairmount Park Art Association, from the Philadelphia International Sculpture Exhibition of 1950, to execute sculptures for the Ellen Phillips Samuel Memorial, he has been working during 1951, 1952, and 1953 on this important commission. His theme is *The Inventor,* an 8½ foot figure carved directly in granite.

The accompanying illustrations are typical of Der Harootian at his best. All of them demonstrate the theme with universal significance. All are built into fully realized form as form—and into the controlled relationships of three-dimensional form design. All are inspired by a profound experience of life. The final realization of content and form in each case is imbued with a just blending of emotion and intellect. Each speaks eloquently the language of the spirit of man and artist.

One exceedingly encouraging item of news is that *Liturgical Arts,* a quarterly magazine devoted to the arts of the Catholic Church, featured in a double page spread the *Descent From the Cross* (Fig. 86) the moment it was completed, before it had been exhibited; the impressive spread of quality photographs was in the issue of May, 1952. A progressive wing of the Church is alert to such important news and is fostering a revival of genuine contemporary art for religious use.

GWEN LUX

It was her statue of *Eve,* commissioned for the Music Hall Theater of Rockefeller Center in 1932, that first turned the spotlight upon the then twenty-year-old sculptress Gwen Lux. A considerable portion of that publicity, it must be admitted, was due, not to the inherent merit of the work but to the fact that Roxy, the prosperous exploiter of near-nude chorus girls, was afraid that a nearer-nude *Eve* would shock his patrons and cause certain box-office losses, and so banned the finished statue, consigning it to the basement instead of the foyer. This reflected prudery made the headlines and, by focusing attention on a genuine artist of considerable already realized achievement and real promise, gave her a useful boost upon a distinguished career. The promise has been amply fulfilled. Prudery, unfortunately, does not always choose its victims so wisely.

Born in Chicago in 1912, Gwen Lux studied in Detroit (1924-25), in Baltimore (1926-27), Boston (1927-28), and with Mestrovic in Yugoslavia for six months in 1929. Asked what this modern master had taught her, she replied, "Anatomy of the human figure and realism as a solid foundation." When asked where she had first discovered and assimilated form design (which has increasingly imbued all her work with plastic vitality), she paused to reflect, then said she hardly knew, since the learning had been so gradual, but she thought more credit belonged to Demetrious, teaching at the Boston Museum School in 1927, than to any other single source. Mestrovic, it seems, did not stress form design. Then, in Paris, on a Guggenheim Fellowship in 1933 and 1934, she learned much from the French moderns, including Mondrian. In Paris also she exhibited with the modern group. Her first one-man show in the United States was at Delphic Studios in 1933. Then followed many exhibits and commissions climaxed with her most impressive and largest showing to date at Associated American Artists in New York in 1946. All but two of the major works there exhibited—thirty-two in number—were produced in 1945 and early 1946.

What are the main characteristics of this artist's copious productions during the past two decades? Diversity, I would say, is what first strikes the careful observer. Diversity of motivation. Diversity of subject. Diversity of style. Diversity of material. No ruts, no exploited clichés, confine the map of her progress within set limits. Sometimes the material, wood or stone, suggests the concept and form—as in the case of a recent series which develop driftwood into elusive birds in flight or fish or animals. Always she is inspired by need, by the purpose or function of the work, by where it is to go. A theater calls for one type of expression, a fountain for another. She is highly sensitive to mood, to environment. Sometimes the feel is for the abstract, again for the real; always atmosphere makes imperious demands. "I build around my figures," she says. "I create my own environmental house for each piece." In a portrait, such as Fig. 90, it is the character of the individual that determines the character of concept and form. Fig. 89 demands openings in the total form, through which the west wind may blow.

Other characteristics are "solidity of form; it is essential," and positive form (the bulge) played against negative (the hollow) and always, of course, form must be controlled into its own deep-space design. Loss of control with its resulting chaos is unthinkable to this artist in form.

"Why do you at times use distortion?" I asked the question to get the answer into her own words. "Take, for instance, the *Evacuée;* why the elongated head?"

"This was done during the War," she answered. "It is a lonely old person—more than one individual; it is all old people reflecting the tragedy of war. Hope is crumbling around them; this tries to show how they feel. The elongation means loneliness, oneness. It is the tension of length, the parts pulling against each other. The exaggeration heightens meaning. The cape over the head spells mystery. I study the contours. The solid form cuts the air to accent both meaning and design. The air space counts as much as the solid form. The concave is a foil for the convex."

Fairly typical of her diversity of concept and style are Fig. 89, where male and female forms echo each other and interrelate plastically, and the serious portrait of Fig. 90, where character portrayal is the main goal. The Lux portraits do extract purified character, each from its different

Fig. 87. *Eve*, by GWEN LUX, 1932.
Commissioned for Roxy Theater.

Fig. 88. *Evacuée*, by GWEN LUX, 1945.

Fig. 89. *Rhythm,* by GWEN LUX, 1945.

Fig. 90. *Portrait of Serge Rachmaninoff,*
by GWEN LUX, 1948.

subject, and preserve it in stone or wood for generations to come. Her other works, I think it is fair to say, dramatize meaning for a like end. I did not know Serge Rachmaninoff but this portrait re-creation *seems* right as a characterization of him.

During the past several years there have been commissions, mainly for theaters; the latest was for the ocean liner, United States.

The work of Gwen Lux has a distinction all its own. It reveals insight and strength in concept and form. Coming from a woman who is anything but an Amazon in a physical sense, its strength bespeaks a sturdiness of both spirit and physique which is certainly Amazonian in character.

DORIS LEE

"DORIS LEE'S HUMOR BRIGHTEN'S A WEARY WORLD," said an *Art Digest* headline in 1941. Ever since that date, up to and including her "one-man" showing of November, 1950, Doris has been continuing the brightening process—for an even wearier world. It is an impressive record.

How does she do it? By a canny sophistication dressing itself up in simple (or primitive) naïveté. Dressing up and posturing, and reveling in the play-acting with an abandon that is pure delight. But is it proper, prompts one's heavy-footed conscience? Miss Lee herself is anything but simple (or primitive) naïveté. Has she the ethical right to dress her paintings in party costumes and let them play a part upon a stage? Is it becoming for her to pretend to be, via the paintings, what she is not? The question is a delicate one, especially for a writer who has been hurling critical broadsides at juries and museums for honors to paintings he considers pseudo-primitives. So delicate is the issue, in fact, that it seems wise to listen to the evidence (and see some scraps of it) before making our decision.

As artist, the Doris Lee record goes back only a little over a score of years—which does make her rise to fame somewhat "meteoric," as the reviews like to say. For the first five of those years she was a realist with a preference for the folksy subject—*Farmer's Wife, Country Post, The Widow,*

Thanksgiving, Noon (with the lovers and their friendly haystack), were typical titles. Never were these mere landscapes or only posing models; they portrayed life being lived—in fields, farm kitchens, and barnyards. Her people were doing their daily chores; she lifted them onto her stage of art and controlled their acts to tell their stories effectively. Forms were robust and three-dimensional; design was functional and as solid as the forms. "What I feel," she said at the time in explaining her work, "is a kind of violence." This was realism in the tradition of the old masters. There was no feminine "weakness" anywhere in sight; the only visible contribution of the woman as artist was in the slant toward subject—the delicious featuring of her men and women from the woman's viewpoint. No pin-up girls, but humans, members of the human family, were her folk-actors and actresses. And it is not exactly amiss to find some relief in art from the posing nudes, to which the masculine brushes are attracted —only by the aesthetic appeal, of course. We are short on women artists with the womanly viewpoint. One important reason for the rapid rise to fame of Doris Lee is that she kept her personal vision inviolate.

It was about 1940 that the Lee style changed gradually from the real subject to the symbol of the real, expressed more in flattened pattern than in complete three-dimensional form. As always happens, this release into the symbol was also a release into a more obvious pictorial drama; the simplification of subject and design heightened the effectiveness. Complexity of form is justified in a profound and complex theme. When the theme is light-weight and humorous, the simplicity of statement adds immensely to its impact and to the easy enjoyment of a more frankly featured design. The Lee themes are not heavy drama; they are frolicsome; therefore pictorial light opera is their logical medium. This is what Doris must have realized consciously or unconsciously as she slowly changed her style.

In 1941, *Life* magazine recognized this rising young artist with a commission to paint Southern Negro women in their home country. The reason for the commissioning was a weird bundle of paradoxes. It was, believe it or not, "To do a series of *sketches* [note this editorial belittling of the artist's function] of Southern Negroes which might serve as a source

Fig. 91. *Thanksgiving Day,* by DORIS LEE, 1935.
Logan Gold Medal and First Prize, Chicago Art Institute, 1935.

of fashion-inspiration for Southern winter resort wear." Can you beat
that? Well, the event transpired. Doris made the character "sketches"
that were choice works of art honoring the native taste of the Negro
women who assembled costumes out of flour sacking, faded, cheap, commercial cotton prints and big gay handkerchiefs—with an eye to color
combinations of originality and charm *which constituted a genuine native art.*
And the commercial designers copied, and the rich playgirls accepted a
ready-made "style" instead of creating their own.

In 1945 and 1947 commissions from *Life* came thick and fast to Doris
Lee and the resulting interpretations of "Life in Hollywood," the "Harvey Girls," and a "Tropic Tour to Cuba and Mexico" took her delightful
dramatizations to millions of magazine readers. Each of these series of
paintings was eminently "quaint and amusing" and had such other
simple virtues as designed symbols that probably went more or less un-
recognized. The quality was uneven among so many creations, but held

Fig. 92. *Siesta*, by DORIS LEE, 1944.
Third Prize, Carnegie Institute, 1944.

Fig. 93. *Costumes for Dragonwyck*, by
DORIS LEE, 1945. From the Series
on Hollywood, 1945, for *Life*.

Fig. 94. *Badminton*,
by DORIS LEE, 1950.

up best in the first two of the series, where the Hollywood costumes and the virtuous Harvey Girls caught the Lee fancy and came through with outstanding folk-tales wrought into genuine art. In the last venture—to the tropical scene—the talent dwindled considerably; control of color and space was lost or went dead, flat or banal in many of the "sketches." Characterization, even, at which Doris is so proficient, in all but one or two cases, lost its zip.

Have I answered my leading question? The evidence seems to say, and I believe does say, Doris Lee has embraced a simplified style which can be called primitive, because of an innate and interacting logic in her approach to art and life. She sees the little dramas, the day-to-day events of little people or big people, and she makes of them a fiesta, gay with waving colors, spaces, and pictured signs that have easily read meanings —of the peace, the harmony, and the smiles which man needs to counteract the harsh clashes of greed and power always striving to down the better ways of life. The chaos of these clashes is the backdrop of our lives. This artist puts on a play for us in front of that backdrop to distract us from its tensions. This could be done innocently or with sophisticated forethought. Doris is not innocent; she knows what she is doing. But the choice of means, I wager, comes innocently. The simple form is the best means. She knows this. She uses it. The earlier and distant primitives have no patent on the primitive in art. We also can be primitives—in pictures, for good and sufficient reason—and gain the power of the simple expression. This woman-artist is an honest primitive.

I don't really mind being called a primitive [says Doris], but I think it is a tag that means different things to different people. To some it means "done innocently"—and as you say, this is not so with me; I am very aware, and it seems to me to be the artist's business to be intentional. I feel that the material for creative painting is deeply within us and only the "pure in heart" can get to it. Knowledge is really only to help release these contents. There are a few exceptions, but I don't think the content of an artist's work changes much even though the means (or style) changes drastically. When you write of a change in my work, I think the reasons you give for it are pretty accurate. I am not trying to mirror a complex world. I'm trying to get a simpler, heightened reality. . . . Why is it when a painter using recognizable forms wishes to simplify, he or she is called a "primitive?"

The paintings shown herewith illustrate the several stages of development in the Doris Lee history. *Thanksgiving Day* represents the many paintings of solid realism of the 1930's. In the famous and prize-winning *Siesta,* of 1944, the compression of subject toward the flatness of the picture plane is well under way; the setting in deep space has dwindled to a single tree and a horizon. Of the several series executed for *Life,* perhaps the *Clothes Designed for Dragonwyck* is the most mature and thoroughly delightful work. This is no flat, primitive naïveté, by the way; here is sophistication with a developed "form" to support it. Here is the Lee philosophy and style at its most rewarding fruition.

Fig. 94 of *Badminton* was chosen for reproduction on the cover of the 1950 exhibition of the then most recent Lee paintings, thereby giving it apparent priority. All the other works in that exhibit were in similar flat-pattern vein. To this critic, these works seem the least important to date —because the "primitive," out-of-drawing distortions have got out of hand, have lost all point. Both setting and figures have abandoned form in deep space—and there are no compensating virtues, aside from the flat symbol. This radical increase of naïveté beyond the humorous seems unfortunate.

The same type of work has continued through 1952 and prompts the thought: Must an artist be pictorially consistent? Can not Doris in some paintings be non-naïve and non-two-dimensional? Can she not at times return to her former maturity, depth, complexity, and sophistication? It is wonderful to initiate the readers of Big Magazines into the validity and delicate humor of the fanciful symbol, but not all of her admirers depend on *Life* for their enlightenment; they also deserve consideration.

CHARLES UMLAUF

As a spectator, I reported for *Art Digest* a certain event in Texas in 1948 approximately as follows:

If there were seismograph instalations distributed among key centers of Western society which would catch and record the vibrations of significant events in art as present instruments respond to earthquake shocks, these new instruments, if they were sensitive enough, would have been

Fig. 95. *Crucifixion*, by CHARLES UMLAUF, 1948. For the National Shrine of
Saint Anthony, San Antonio, Texas. Donated by Marion Koogler McNay.

set vibrating in many countries by a ceremony which occurred on a cold, windy hilltop in the outskirts of San Antonio, Texas, on the afternoon of Sunday, October 17, 1948. The event was the dedication of a statue of the *Crucifixion* by Charles Umlauf, at the Shrine of Saint Anthony, donated by Marion Koogler McNay and unveiled and blessed by the Archbiship of San Antonio, His Excellency the Most Reverend Robert E. Lucey.

History was repeating itself in this dedication of a Crucifixion, as history has a way of doing; many a statue of Christ on the Cross has been dedicated on many a hilltop in the past 1900 years. But the things which make this event important and mark it as a carrying on of the supreme achievements of religious art are the facts that it grew honestly and unpretentiously out of the soil of its own community and that the triumvirate of necessary contributing factors to significant production were present.

There was the generous, informed, and courageous patron. There was an outstanding local artist imbued with a full realization of the profundity and historical continuity of the modern creative renaissance and equipped with the technical mastery of expressive form and form design necessary to the realization of his conception. And finally, the element of need, of usefulness, was present. The Shrine of Saint Anthony serves a settlement of under-privileged Mexican-American workers for whom their Catholic religion is not only the protective mother but also their only release from a hard, grinding materialism into the life of the spirit.

The Umlauf statue achieves that rare blending of the real and the ideal which marks the perfect symbol. This is not the tortured, suffering, individual man. It is crucified spirit inhabiting Man. It is the drama of the Christian story standing for all human suffering and sacrifice. The art of designed form universalizes the story, turning it into drama. The idea, the ideal, transcends the flesh. The dull-rich gray of the silver-aluminum metal on its black granite base enhances this detachment from the physical. The position on the crest of a low swelling hill seems to echo the delicate balances of meaning and form; this Christ is close to earth and living men, yet not earthbound.

Fig. 96. *Head of a Saint*, by CHARLES UMLAUF, 1950.

Fig. 97. *Lazarus*, by CHARLES UMLAUF, 1950.

It was the vision and strong convictions of the late Mrs. Marion Mc-Nay[3] which caused this work of art to be produced. Herself an artist and collector of French modern paintings, she was devoting her life, her fortune, and about half of her large, rambling home (in which she endowed a flourishing art school) to bringing a living art to her home city of San Antonio. She keenly enjoyed the constructive experience of initiating the plan for this crucifix, of knowing it would be of profound value to the Church, of commissioning a sculptor in whose work she had confidence, and of helping by consultation (but not dictation) in the planning. By doing these things she was making cultural history, instead of only worshipping at its shrine. She was *participating* instead of only *collecting*.

The vibratory significance of this event reaches far beyond the merits of the one specific work. It lies in the fact that liturgical art is here, again in our time, returning to the grand tradition of creative art.

In January, 1951, an exhibit of Umlauf sculptures, produced in 1949–50 with the aid of a Guggenheim Fellowship, was shown at the Mortimer Levitt Gallery in New York. It was an impressive showing on two counts —for the physical bulk of the work (twenty-seven pieces in two years), and for its distinguished evidence of the carrying on of the Grand Tradition of timeless sculptural art. For all of these creations were imbued with the same pulsing life, of concept and formal harmony, as was the previously completed *Crucifixion*. In fact this sculptor learned his formal harmonies along with his schooling (from 1929 to 1937, with interruptions), in spite of certain conflicts which persisted quite needlessly into those years. His vision and power to extract his own meanings from life and art must have been born in him to a considerable degree and then effectively supplemented by his inheritance from history and the modern rebirth. Such influences have been assimilated, as should always happen but often does not. There is no mere imitation of externals; the Umlauf drive to expression is always from within. He understands the past. He extracts from it essentials. And these include the right to experimentation in the present. His living art may be nourished by the past but it grows out of

---

[3] Mrs. McNay died about a year after this dedication ceremony.

contemporary experience. Automatically he re-evaluates tradition. Such is the normal function of all creative art.

Undoubtedly the most noteworthy element about the Umlauf choice of subject-matter is his constant preoccupation with the religious motif. He is not interested in a personal religion, he says, but was inspired by the early Christian art in the Chicago Art Institute during his student days therein, and by the religious side of African and Asian sculpture. "I believe a genuine art should have spiritual content in the religious sense," is the way he puts it. Thus it appears he experiences religious feeling in an aesthetic rather than a ritualistic sense. The spirit of religion evokes the spirit of art. The difference between this motivation and the manufacture of correct but externally conceived religious subjects for the Church is abysmal. The Catholic Church, since the European Renaissance, has allowed itself to sink to the level of using a commercialized, stock-pattern art merchandise; hence the revival of a genuine liturgical art which again deals with spirit rather than matter and which is again beginning to be used by the Church, both here and in Europe, takes on immense significance.

In addition to the *Crucifixion*, the *Head of a Saint* of Fig. 96, and the *Lazarus* of Fig. 97 are outstanding examples of this important revival.

Umlauf, however, also extracts spirit and meaning from non-religious subjects. His animal studies catch the form-spirit of snakes, burros, and bulls. His portraits and studies of children mold essential character into designed form. Charles Umlauf, of Texas, is one of those leader-artists who is making international cultural history today.

JACOB LAWRENCE

The life story of Jacob Lawrence demonstrates once again that the blot of racial prejudice which mars our national record is not all-inclusive. A genuine talent can break through the barriers and win support, recognition, and acclaim, and sometimes is helped along the difficult way rather than repressed. We need a credit mark such as the success story of this Negro artist to help us in trying to balance our cultural ledger. The

Fig. 98. *You Can Buy Whiskey for Twenty-five Cents a Quart*,
by JACOB LAWRENCE, 1943. From the "Harlem" series.

story, therefore, is bilateral in its social significance. Society has aided an important artist to find himself and develop his powers. He has helped his country in providing it with that opportunity. Mutual felicitations are in order.

Born in Atlantic City, New Jersey, in 1917, Lawrence grew up in Philadelphia and New York where he attended public schools, taking the usual required art courses, all of a practical nature. His family arrived in New York in the early 1930's, where he was just in time to experience the rigors of the Great Depression. Only for him the Depression was hardly rigorous. He attended free art classes at the 135th Street Library, moved on to the WPA Art Project Schools, through the CCC Camps, won a scholarship at the American Artists School, worked on the Federal Art Project in the easel painting division for eighteen months from 1938, had several one-man shows, received a Rosenwald Fellowship in 1940, which lasted three years and allowed him to go South and study the problems of his race by direct contacts and experience. Out of these years of research and study came his first group of social-comment paintings—the "Negro Migration" series—to win wide recognition. He had done several series before this and had plans for the Migration theme well developed by the time the Rosenwald funds allowed him a year of steady work to produce the sixty paintings comprising the set. These were exhibited in 1941 at the Downtown Gallery, then purchased, half by the Museum of Modern Art and half by the Phillips Memorial Gallery.

> I was always interested in Negro history [said Lawrence]; contemporary Negro life was the only thing I knew to do. Naturally I was interested in the problems of the Negro people. I just divided the subject into two parts —how things were in the South and the reasons why people migrated. I did plenty of research in books and pamphlets written during the migration and afterward. I took notes. Sometimes I would make ten or twenty sketches for one incident. By the time I started work on the Migration I was more conscious of what I wanted to do. I was looking consciously at things and for things. I wanted to tell a lot. This was the only way I could work and tell the whole story.

This series was held almost entirely to flat pattern.

Then, from 1941 to 1943, came the "Harlem" series in twenty-six gouaches. The life of Harlem was projected in simplified dynamic symbols which carried their messages to the observer with intensified dramatic force. Symbols were kept flat, but in three-dimensional arrangements, as vividly illustrated in Figs. 98 and 99.

Then enlistment in the Coast Guard for the war years resulted in a series portraying that life amidst "the greatest democracy I had known to date." The "War" series, containing war subjects other than those based on sea life, was shown at the Downtown Gallery in 1947. It should be kept intact as a war sermon in paint because its impact is more terrific than any related sermon in words. The symbolic story was not grandiose; it stuck to the simple facts of specific subjects—two praying women, tiers of bunks occupied by soldiers *Shipping Out,* beachhead operations, the loneliness of a foxhole, the tension of an attack, the effect of a letter or a casualty notice on a mother or sweetheart back home and, finally, *Victory* as embodied in one tired but stolid soldier, and *Going Home.*

Fig. 99. *Catfish Row*, by JACOB LAWRENCE, 1947.

Fig. 100. *Vaudeville*, by JACOB LAWRENCE, 1952. From the "Theater" series.

The year ending in July, 1950, Lawrence spent as a voluntary patient in a mental hospital in Queens because of nervous difficulties, neither particularly complicated nor unique, which became so much of a burden that he sought help in their curing. While there, inevitably he made paintings—a series of eleven this time—which capture the frenzied absorption of patients seeking release from tension in the "occupational therapy" pursuits of weaving, sewing, gardening, and the like, the concentration of those haltingly disclosing dark secrets, the desperate attempts to lose themselves in the entertainment of square-dance or concert. One called *Depression* shows three men wandering listlessly about, each sunk in his own introspective agony. All these processes of recovery interested Lawrence; he "felt them through his eyes." His respect for psychiatry and his compassion are told in these paintings.

The Lawrence paintings are symbolic; never are they replicas of actual life or scenes. So arbitrary are their symbols, frequently becoming flat-pattern shapes set in three-dimensional deep space, that the detachment from the literal is greatly heightened and freedom of design greatly enhanced. Invention, in other words, is rampant—the inventions of a burning genius with a deep emotional and ideological drive. Colors are played, usually in one or two dominant notes of raw or near-raw pigment, contrasted to delicate grayed areas plus powerful blacks and browns. Textures then enhance color; this artist is not afraid of textures, though he has only discovered them in recent years. By means of them, with uncanny logic, Lawrence lifts color areas and their subjects into restrained or violent prominence and diverse sensation-appeals. The four off-square panels in Fig. 99 are examples of such exploitation of textures.

So congenial to Lawrence is the flat-pattern symbol, often technically crude but always ideologically powerful, that one cannot but speculate on his future development. Will he be tempted to abandon his relatively simple plastic means for the greater realism of three-dimensional form? Or will he refine two-dimensional pattern? The latter course seems to be indicated by well established habit and by his basic goal.

The Lawrence paintings produced in 1951 and 1952 substantiate this indication. In them he has refined and amplified two-dimensional pattern by a kind of telescoping or compression into three dimensions. His flat or near-flat symbols overlie each other, thereby receding into the deep space of a scene. But always they acknowledge and decorate surface. This is plastic painting in its most obvious sense. Yet within the obvious he gets a high degree of complexity. A series done in 1952 on the general theme of the Theater illustrate this development. Fig. 100 is one of this series. It uses only two superimposed planes, whereas others add many more. Color, of course, adds greatly to the impact; the comedian at left is in soft, grayed greens, the one at right in near-black purples; the background is almost strident in slightly grayed primaries.

In my work [says Lawrence] the human subject is the most important thing. I want to communicate. I want the idea to strike right away. My work is abstract in the sense of having been designed or composed, but it is not abstract in the sense of having no human content.

Design is functional and secondary with him, the artist is here saying. But it is always instinctively present; that is what matters. And the relative proportions of content and form seem right for him. If Lawrence essays future excursions into the realm of obvious visual reality, he will have tremendous problems to solve and, unless the solutions are adequate, he may lose control of the sub-surface realities which give vital force to his present canvases. The issue is a tough one to solve for any artist who has found himself in the abstract or semi-abstract idiom.

Questioned about these possibilities and his future direction, Lawrence replied:

I want to become more universal in approach. I don't want to limit my painting to any one field, such as that of the Negro. I want to grow into the universal, to have the picture bigger in content, to gain a much bigger statement when complete. Some things look small when complete, some look big. I have to grow to this; I am aware of it all the time. Ten years ago it was much easier to paint a picture than it is today. Now I can't paint easily; I have to think about it much more.

In spite, however, of this desire for growth, the artist said he felt he had recently been getting too much depth (into too deep water, did he mean?); he wanted to "go back and capture flatness again." This statement seems to indicate an affinity for and satisfaction with the duality of flattened deep space. It is a worthy field of vast potentialities. It need not limit

Lawrence; its boundaries are not static. Design, within it, can always be expanded, as can symbolic meanings. Since it is congenial, why not explore its deepest galleries?

ELDZIER CORTOR

Eldzier Cortor was born in Richmond, Virginia, in 1916. He studied at the Chicago Art Institute from 1936 to 1938, at the Institute of Design in Chicago from 1942, and at Columbia University in New York in 1946. He began exhibiting in 1940 and has been winning deserved recognition, honors, scholarships, and publicity ever since.

In 1942 and 1943 he was already creating masterly drawings like Fig. 101 and paintings like Fig. 102, in which character, form expression, and functional design blend into the perfect whole; already these were classic works.

In 1944 and 1945 Cortor received Rosenwald Fellowships to travel through the Southeastern coastal regions of the United States to gather material for a series of paintings depicting characteristic aspects of the life of the Gullah Negroes. The paintings in this series were done after his return to Chicago, from imagination and memory, fusing his various impressions of Gullah women seen in South Carolina. Backgrounds of posters are typical of the Southern habit of papering walls with newspapers, old magazine covers, and calendars, but the choice and arrangement of these materials is imaginative and derives entirely from his own designed conception. Cortor does not like working directly from posed life models; he feels it restricts him. Commenting on this painting, the artist said:

> As a Negro artist I have been particularly concerned with painting Negro racial types, not only as such, but in connection with special problems in color, design and composition that interested me. I felt particular interest in painting Negroes whose cultural tradition had been only slightly influenced by Whites. This series of pictures reflects the physical and racial characteristics of the Gullahs. I hope the assimilation of their background and mode of living has added, not only to the authenticity of the paintings, but also to their intrinsic value.

Here is an art rich in symbolic characterization of a people, in integrity of concept and execution and in masterful design. On all counts it is a

Fig. 101. *Two Nudes*, by ELDZIER CORTOR, 1943.

Fig. 102. *Affection*, by ELDZIER CORTOR, 1942.

Fig. 103. *Room Number VI*, by ELDZIER CORTOR.

Fig. 104. *Southern Souvenir*,
by ELDZIER CORTOR, 1948.

highly significant contribution to American and international production.

Of *Room Number VI* (Fig. 103) Cortor commented:

> This is one of a series of paintings of rooms depicting scenes in the lives of people of the slum areas. It shows the overcrowded condition of those who are obliged to carry out their daily activities of life in the confines of the same four walls in the utmost poverty. I attempted to combine the figure studies, the bed and the other elements of the room in an interesting pattern.

An outstanding characteristic of *Room Number VI* is the interplay of textures—of wall, floor-boards, newspapers, checkerboard quilt, smooth sheets and smooth bodies and stove, with and against each other. Also there is the interplay of movements—the tall vertical figure against the quick, angular ones of the bodies on the bed and these contrasted to the counter-movements of newspapers on the floor, with the small vertical of the echoing milk bottle. Again, the stove and its pipe and the vertical leg at left echo the vertical woman, and the active little doll is a repeat of the activity on the bed. All parts relate. All combine into the harmonious whole. Design unobtrusively dominates subject.

In *Southern Souvenir,* of Fig. 104, the above-mentioned virtues are heightened in a more subtle impact. Against the two women—and quite apart from certain enhancements of color—note the amazing visual melodies which this resourceful artist plays. The daring off-center positions of the two main actresses. The counterpoint—of railings (a formal note), of the controlled diversity of spacing in the shutter slats, the diagonal rope with its dripping seaweed (?), the abstract, intriguing shapes, the near-white wall posters, the partly obscured smooth round bodies; again all welded into the perfect whole.

One highly original aspect of many of the Cortor paintings springs from his belief that the half-seen is more interest-compelling than the total subject. Parts of many a subject he will call upon to serve as a tantalizing provocation for the whole. And it works. Imagination is brought into play. There is audience participation. There are overtones that catch the roving eye and stimulate speculation. Artist and observer enter into a kind of partnership. And the rareness of this trait in pictures adds to its appeal.

I think Mr. Cortor can be quite sure that his "assimilation of the background and mode of living" of his chosen subjects will add to the authenticity and intrinsic value of his paintings. Such *assimilation,* incidentally, plus his interest in "color, pattern, design and composition" and plus his marked ability to weld all these elements into his own pictorial drama, is the compelling reason for his inclusion in these pages.

PAT TRIVIGNO

Late in 1949 I saw on the walls of a New York dealer's gallery a painting entitled *Gothic Sentinals.* The signature upon investigation proved to be Trivigno, a name unknown to me. But the work was so arresting, with its lively shattering of precedents relating to the time-honored decorum of saints carved in stone to guard cathedral grand doorways, that I immediately realized I was faced with one of those challenging situations where an observer or critic must make a new decision about merit. Here were saints who had come alive and were disporting themselves with an emancipated unconventionality which was quite shocking. Their heads and bodies were turned into informal positions, their hands were making gestures, which metamorphosed them from historical symbols to individuals, each eloquently expressing a personal reaction to his imposed saintly function. Yet the feeling of the architectual setting was preserved; the niches and hints of the building and the small houses of the neighboring community were still there; these events were obviously transpiring on, or just in front of, the wall of the cathedral. It was as if these actors in a drama had stepped out of their prescribed roles and positions for a brief moment—to relax and discuss matters. The discussion was serious, the religious spirit was still there; some heads seemed to express suffering or resignation, some deep thought. Hence there was no flippancy on the part of the artist in his bold smashing of saintly propriety. He was as serious as his liberated saints.

Colors, restrained mainly to grayed greens, supported this serious at-

Fig. 105. *Captives,* by PAT TRIVIGNO, 1948.

Fig. 106. *Gothic Sentinels,* by PAT TRIVIGNO, 1949

mosphere. All elements were under full control; no chaos marred the unity of the picture; the artist obviously knew his design. So this was an original expression of a weighty theme (content), hand-wrought into adequate and harmonious design (form). But these are the stuff out of which enduring art is built. I must then be in the presence of a significant work of contemporary creation which demanded, on native merits, serious consideration. To confirm that suspicion did not take too long.

I describe this event at so much length because it indicates how an observer, when not distracted or prejudiced by fame, can join the artist's adventuring in production by a like adventuring in appraisal. Observation, in other words, can share dangers, and rewards, with the artist; he who merely looks at pictures can thereby enter into a limited but significant partnership with him who creates.

In October of 1950, Pat Trivigno made his formal debut in New York in an impressive one-man showing of some twenty-one paintings, and initial impressions were amply confirmed. The young artist (he was born in New York in 1922) came from his teaching position with Tulane University in New Orleans for the opening.

Trivigno, it developed, was another of those fortunate silver-plattered youngsters, so far as his art training was concerned; he began his art study in the opening class of New York's High School of Music and Art, where the teaching was in tune with modern developments and he accordingly was not compelled to waste one or more years copying the surface data of casts, models, and still-lifes. This happy beginning was supplemented through the following years at Temple, Iowa, and Columbia Universities —apparently without undue conflicts. And this educational record has paid off handsomely. An artist of genuine achievement and great promise has emerged from his native chrysalis in a mere dozen years.

The *oldest* work in this show was done way back in 1948. It is designed realism (see Fig. 105). Here, in his "early" period, this artist demonstrates that he can paint real forms, not as posed models, but as living organisms performing their allotted functions in real life. Caged monkeys and their thwarting bars are certainly well dramatized in this mature design of interacting bodies and movements. From such realism, Trivigno pro-

Fig. 107. *Andante*, by PAT TRIVIGNO, 1950.

gressed into greater degrees of abstraction in all his creations in the fertile years, 1949 and 1950.

"Representation itself is not the thing that I work for," says this painter. "It is the spirit I want. To get the spirit I begin with the abstract and its design. The painting called *The Dance,* for instance, was an abstraction for three weeks as I worked on it; only then did the bodies of the dancers emerge." And the said painting, I had already observed, certainly *was* the spirit of the dance. It was a small piece but that spirit carried across the room; the bodies, vague as such, were but the vehicles for the rhythmic movement of the theme. And so it was with all the other paintings; their spirit brought drab gallery walls to life.

One called *Escape to Nowhere* dramatized by means of a semi-abstract fleeing woman, her arms thrashing the air in anguished movement, the futility of the attempt to escape war's desolation. Born in an observed fragment of World War II, in which the artist played his part, the memory lived until it found expression in this "inspired" work. Inspired from on high? No. Inspired by a direct, personal experience burned into memory by its tragic significance.

In *Andante* (Fig. 107) this artist has achieved that most rare and difficult task of painting musicians in a way that subordinates individual human bodies (the physical means to the music) to the functioning *group* which is its direct source. And the group, without conflicting impressions, at once conveys the familiar concept—symphony orchestra. It does this by giving out the feeling of essentials—the gesticulating leader played up oversize, as he is in musical fact, the synchronized bows, always a dominant visual motif to the concert audience, and the musically-inspired positions of heads and bodies of the players—another pertinent visual fact, infinitely more important than details of dress in the individual players. The facts here stressed, in other words, pertain to and express *music*. The familiar visual aspects of a playing orchestra—those closely associated with the resulting music itself—are so effectively dramatized that one easily imagines he is hearing the Beethoven Fifth Symphony. The moderate distortions contribute to this potent necromancy. It is interesting to note the similarity of this and the Max Weber approach to the musical theme.

The work of Trivigno produced through 1951 and 1952 has gone more abstract, the symbolism more amorphous and thereby more obscure. The artist's integrity of purpose remains as valid as ever, I am convinced, but the anomalous statement hardly strengthens the impact of that purpose —as this critic sees it.

HOWARD MANDEL

Howard Mandel belongs to that fairly large, but not crowded, group of younger artists who have something to say worth the saying and are hammering (or brushing) their concepts into expressive form of originality and power. Of such ingredients significant art is made.

The Mandel concepts are based on life experiences that include four years in the last war. For him, therefore, all veils and masks are stripped from the players in the vast drama being carried on so precariously in our *House of Cards*. He sees men in war turned into dehumanized machines —and makes tangible his vision. He observes the masked parade and the unmasking at *Midnight* when the party ends.

He envisions frustrated angels representing man's ideals—and the tragic loss of contact with them. And the resulting creation is called *Saints Deposed*. He knows pleasure and disenchantment—and paints them. He

Fig. 108. *Saints Deposed,*
by HOWARD MANDEL, 1949.

Fig. 109. *Midnight,* by HOWARD MANDEL, 1950.

perceives, in fact, many things and transcribes them onto canvas in his own complex, yet subtly restrained and compressed, way.

Mandel is one of our young artists (born in 1917) who has not been corrupted by the siren call of the easy escape into the emotional spree. He has taken his art seriously, has digested, or is still digesting, the many influences which, as he puts it, "are alive, strong and omnipresent. Perhaps there should be a new category for us. We are interested in many things and moved by many an impetus—a mood, the quality of light, a literary idea, symbolism, or a combination of all." His seriousness is two-pronged. In addition to facing the profound problems of the artist and striving to solve them adequately, he has the never-to-be-forgotten background of those four war years, from which he emerged, by the way, with the rank of Major. Faces in the Mandel paintings are serious or tragic; a smile, it seems, is out of bounds for his brush and highly conspicuous by its absence. Even in lighter themes, like *Bird Lover* of 1951, the bearded man stares straight ahead with brooding, melancholy eyes.

Mandel has found a plastic means of expressing his thoughts and moods that is his own—no mean achievement this, considering the many influences which have been his inheritance. His figures are semi-abstract symbols with just enough tie to reality to preserve character and express action, mood, and meaning. His stage sets, of houses, streets, rooms, are in keeping; they are torn apart, opened up, reduced or enlarged in size to meet the imperious demands of the play. All parts are then woven into a remarkably complete design. Nothing is vacuous; there is no chaos or blundering; all is under control. Content and form, the prevailing art recipe of the ages, are blended into a unified whole. From such a marriage, enduring art is born.

The years 1952 and 1953 were spent in Paris and in travel through Europe; dividends on this investment of work and study are already evident.

EUGENE BERMAN

The self-chosen label under which Eugene Berman works is Neo-Romantic. Born in Russia in 1899 where, at the age of fifteen he studied

Fig. 110. *Portrait of Rico Lebrun,*
by EUGENE BERMAN, 1943.

Fig. 111. *Dark Muse,* by EUGENE BERMAN, 1944.

with an architect, Berman reached Paris in 1918. There he was inspired by Picasso's Blue period, and dismissing the clamorous world of the Fauves, went on to Italy in 1922 for the first of a series of trips to that architectural world capital. Here the architect-inspired love of Italian architecture took deep root and grew into the major motivation of the following decades. A melancholy humanism graced his architecture-dotted landscapes and cityscapes in disrepair. The marks of time upon noble architecture, the decay and apathy of a race that inhabits ruins, played an increasingly important part in his paintings. "If Berman's melancholy at first seemed personal," wrote James Thrall Soby in 1941, "or at most national, it has lately come to be almost universal in application. His landscapes in ruin are now reality itself; in real life his home-less, destitute figures pause wearily in the bare fields of all Europe." And this was before World War II. His vision was nostalgic, human, and pro-phetic.

Berman's American debut was in 1932 at the Julien Levy Gallery and, in 1935, he came here to stay, except for the frequent migrations back to Paris and Italy that have continued to date.

Architectural preoccupation led to the theatre by 1936, and the record of stage and ballet settings is long and impressive. Even literal-minded Hollywood could not down, but profited by, his flair for the bizarre, spectacular and romantic.

The romantic theme, variously costumed and with amazingly diverse settings, has endured through the years. The psychological investigations of the Surrealists left him unconcerned. The visible drama of life has torched his imagination and guided his improvisations. Mr. Soby, who was his first American patron and protagonist, has concisely summed up his career in these words: "Berman is the arbiter of a poetic order of great dignity, the creator of his own intelligence and emotion."

One aspect of the Berman paintings in the 1940's that puzzles the un-informed spectator is the spattered, almost moldy treatment of picture surfaces. The artist explained this in 1949 by saying it symbolized for him "all the bullet holes with which the world's walls were peppered during the war, as well as our whole moral and spiritual degradation."

EUGENE BERMAN   181

Fig. 112. *The Temptation of St. Anthony,* by EUGENE BERMAN, 1946.

Fig. 113. *The Obelisks,* by EUGENE BERMAN, 1949.

Obviously there is logic in this realized reasoning. But when the spatterings invade a still-life of watermelons and the portrait of Reco Lebrun (Fig. 110), one wonders if the logic is not stretched to the breaking point. *The Dark Muse* of Fig. 130 is a welcome relief on this point and indicates that a rule can also be honored by its occasional breaking. Our spiritual and moral degradation is not "whole."

The eloquent humanism of this artist's philosophy and paintings is a timely reminder to our currently confused art world that the age-old virtues endure even into and through a period of strident reversions to the easy allurements of chaos. The virtues "of a poetic order of great dignity" —will not perish, Berman assures us, from the face of the earth.

The Temptation of St. Anthony of 1946, executed for the same Competition in which Max Ernst won the award, fairly seethes with symbolism in addition to the pock-marking of bullet holes; it is a more or less open book for all to read who can. Man ironically bows down to obscurely pedestalled Woman; the serpents writhe, the bats flay the air, skulls, weird birds and the tattered trappings of elegance all announce their meanings. And the whole is disciplined into the work that is art.

The Obelisks of 1949, carries on the long tradition of the melancholy of the Berman human drama in the architectural stage setting. Is this set of scenery itself becoming a bit tattered? Has it outlived its usefulness? Is a new set, and perhaps a new drama, in the making?

In the years since 1949 the drama, at least, has shifted from the painted picture to the stages of Metropolitan Opera and television. In 1950–51 Berman created the stage settings and costumes for *Rigoletto* and in 1951–52 for *La Forza del Destino*. And in the latter years he did the settings for *Amahl,* the opera by Menotti based on the Birth of Christ which had two performances on television. This collaboration between an artist of originality and power to invent and the art of drama is highly significant and should occur much more often than it does.

In 1951 Berman turned to lithographic illustrations for a book, *Viaggio in Italia,* in which his love of Italian baroche architecture and the melancholy actors on his pictorial stage continued with undiminished zeal. It will be interesting to watch for future directions.

RUTH REEVES

The law of survival of the genius of a race sees to it that enough leader-artists manage to survive and function at least fragmentarily in each age and country to save the racial culture from extinction. The margin of safety between fruition and extinction has varied greatly throughout history. In some periods, including most of those called "primitive," where simple pleasure in a man-made thing of beauty has insured its production without conflicts of profit and prestige, fruition has been automatic. In others, it has been encouraged by various patrons—a de Medici family, the Church, a King, or a State, and distinguished products have been born. In still others, indifference and neglect plus a materialistic philosophy have cut production to a trickle—on which trickle the cultural reputation of a country precariously hung. This gamut of experience has existed within nations as well as within the total period of history. It has run its course within our nation.

The story of Ruth Reeves illustrates this gamut of cultural ups and downs in that section of our recent history covered by the twenty-odd years of her personal striving. The story should be expanded into a novel with the usual conflict theme, which makes such good reading, shifted from sex to culture.

The record of her early strivings and minor successes reads much like that of any genuine artist—except that she, being a woman, had to assume the double burden, which man escapes, of managing both home and studio. Her married name is Mrs. Donald R. Baker, and three talented daughters testify to her success in this form of creative production.

Her love of textiles was born in her and the turning to them as a profession was foreordained. At first she created them just for love—choice patterns that pleased her sensitive soul—scenes of the home and baby's bath with neighbors coming in to chat. (See Fig. 114, made to hang at her own window.) Slowly orders came in for single commissions, mostly from individuals for their private use, gradually from a few scattered manufacturers for the textile trade. Her reputation grew steadily, until by 1926 she was already more or less known as the foremost artist-textile-designer in the country.

Fig. 114. *Textile*, by RUTH REEVES.
One of her earliest fabric designs
made to hang in her own home.

Fig. 115. *Life in Rockland County*, by
RUTH REEVES, 1926. A rug design. The rug was
produced by W. and J. Sloane, size 6' x 9'.

In that year plans were announced by the American Federation of Arts for an International Exhibition of Contemporary Industrial Art, featuring glass and rugs, to tour American museums during 1929 and 1930. Ruth Reeves (taking the initiative instead of waiting to be asked), went to W. and J. Sloane and offered to create a major rug design to be produced by them in a hand-knotted medium for this exhibition. Tempted by a place in the exhibit and the attendant distinction, Sloane accepted the offer, in spite of their complete preoccupation with commercial and antique furnishings. The artist was paid nothing for a design entitled *Life in Rockland County* (her home county); the rug was made up in size 9 x 6 feet, entered and exhibited. Without doubt it was the most original and distinguished indigenous rug to be designed and produced in this country within, to be safe, let us say, the past half century. I have no record of its listed price but, considering medium, uniqueness, and artist, $2500 would have been reasonable.

The rug toured museums for a year, then came back to Sloane. Four years later I investigated to see what had happened to this masterpiece, assuming that some museum would have purchased it because of its historical and cultural importance. I found the head of the Rug Department. Yes, he remembered the rug. They had had it around for some three years but could not sell it. Accordingly, just a few months previously, they had closed it out to Wanamakers in Philadelphia for $50. (See Fig. 115.)

In the following year, the Federation (which deserves great credit for these events) staged another International Exhibition—of Metal Work and Cotton Textiles. Again Miss Reeves approached Sloane. Would they produce a set of her textile designs for this exhibit? Figuring that the publicity and distinction values justified the former money loss, the answer was affirmative. Since the set was to be primarily for exhibition they would impose no restrictions; she could please herself in the designs. The financial arrangement was satisfactory; the firm paid $6000 for a series of eight designs, each screen-printed by her on cotton in 300-yard lengths, each with three color schemes.

The set with its Americana motifs—titles included *Flora Americanae,*

Fig. 116. *Tribute to Emily Dickinson,* by RUTH REEVES, 1927. One from the set of textiles designed and produced by screen printing in 1927 for W. & J. Sloane and exhibited under the auspices of the American Federation of Arts in its National Exhibition of Cotton Textiles.

Canyons of Steel, Play Boy, Electric, and *Homage to Emily Dickinson*—entered the exhibition, toured museums for another year, was featured in a large and dramatic showing at the Sloane store, received copious publicity— and undoubtedly clinched the Reeves reputation as our foremost artist- designer of printed textiles. (See Fig. 116.)

A few months after the close of the Sloane exhibit there were reports that the firm was no longer showing the materials. Again I investigated. "Yes, we have closed out the set," an executive explained. "Why?" "Well they didn't pay; sales were too small." "What do you mean by 'too small?' How large must sales be to pay?" "Oh, we figure an item must sell five thousand yards before it becomes profitable. The Reeves designs did not sell a total of five thousand yards for twenty items. So we closed them out." And a few months later reports filtered in that Sloane had spread the report in the trade that Ruth Reeves "was a commercial flop." For a number of years thereafter this leading artist was unable to obtain a single other major commission from American industry.[4]

The struggle to exist then led Ruth to the Carnegie Institute of Washington with a plan for a subsidy. Not daring to suggest support for her own uncompromising creations based on the life around her, she tied her plan to inter-American relations and research into historical art. She proposed a year's trip to Guatemala to study and collect its native textiles, then to design a set of contemporary textiles based on the native ones, or "inspired" by them, to be produced here. The Carnegie Institution accepted the plan and appropriated $10,000 to carry it out.

In due time the venture was completed. The adapted designs—"an artist presenting another culture's art through her own concepts," as Ruth calls this kind of "fortuitous" event—were shown in a Radio City gallery and also, with a great fanfare of publicity, at Macy's in New York City. In the latter, the Carnegie Corporation was prominently featured in full page ads—*and the artist, Ruth Reeves, never even mentioned in connection with the designs on sale.* This occurred in 1935 and 1936.

The idea which rapidly developed into *The Index of American Design* was born in the fertile mind of Ruth Reeves in May, 1935. It was first put into words at a chance meeting with Henry Varnum Poor in the Picture Collection of the New York Public Library, to which both artists had come for pictorial data they were both unable to find, about the American historical scene. So obvious was the need, so vast the possibilities of a pictorial recording of American achievements in design, that the idea grew into a plan for Government sponsorship. Others were consulted, including Mrs. Pollak of the WPA Federal Arts Projects, and added their ideas. At Mrs. Pollak's request Miss Reeves outlined a statement of the plan which was presented to the Arts Projects, accepted, financed, and

[4] During the Sloane exhibit I induced the firm to give me a full set of the Reeves textiles to show throughout the country as part of a lecture exhibit. This set I still have. Miss Reeves told me in 1945 it is the only complete set she knows to be in existence, except one which was purchased by the Victoria and Albert Museum in London. Her own set became scattered, and no American museum or other agency, so far as she knows, purchased or preserved the group.

Fig. 117. *Fabric Wall Hanging,* by RUTH REEVES, 1949. A specially commissioned wall hanging for Mr. and Mrs. Harry Tschopik.

Fig. 118. *My Three Daughters,* by RUTH REEVES, 1949.

Fig. 119. Contempora Silk Scarf, designed by RUTH REEVES, 1948.

Fig. 120. Contempora Silk Necktie, designed by RUTH REEVES, 1948.

hundreds of artists then on relief were put to work on the immense task, with artist Reeves engaged as National Superintendent—a post she held till the autumn of 1936.

Fourteen years later, the great enterprise was memorialized in a book, *The Index of American Design,* by Erwin O. Christensen of the National Gallery of Art, which now houses the collection. In his foreword, Holger Cahill, made National Director in New York City after the plan was organized, lists Ruth Reeves as one of several persons responsible for the *Index* but, most unfortunately, with unfair audacity, shrouds its early history with group credits which deny to Ruth Reeves the due honor of having been the first to conceive this vast project for Government. An artist should receive full credit for ideas.

In 1940 and 41, a John Simon Guggenheim Foundation fellowship was awarded to this artist for creative study among the Indians of the Andes Mountains of Peru, Equador, and Bolivia. This meant surcease from financial worry for a blessed eighteen months of self-development —an event of marked credit to the Foundation, even if, again, the scene of the said development must perforce be remote and circuitous. During the war, Ruth taught at Cooper Union to keep the wolf from her artist's door.

In reviewing this report on her case history, Ruth made several significant remarks. The one great moment of freedom to carry out her own uncensored textile creations, as offered by the Sloane commission, came about, it seems, by a fluke. "There actually was no restriction," she explained, "merely because a new fabric department head with whom I dealt broke his leg the summer I was working on the designs and so had no opportunity to investigate what I was doing. When I made delivery, this man was so shocked at the thought of Sloane's sponsoring such modern designs in public that he tried to turn back the whole yardage to me on the ground of printing mistakes. Only my contract saved me."

Then she tells how, during the War, various people in the trade again and again gave her good reasons why she should be satisfied with teaching and not attempt production. " 'I should not use my fabric-designing efforts toward making people want to buy priority-scarce commodities,' they told me. Or, if I would only elect to design the type of fabric for which there is a popular demand, I could easily support myself. In short, to quote the late General Patton's appeasement policy in his occupation of Bavaria, 'We have got to compromise with the Devil a little bit to get things going.'" Then, after a moment's thought, she continued, "This is the tragic mistake, I believe, that good designers make when they lend their talents to converters of fabrics and produce designs which, it is assumed, will be best sellers in quantity production. What I planned to do would have been a stern rebuke to manufacturers and retail stores that try so hard to get the public to buy new goods that they stage periodic affronteries based on historical design lootage. We artists have been supine about these things to an unforgivable degree."

In the years since 1946 Miss Reeves has been able to produce for the trade somewhat more frequently than in the earlier two decades. She has designed a distinguished series of Christmas cards, produced by American Artists Group, publishers, of New York. She was instrumental in starting a small firm to produce silk scarves (Contempora Scarves), and later, neckties, designed by genuine artists, even investing a considerable sum of her own savings therein. Gradually the businessmen involved lowered standards (to meet the popular taste); consequently, perhaps, after several years of impressive publicity and sales the enterprise faded out (without returning her investment).

She has had a fair number of commissions, among which a private one by Mr. and Mrs. Harry Tschopik, Jr., of Tarrytown, N.Y., indicates what would be normal procedure if we were more culturally mature. This special design was based on ancient Peruvian, Spanish, Colonial, and current Andean artifacts which the Tschopiks brought back to the States and used as *objets d'art* in their home. Miss Reeves took the decorative motifs in these objects and transposed them (by a process of redesigning into her own translation) into the screen-printed wall-hanging of Fig. 117 to go into the living room where the original objects were shown. If a design of this type merely copies ancient or other motifs, or is transposed by a commercial designer, the imitative result will automatically be one more evidence of our art decadence. A genuine artist, however,

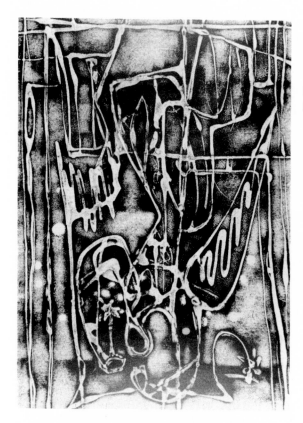

Fig. 121. *Allegory,*
by RUTH REEVES, 1951.

by a re-creation of such data into her own terms, as dictated by her own sensitivity, can achieve an original work, as would happen if source material were taken from nature or life. Ruth Reeves has in this case so achieved.

In addition to the examples here shown, a great many of the Reeves textile designs through the years have been highly sensitive, authentic, and original abstractions. Whether they tell a story or play pure visual music, the creations of this artist are always the result of her own reactions to the varied stimuli in the life about her. An alert mind, a quick eye, and a supersensitive soul capture sensations and transmute them into works of living art. See the print, *Allegory* (not a textile), of Fig. 121.

Such is the record. The point in this dramatic story of a sucessful battle for survival, which needs careful consideration by the American people, is that an artist of high talents in a special but widely useful field has been allowed to function freely and at her best only once in some twenty-five years, and for the balance of that time has had to submerge and side-track her special abilities with research, teaching, and other tasks in order to live. To date there has been no agency, profit or non-profit, in this richest country in the world, concerned with protecting, fostering, and equipping with production facilities this "natural resource" in the art of printed textiles. As a result the country is tangibly poorer; it has lost many distinguished creations which might have been produced during these fertile years. And which, of course, can still be produced when and if conditions change.

PART III - ABSTRACTION AND/OR THE NON-OBJECTIVE

Since a considerable number of artists believe that the profoundest meanings can only be expressed via abstraction, we shall follow that presumption in the present plan of arrangement. The complete follows the partial abstraction.

I-ON ABSTRACT PAINTING

If the abstract in art is a release into profundity, symbolism, and design, and if profundity gains as it ascends in pictures from the province of the obvious fact into that of spirit with its non-obvious language, then this is the right moment in our developing scheme to observe abstract painting. In its dual role of playing pure visual music and symbolizing the deeper realities, it can go, in the hands of a profound artist, beyond the reach of designed realism and yet it does not delve into the fantasy of surrealism. There is an ebb and flow in the affairs of men, including artists; some will be attracted, some repulsed, by the same development in a given era, or at different times in their own journey through life. Abstract art is no exception to this rule.

> When an art dies [wrote Wyndham Lewis back in 1940], there is no announcement in the newspapers, as in the case of the demise of an eminent citizen. So no one knows that it is dead. It is still spoken of as if it were alive and kicking. This article is a sort of obituary notice. It is written to announce the death of "abstract art." . . . Braque's abstract bric-a-brac is fast becoming junk. The most amusing collage will fetch nothing in Europe. Brancusi's egg has gone to join the Dodo's. Picasso's latest spawn is merely reflex action, from a lower center, that does not count any more than the stampede of the chicken after its head has been severed. A little *kicking* goes

on, of a morning, in Monsieur Léger's studio, no doubt (for *he* is still alive, of course). But all such activity today—however corrupt and involved with natural form—belongs to a movement that is dead.

So said abstractionist Lewis at a moment in history when a powerful revival of interest in the abstract was just getting underway. What he meant subconsciously was, of course, that the abstract motivation had run its course *in him*. It was his resources that had come to an end, not those of the movement he condemned. Since those words were printed, it is the revolt against the limitations of "natural forms" that has steadily accelerated, until it is safe to say that from a third to a half of a national painting exhibition will deal with a major degree of abstraction.

It was only two years later, in 1942, that Clement Greenberg, for instance, was saying about the abstract,

> Here is art in movement; new possibilities are being plumbed that burst the confines of the set easel picture and sculptured piece. . . . At the sight of the cubist paintings by Gris, Picasso and Braque, one wonders how it was ever possible to say that cubism is a dry, intellectualized art without emotion, for these pictures with their brown tones and vibrating planes communicate the pathos of their moment and place with an eloquence more than equal to that of Apollinaire's poetry.

And so it goes. The same Greenberg, by the way, since about 1950, has been proclaiming the "action painters" with their abandonment of almost all the cubists stood for, except emotion, as the avant-garde. The fact that some artists and critics have reversed trends and swung back to the obvious subject, or to chaos, does not disprove the lure of the profound statement; it merely announces the law that pendulums must swing.

In a recent interview Georges Braque was asked if he was consciously abandoning abstraction in his later paintings. In answer he drew a line suggesting the profile of a woman's head. "Look at this line," he said. "Is it abstract? Is it a profile? Where does abstraction begin? Where does it end? I have never been able to find out what it really is."

Not a very helpful comment, this, from a modern master of abstraction and its plastic design. He who should know leaves those who want to know out in the cold on their own resources to make their own decisions. Shall we be equally modest? Or shall we pursue the question about the nature of abstraction in art and self-assertively make our own decisions? The former is easy. The latter difficult. Suppose we choose the difficult way.

Setting aside the question of where abstraction begins and ends, what is its nature and purpose in the art of the picture?

To abstract is to take from, to extract. To extract from a subject some phase of its many characteristics which suits an artist's purpose and to organize that material into an expression is to create a new entity under the sun. Such a creation will stand as a symbol of the object, or some part of it, and will be more or less recognizable as it is more or less real. It is this function of extracting meaning or quality from some concrete source that is the important matter; the degree of the recognizability, or the abstraction, is relatively unimportant.

Such extracted material can be freely bent to the artist's will. It can be played with. It can be designed. Its colors and spaces and textures can be enhanced, dramatized. Intangibles can be given a new identity. Sidney Janis argues that whereas surrealism stems mainly from the romantic emotional stream and may be emotional, spontaneous, intuitive, subjective, and unconscious, the abstract art of today follows the classic line from cubism through futurism to abstract art and for the most part is intellectual, disciplined, architectonic, objective, and conscious. This distinction between the two streams may apply if he has in mind certain artists who exemplify each. But it need not apply. Abstract painting can be lavishly emotional and spontaneous and thereby release creative powers that are excluded from intellect. And it can be subjective as well as objective in its source of inspiration. Disciplined, yes; the emotions need to be pressed into an art form by conscious mind controlling their exuberance; but this must be done without undue damage to their felt relationships. Architectonic control implies such a judicious ordering to gain the dignity of the enduring form. The point is, abstraction can be about anything, both in its content, if any, and in its form. It can have any degree of meaning. It can be geometric or amorphous in character. It is a release into a limitless symbolism. But perhaps its most important single characteristic is that it invites the emergence of design as pure visual sensation.

In a broader sense the general impact of abstraction on the art of our time is notable because of the opportunity it offers artists to implement a steadily changing and expanding concept of the meaning of reality, and a growing quest for a language of symbols and images to express its deeper truths as these are individually discovered. The sense of need for this quest and for a modern iconography to express its findings has been spreading among artists during the last two decades as is amply indicated by the steady gain in the number of abstract and semi-abstract works entering exhibitions. When you ask an abstract artist why he paints that way the almost invariable answer is to the effect that he is weary of painting the obvious and hungers for the deeper realities. Some will add the sensory satisfactions to this goal but others, surprisingly enough, will overlook these, or take them for granted, and stress only the desire for the more profound meaning.

The more profound meanings of semi-abstract and abstract symbolism, when they are present in a work, come under the head of subject, and interpretation of subject is a happy hunting ground for the intellects of any and all comers—the findings of any one prospector presumably being authentic, at least for himself. This fact should give the professional critic pause before he invades the estate of subject, for the truth applies to him as well as the layman. The present critic will try to maintain a becoming humility in this respect and concentrate his self-assertive opinions on that other wide-ranging estate of the art of the picture where reactions are more universal in their authority. The sensory response to the music of sound certainly is more universal than ever has beeen the intellectual re-sponse to ideas; the same should hold for the music of color and form.

NON-OBJECTIVE PAINTING

The term "non-objective painting" is another way of saying complete abstraction. The Solomon R. Guggenheim Collection of Non-Objective Paintings, in the person of Hilla Rebay, its former director, has greatly expanded and particularized the obvious meaning of the words, however. I quote:

> Non-Objective art is the cosmic sense, beautified by genius. Its lawful arrangement is the eternal rhythm that one perceives and feels but cannot see.
>
> Non-Objectivity is intuition made audible and visible. Its experience is the culmination of culture. It cannot be given. It must be acquired. Genius is born to it. Non-objective art in music and painting represents the spiritual height. . . . The intellectually conscious approach prevents spontaneous joy and a sensitive reaction to the wealth of creation.

If you can delete the romance from this short extract from a long article, Miss Rebay is right, especially in the last sentence. The point is, the essence of her argument also applies to genuine abstract art; it need not be limited, as she limits it, to the non-objective. The Museum of Non-Objective Paintings deserves great credit for its educational featuring of distinguished work—mainly, heretofore, from European artists, with Paul Klee, Vasily Kandinsky, and Rudolf Bauer justly featured. The Museum's new building, designed by Frank Lloyd Wright, is on its way to completion in New York and will break new ground in museum design. And its new Director, James Johnson Sweeney, is breaking new ground within its walls by declining to make a rigid distinction between abstract and non-objective; quality is his guide. Lovers of distinguished art the country over are looking to Mr. Sweeney to assume leadership in his support of contemporary art—a leadership that is desperately needed in today's art world.

Abstraction, then, can be summed up as a magnificent release—a release into profundity, symbolism, and design.

I shall make no attempt to outline the growth of the Abstract Movement from its revival in France—(historically speaking it is anything but new)—to its transplanting to our shores after 1913, nor of its rapid development here. Rather I shall select a relatively few artists who in eminent degree have brought to their experiments and high achievements, in this domain of the spirit, the art of the ages to temper their subconscious and emotional adventurings, thereby entrenching them securely within the Grand Tradition. Since the list of successful experimentation is far too

long to allow a critic to do justice to all, and since it is constantly growing, thereby demanding annual revision, the few will have to represent,
for this volume, the many. Future surveys must constantly amplify the
list by giving credit where credit is due.

II-OUR ABSTRACT PAINTERS
AND SCULPTORS

STUART DAVIS

To get our bearings in the arena of contemporary art, it is only necessary to examine again the words and deeds of those artists who have resolved their chaos into mature expressions of the grand tradition. No other of our seasoned creators could serve that refresher-course purpose better than Stuart Davis, one of our deans of American abstract painting.

Back in 1915 Davis was already in revolt against his Robert Henri inheritance of stark realism. Emotional distortion with its free improvisation was his means of escape. He was floundering then—away from something he knew to be inadequate, toward he knew not what. So have many artists floundered before and since. But he made no haven of that unhappy state. He found a way out. That way was the discovery of essences rather than appearances. Fig. 122, of 1930, one of a series of early improvisations, illustrates the middle period of that quest; the symbol has replaced the replica and the organization of color, space, form has come into its own. Thereafter the search for inner realities continued with ever-increasing range and intensity—and has been highly successful.

Davis is an educator and protagonist of modern art as well as a producer. In many visits over the years to his old Seventh-avenue studio I have interrupted him slaving away with pencil and paper, performing his self-imposed obligation to society by organizing words into letters and articles for such of the public prints as they could break into. And these words, with their clarified ideas, have forced their way into many and diverse printings; the breaks have probably been more frequent than those achieved by any other practicing American artist. Many liberal magazines have welcomed them, including *Harper's* (1943), and even the International Business Machines Corporation magazine, *Think* (1945). They have also penetrated at times the insidious censorship of our business-controlled means of mass communication—"that subtle and far-reaching censorship which acts as a termite blitz against the very foundations of the spontaneous impulse to create free art," as Davis calls it —as well as many art pages of New York and other newspapers. The penetrations, however, have not included *Life*. In its four-page article about Davis (Feb. 17, 1947), that magazine *interpreted* the artist in a trite and supercilious fashion which brought the "artistic jargon of high-brow esthetes" down to the assumed intelligence level of the man-in-the-street. Let me illustrate the Main-street "jargon."

> Fundamentally there is nothing very mysterious or difficult to understand about the work of an abstract painter like Stuart Davis. He goes about painting a picture in very much the spirit grandma had when she was making a patchwork quilt, placing squares and oblongs of color where they will contribute tasefully to the overall pattern. Being a professional, he is somewhat more skillful and imaginative than grandma; he knows how to produce striking contrasts and how to lead the eye through *interesting little adventures* in observation. [Italics are mine.]

In contrast to this sugar-coating, here is a sample of Davis's "artistic jargon" which explains the modern viewpoint, including his own, about as well as it can be expressed.

> From the great variety of approaches toward the same basic subject-matter in art throughout the centuries, the artist has learned that "art" is not the pursuit of some ideal canon of beauty. He sees instead that it is a struggle to realize spiritual values innate in himself in relation to the world in which we live. He accepts the environment of today with its new lights, speeds and spaces, as his subject-matter. His purpose is to create forms that em-

body the psychological content of his perceptions and emotions in response to that subject-matter. It is certain that these forms will not be replicas of external form, light, color and space in nature, because such forms would not express the psychological reality which gives art its enduring meaning. In the very nature of the artist's purpose the forms of his subject-matter are organized in a way that has no objective counterpart. They are organized in a way that expresses the psychological temper of some aspect of the society he lives in and of his own temperament in relation to that society.

Is this "high-brow jargon" really over the heads of all the grandmas and grandpas of the country? And of their collegiate sons and daughters? If so, something should be done about it. Would it not be more intelligent and flattering to the low-brows if that something were intellectual meat straight from the authority-in-the-case for them to chew on? If that section of the public which will read any article on art is not as dumb as the editors think, this kind of editorial dilution is unnecessary and puerile.

For many years Davis has been arguing that abstract art is realistic and has meaning, in addition to its other values. He has in fact, in his own work, given this phase of the abstract priority over its more obvious sensory qualities. Back in the 1930's he was explaining thus:

> Why is abstract art realistic, and what does it mean? What is meaning? Meaning is objective process, a real happening, which is proved by its social communicability. Meaning is a quality found only in association with experience common to many people. For an event to have meaning for us, we must have had experience with the objective elements that compose it. Abstract art is realistic and has meaning because it expresses common experience.

Davis would doubtless be the first to admit that many people realize inadequately, or in some cases not at all, the nature of their common experiences which tie in with, and can only be expressed by, the abstract. Every one admits that a radio exists, yet it is the essence of abstraction. Emotions, feelings, moods are common experiences, yet quite intangible. "To regard abstract art as a mysterious and irrational bypath on the road of true art," says this artist, "is like regarding electricity as a passing fad."

Davis, however, does find time to paint as well as explain; he has been implementing such words as the above since 1912. Even in 1910, while he was studying with Henri, his revolt had begun—against the "saccha-

Fig. 122. *Still Life with Flowers,* by STUART DAVIS, 1930.

Fig. 123. *Ursine Park,* by STUART DAVIS, 1942

Fig. 124. *Seme,* by STUART DAVIS, 1953.

rine Fifth Avenue vulgarity of the Academy." Then came the Armory Show of 1913 which he calls the "greatest single influence on my work." In the intervening years his growth has been consistent and always solidly based on the enduring values. For the past two decades that work has won a place for him in the forefront of our contemporary art.

No critic should presume to explain for others mature paintings like *Ursine Park* and *Seme*. Much better it is for each observer to acquaint himself with the philosophy of the artist as expressed in his words and then read into its symbolism his own meanings, enjoying to the full in that process all possible sensory aesthetic excitements.

Stuart Davis, in the summer of 1952, was one of four artists chosen by a committee of museum curators and art historians to represent the United States in the International Biennale Exhibition in Venice, Italy.

GEORGE L. K. MORRIS

George L. K. Morris is one of those relatively few moderns who has achieved mastery in his field of abstract painting and has also been able to "pacify" (he likes to use this word in describing the artist's problems of organization of the diverse and conflicting pictorial elements)—the ideological chaos which rages about him and all of us in the works themselves and in the words relating to abstract art. He has thought through the motivations and processes of this important art and put them into the record in print and speech in a way which clarifies rather than adds to the confusion. Let me illustrate by several quotations:

> Somewhere in his journal, Delacroix observes that painting is the most difficult of the arts because it demands not only erudition like that of a composer but execution like that of a violinist as well. Regardless of the validity of such an appraisal, it is pertinent to emphasize this dual aspect of the painter's task.
>
> There is of course no reliable method of tracing the evolution of an art work through either of these stages. Even the most rational artist leans so heavily upon unconscious intuition that he himself can rarely tell where one process ends and the other begins. Suffice it to say that somewhere during the progress of every painting there is an interval which culminates in the emergence of the image (wherein the artist is functioning as com-

poser) and a second period (the artist as performer) during which the creator draws upon his technical skill and qualitative sensibility for the credible rendition of this image.

Abstract painting obviously fits closely into such a musical parallel because the abstractionist, in his renditions of form and space, can shake himself thoroughly free. No spot or line needs to be fixed just because it would seem to belong there in nature. And, during the second process indicated above, a virtuoso-technique can deliver expressive content most directly when there are no naturalistic problems to demand simultaneous realization. . . .

Good art emerges in quite unexpected ways as a direct expression of the personality producing it. It is on quality alone that any work must stand, with a right to be judged by itself and without relation to anything else.

It is difficult to penetrate the creative process beyond such general specifications as these. And, in the later stages particularly, it will be seen that the abstract painter does not differ so much from any other artist after all; there are the same requisites; a new freedom releases new potentialities. And, during an epoch in history such as this, when everywhere the mind seeks some order for its broken cultural fragments, the abstract art work takes on a new significance. It has the "look" of its time, the ability to hold its place among the mechanisms that characterize the new civilization we are just beginning to know. And most of all it provides an area within whose bounds human emotion and plastic energy have combined to provide a space where every element must be understood, every tension held within an ordered limit.[1]

This is a formal statement of the artist's creed that is intended to apply to all abstract art. It does so apply. But it also, as is natural, specifically fits Morris's own work. And his abstractions fit it. He uses all his faculties of conscious mind and unconscious intuition, all his erudition to compose, and all his technical capacities to execute, "like a violinist"—to achieve his goal. He allows the new freedom to realize new potentialities which do bring order into our broken cultural fragments (if we are alert enough to get the messages) and thereby take on fresh significance. He challenges the observers of his paintings to comprehend how he has combined human emotion and plastic energy in ways that characterize the new civilization of which we are a part.

[1] The above is taken from an article by Morris on "Aspects of Picture-Making" in the book, *American Abstract Artists* (New York: Ram Press, 1946).

In conversation recently, Morris in effect paraphrased these formally worded goals by an immediate and personal statement. "It is as if you throw spots on a wall," he said, "and then by some magic they acquire an order. Technique, in the sense of all the skills, is obliterated. It is a terrible task to bring it off, this order, into a consistent spirit, when all the influences of life and so many in art are pulling in different directions. All great works must have a sense of immediacy of creation; even if there are months of work in them, they must look as if done in a second. The best of primitive art has this feel of immediacy and this consistent spirit. We have to match the primitives on these counts without imitating them and then carry on from there into our own idiom and our own expression." Note that Morris says technique is to be "obliterated"—but not abandoned.

Morris has been called an intellectual painter, a modern academician, a "sterile formalist," and the like. "This is skillful, knowledgeable, painting," said one art critic in 1948, "You may, however, find it, as I did, rather decorative than expressive." I deny all such charges. Morris is an intellectual, admittedly. But I find a just balance in his work between conscious mind and the unconscious intuition and plastic energy which transcend it. Morris feels as well as thinks. And at a time when undisciplined emotion is rampant in some quarters, we need to be pulled back, in our production and our thinking, to such a just balance. Finally, to reduce the potentialities of the word "design" into its conventionally accepted diminutive "decorative," or "mere decoration," is to measure the sensitivities of the critic rather than the work.

On a symposium in 1951, where devotees of the chaos of the emotional spree were represented, Morris spoke for all mature artists in the eloquent statement of a creed quoted in Part I, under the heading of "Order Versus Chaos."

That statement did pull back to basic issues about as forcefully as is possible in words. It should be emblazoned somewhere for all devotees of enduring art to see, read, remember, and pass on to others, especially the youth of today. A parting of the ways is indeed involved. It is salvation or disaster we must choose.

Fig. 125. Orvieto, by GEORGE L. K. MORRIS, 1944.

Fig. 126. *Saks Fifth Avenue Window,*
by GEORGE L. K. MORRIS, 1950.

Fig. 127. *I R T,* by GEORGE L. K. MORRIS, 1936--1953.

George Morris, in May of 1950, had one of those opportunities which come all too rarely to genuine artists, of using his talents in a "practical" way. Artist's Equity and Saks Fifth Avenue, the department store, made a deal whereby each would advertise the other by means of windows on Fifth Avenue to be designed by Equity's artist members. Nine windows were so designed. In seven, two artists collaborated; in only two did an individual artist have solo responsibility and Morris was one of these. His window was an outstanding achievement of the dynamic control of interacting planes made up of small geometric shapes—the dynamism resulting from clever contrasts of size and movement rather than color. A naturalistic manikin displaying a dress was required by the store in each window, thereby destroying the unity of any abstract design. Morris alone revolted, substituted an abstract head on his manikin, and saved the integrity of his window and his art. (See Fig. 126.)

The Morris paintings here shown certainly have a sense of rightness about them; they belong to our time. As to "immediacy," they do not look as if "done in a second"; rather there is evidence of months of work behind them to gain the perfect harmony of all parts. Colors are restrained and often accented with grays and blacks. Fig. 125 shows a masterly amalgamation of diverse, richly textured spaces. Figs. 126 and 127 experiment successfully with checker-board effects playing with the illusion of deep space that actually is firmly held to the picture plane. About Fig. 127, the artist has this to say:

> I R T takes a Subway Station, to me the most unpleasing, disordered and cacophonous spot I know of, and expends every effort toward making an abstract rendition of it that will be in one way ordered and classical, and in another suggest the harshness of the subject.
>
> One idea behind all my recent work is to create a sort of union of opposites—both in structure and mood. In structure, it is to make a controlled projection into space by means of perspective, symbols and a back-plane—and at the same time to have a rhythmic play on the picture surface so that the eye can, as it were, always be in two places at once—back in space if looked at one way, or on the canvas level in another.

Abstractionist Morris is offering his fellow citizens sensory experiences with profound values somewhat hidden within them. The obscurity is due, not to any wish or fault of the artist, but rather to certain limitations of our aesthetic climate. Climates, however, do change.

JOSEF ALBERS

It takes an unusually sensitive eye to "get" the refinements of sensation which Josef Albers presents to the observer of his prints and paintings. These sensations deal with the usual elements—color, space, line, texture, and form—but not in the usual way. His vision is attuned to the refinements of harmonic relationships between two or ten colors, or spaces, or organic interaction of planes, with a sensitivity comparable only to the similar tonal refinements of a Chopin or a Brahms. Hours, perhaps days, or even months or years, will be spent in shifting a line or a space to that exact position in relation to the frame and the spaces around where it will "sing" the perfect harmony.

Colors must integrate and correlate perfectly. Lines will play an important part as soloists, or as boundaries, and / or as foils for the spaces of planes. Textures are used sparingly, mainly for their enrichment of planes; never are they exploited above other actors on the pictorial stage; it is spaces, colors, lines that most attract this artist. And the dynamics of the angular shape and straight line—the ruled line rather than the free-hand—are more frequent than the suavity of curves. Says Albers:

> These abstract compositions are, as the term "tectonic" defines, constructed. They are built with elements which are produced preferably by mechanical means and which are arranged in an emphasized mechanical order.
> These results promote ruler and drafting pen as proper means for graphic expression. They prove it unjustified to evaluate and reject lines without modulation as an inartistic means for graphic art. In this way they oppose a belief that hand-made is better than machine or tool-made; or that construction is anti-graphic, or unable to reveal and to arouse emotion. Each way has its possibilities. Most emphatically is this true in this time of industrial evolution.

Albers is related to Mondrian in this preference for the severe, pure design but, unlike that other highly sensitized nature, he does not confine himself within the rigidity of the right angle. He enjoys the diversity of non-parallel, crossing lines, and planes of oblique directions, for the

Fig. 128. *Lowers*, by JOSEF ALBERS, 1930.

Fig. 129. *View*, by JOSEF ALBERS, 1933.

Fig. 130. *Brick Mural*, by JOSEF ALBERS, 1949.

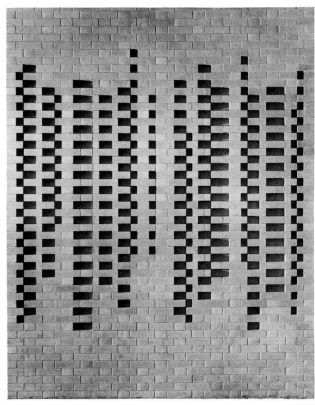

wider range of sensations they offer. He believes that surprise and the shock of contrast give a keen edge to aesthetic pleasure. The shocks which Albers offers, however, are gentle ones; there is never the sensitized emotional brutality of a Rouault. But the emotion is there, nevertheless. So is intellect, but not in cold-blooded isolation. The two extremes have learned to co-habit in the art of this man in perfect adjustment to each other and it is this adjustment which carries over so adroitly in his creations.

The above quotation presents but one facet of a far-reaching philosophy of art and life owned by Joseph Albers. In presenting his beliefs he is, fortunately, highly vocal. From his voluminous writings I extract a few of many "truths" which, I think, will stand considerable acidic testing:

> I think we have to shift from the data to the spirit, from the person to the situation, or from biography to biology in its real sense. As regards art results, from the content to the sense, from the "what" to the "how"; as regards art purposes, from the representation to the revelation. . . .
>
> To speak in professional terms: We should discover, for instance, that music, too, has to do with proportion and the values of line and volume: also that literature can be static or dynamic, and can have staccatos and crescendos, and poems can have color: that the play on the stage has not only dramatic climax but also optical and acoustical ones; that there are musical qualities in all art—that every art work is built (i.e., composed), has order, consciously or unconsciously.
>
> To say it essentially: Everything has form and every form has meaning. The ability to select this quality is culture. If you agree with me that religion worked out only on Sunday is no religion at all, then we must be united in this opinion, that seeing art only in museums, or using art only as amusement in lazy hours, shows no understanding of art at all. If art is an essential part of culture and life, then we must no longer educate students and public to be art historians or imitators of antiquities, but for artistic seeing, artistic working, and more, for artistic living.

Albers was one of the first of those German artists who imported the philosophy and methods of the Bauhaus of Weimar and Dessau to our shores and practiced them in sixteen years of teaching at Black Mountain College in North Carolina and later at Yale University. The fact that his art was imported, however, is relatively unimportant. "Music," either visual or aural, is an international language; its source does not fundamentally matter. The source of abstract art is the cosmos, or the turn of a head in light, or a flash of insight in a reflective mind—and these events can happen in Weimar, Black Mountain, or New York with equal authority. Albers is an international artist and one of that important group now at work in his adopted country for the benefit of his fellow world-citizens.

I. RICE PEREIRA

Here is an artist—a painter of abstractions—who sees herself as a citizen of the Universe rather than merely Greenwich Village or the U.S.A. Also she sees her art as universe-wide in its implications. I assume this—she has made no such direct claim—because she draws sustenance from the great universal—*light*—and then bends that universal to her will. She manipulates light. As artist, she changes its source from the sun to her painting. The colors she so carefully allots to canvas become the source of light, or, in effect, are light. They give forth sensations to the observer, as light in color. Thus, if I understand correctly, they amalgamate with universals. But let her explain:

> In terms of relationships, man can only make a continuity of perception in terms of his own universe. His perceptions reach out into infinity, but, in order to make a continuity in terms of experience so that the flow of his perceptions does not stop, he must do this in a circulatory movement. That is, he must go back to his own symbol, the SUN—that is the symbol of his own constellation—in order to make a complete circuit back to his position on earth. Otherwise his perceptions become frozen from extension.
>
> Man needs the reconciling symbol of the Sun to restore his *equilibrium* to *reality*.
>
> The Artist can pave the way for Man's perceptions of a conscious reality of new universal ideas. He has the vision and can create the symbols. The Artist has the key to Man's continuity in reality. The Artist can restore equilibrium so Man can sense the universe without losing his balance. If the Artist senses these new dimensions and is able to establish his own relationship to them, he will discover his own language in space and time. But he cannot do this unless the constant (LIGHT) is given its proper position in relation to Man's perceptions of reality. The LIGHT must be taken from its fixed position and become fluid. It is the constant that will make the continuity in human experience.

Pictorially, academic vision is a discrepancy between THINKING and FEELING—because we *think* that vision and light are on the same plane as the spectator. This is a prescribed logic made by man and his *feelings* do not fit the formula. They do not fit because his feelings *sense* that the light is in his own depth of inner reality and out beyond outer reality. So his perceptions cannot grasp reality, or make a continuity or synthesis between inner and outer experience.

Deep stuff, this. What do the big words and big thoughts mean? As Miss Pereira read them to me from a long article explaining her philosophy, I was convinced of two things. They had profound meaning to her and did express her philosophy and they were pregnant with meaning for us who are less initiated into their implications as applied to the art of painting. In other words, the philosophy, backed as it is with a decade of experience in creating abstract works that command respect on their obvious merits, must also command respect for merits which are certainly not readily obvious. It behooves us, therefore, to dig into the tangible creations and try to discover the intangible meanings to the best of our ability.

Irene Pereira has been fortunate in one respect; she did not waste a long period of youth in academic training in skilled copying of surface truth. She studied for four years in the night school of the Art Students League (paying her own way by daytime earnings), mainly with Richard Lahey and Jan Matulka; the years were 1928–1932. Here she evidently learned the fundamentals of a creating art buttressed by her native and developing organizational power over color, space, form, and texture; the early painting, *The Embryo,* of 1936, testifies to this basic training. (See Fig. 131.) By 1942 she had found her place among the textured squares, rectangles, and diverse lines which have held her in willing bondage ever since—with but few such experimental diversions as the *New World A'Coming* of Fig. 133 (1948). *Composition in White,* of Fig. 132 (1942), shows the early and relatively simple play with these elements; note the steadily increasing complexity in nearly all works through succeeding years. Note also that even in this early creation, depth in space was combined with flat pattern to gain profundity—and the plastique of painting.

In 1947 Miss Pereira explained her painting differently. Already she

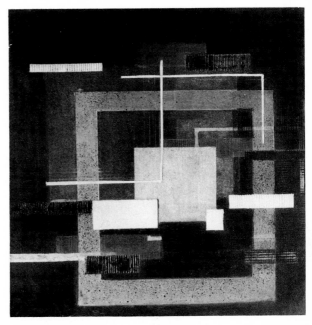

Fig. 131. *The Embryo*, by I. RICE PEREIRA, 1936.

Fig. 132. *Composition in White*, by I. RICE PEREIRA, 1942.

Fig. 133. *New World A'Coming*, by I. RICE PEREIRA, 1948.

was concerned with universals, but her terms of reference were people rather than the universe. Of *Red, Yellow and Blue,* painted in 1942, she then said, "I endeavored to explore the formal and design possibilities of painting with emphasis on structural ways of expressing space. Also to stimulate a visual and tactile awareness of paint quality by textural effects." The shift of emphasis to *light* had developed gradually from about 1938; it was a shift of the major role, not an abnegation of the earlier values, which had already earned her a place within the Grand Tradition.

Evaporating Night (1951), of Fig. 134, has increased in complexity of colors, spaces, textures to what would seem to be the utmost limit possible of expression on a single plane. And yet all parts are cleanly and clearly realized in their infinite variations; here is discipline of feeling, emotion, sensitivity. For these designs grow from within out according to an inherent necessity. They are not cold-blooded intellectualizations.

> My painting is automatic, too [explains the artist]. I know the goal—dedication to light. I can only feel the next step in each work as it develops. It is a feeling rhythm. It has an order—and never makes an error. It organizes itself. I can only analyze the plastic construction at I work. A lot of it has to do with unfolding depths and transparencies. I let the thing flow. Suddenly I understand something. It is a terrific shock. Then I can find myself in words—automatically.

Here is another statement of that age-old creed of genuine artists expressed in personal terms. Its essence, in general terms, should be blazoned over the door of every art institution in the land in six foot letters until its logic stops short in its tracks the current wave of exploitation of *undisciplined* emotional release into chaos which has chiseled its way onto part of our art stage. Discipline need not be by rigid external law; it can be by internal necessity—by a law that is absorbed and works automatically. But the law, the self-discipline, must be there before art is born. Miss Pereira feels strongly on this subject. I could be quoting her in these remarks.

In *Light Is Gold,* of Fig. 135 (1951), complexity of color in light (or light in color), and of linear motifs and the familiar rectangles, is again greatly increased by the overlaying of painted or colored transparencies. And the diagonal becomes a welcome foil for the prevailing verticals and hori-

218   I. RICE PEREIRA

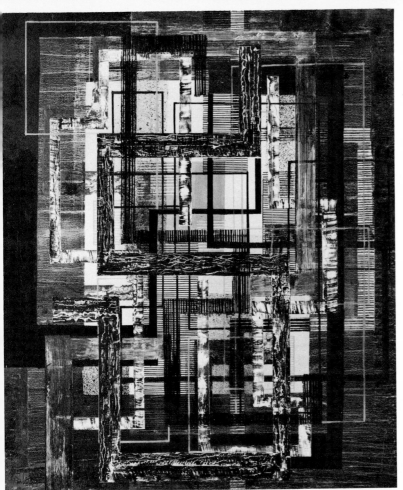

Fig. 134. *Evaporating Night,*
by I. RICE PEREIRA, 1951.

Fig. 135. *Light is Gold,* by I. RICE PEREIRA, 1951.

zontals of nearly all of the Pereira paintings. When asked why she depended so heavily on the right angle, the artist had no ready answer; it was as if she had not thought about this characteristic. "I don't know," she said. "It seems important to preserve the rectilinear. I do it by instinct." Light does appear to emerge from these multiple-layer works; one can glimpse her reason for the emphasis thereon. And we do know about the prism, the spectrum, and that all colors are in the light beam. Perhaps this universal law in nature does demand wider applications to art than it has yet had. Perhaps artist Pereira is pointing a new way of revolutionary implications.

In the meantime we can enjoy the paintings for the delicate, vigorous, and always sensitively controlled waves of sensation they give forth. The broad meandering band of solid black pulls forward, forcing bright colors and many intermediate tints to recede to different depths. Line groups in great variety and many textures (as in Fig. 134) pull fore and push back. Long solo lines, in black and colors, interweave and unify, as do also the bands of textures with color. As Abstract painting this work probably demonstrates the theme of unity amidst diversity as thoroughly as any we could find in the contemporary American scene. It is distinguished, rewarding, Abstract art.

"Art is a living, fluid thing," says Pereira, "that moves in space and time. The real artist is able to make it so live. Otherwise a painting becomes merely a reflection of an object."

The retrospective exhibition of the work of I. Rice Pereira at the Whitney Museum in New York from January to March, 1953, was a well-earned tribute to an important contemporary American artist.

SEYMOUR FOGEL

Seymour Fogel's is another lusty talent, as he is a lusty man. His paintings boil, swirl, writhe. They tear the canvas with a power of movement that only his husky muscles can hold within the frame. They are related to what one imagines nuclear fission must be; the atoms of emotion are split before our eyes and chase each other in endless circlings of check-reined turmoil of color, space, and line. A seething spirit translates itself via hand and brush into an indelible record for all to perceive who can respond to unadulterated emotion. There is no excess cerebralism evident here to mutilate the direct power of this emotion; it is passionate painting.

But, unlike the passion of Rouault, this passion cannot even tolerate the restraints of the recognizable symbol. It makes its own symbolism. Its meanings are within itself. Fogel puts it this way:

> Most of us walk on the surface of things and never see or sense the wonders all about us—wonders which are facets of an underlying, eternal truth. When an artist discovers for himself an element of this truth, he paints because he must. He paints with no thought of the hazardous preoccupation with tomorrow, nor the doctrinaire concepts of today. My paintings are my test-tubes in my laboratory. Each is a separate analysis of something newly discovered.

What does this dynamic artist mean by "truth"? He means, I gather, the essence of a thing, or things, as that essence is ultimately realized after surface distractions have been cleared away. Says Fogel:

> There are elements of truth in everything. There is always an underlying truth somewhere that relates to each of us. The need to see what is beautiful in a thing, or a fragment of a thing—in a bone, a rock, a hole in a rock, a blade of grass, a skyscraper or a spider-web floating in the wind, forces me to try to express my feeling for that beauty as I see it, on the flat plane of the picture. My paintings are not abstract. They are what I see. This inner drive, this compulsion to find that which is true for me, this search for bedrock, leads me to believe that the key to truth can be found plastically as well as scientifically.
>
> To translate these reactions to the spatial needs of a two-dimensional picture, the artist has to pull, to manipulate spaces, colors and linear movement to meet the need of the picture plane. This is plastic design. But I like to forget all terminology, whether or not it is understood. I want to deal with the things themselves. I don't want design to be sensory; that is a by-product. Visual music does have validity; I admit that. But to me design is a means. I use it to help nail down the validity of the thing.

Figs. 136 and 137 will illustrate the words this artist speaks. Movement is here the dominant theme—movement supported by swirling colors, spaces, and textures—and this holds true of the bulk of Fogel's copious works. They sing their harmonic songs of deep meaning, with

Fig. 136. *Labyrinth*, by SEYMOUR FOGEL, 1949.

Fig. 137. *The Flagellants*, by SEYMOUR FOGEL, 1950.

the meaning and the music of the aesthetic song justly balanced. What more can we ask?

The outdoor religious mural of Fig. 138, completed in Austin, Texas, in 1950, where Fogel migrated some years ago from the sophisticated art life of New York to teach in the University of Texas, is an outstanding work of mural art. Symbols expressive of the first verse of Genesis are readable as meaning—the single-celled creatures and fish at base right, bivalves and plant life at left, nebulae, constellations, comets, the primordial elements of earth and the heavens, the Creation Light, the dove of the Holy Spirit, all merged with soaring curves into a symphonic whole. The church people and the community have approved. An artist has demonstrated that religious art can be "more contemporary and meaningful than is a display of saints." The mural decorates the entrance to the new University Baptist Student Center.

Driftwood Structure, of 1951 (Fig. 139), heightens the role of textures to a mellowed equality with line-space-movement in the Fogel repertoire, indicating that the artist is not content to dwell peacefully within one formula. Lines, in diverse lights and darks, merge into and emerge from textured colors with a net result of subtlety and surprise.

The latest achievement of this artist-dynamo is another mural—for the swank and ultra Petroleum Club Cocktail Lounge of Houston, Texas. One can think of oil millionaires as being "swank" without mental strain, but hardly "ultra." Something must have happened in Houston when millionaires, architect, and decorator agree that distinction can be achieved by using a contemporary style and a native artist for its expression, instead of importing both from distant (and respectable) times and places. Various other clubs, colleges, and house-owners (including the owner of a certain white house in Washington, D.C.) might well take note. The mural is 16 by 13 feet, on a curved wall, painted with ethyl silicate—and is a complete abstraction. About it, and mural art in general, Fogel says:

> The mural artist of today who believes in the necessity of achieving a renaissance of his art, faces a three-fold task. On one hand he must prove to a dubious architect that his esthetic contribution as an artist is important to architecture; on another hand, his means, both in form and technique,

Fig. 138. *Genesis*, by SEYMOUR FOGEL, 1950. An outdoor mural for the University of Texas Baptist Youth Center, painted in Ethyl Silicate.

Fig. 139. *Driftwood Structure*, by SEYMOUR FOGEL, 1951.

must be flexible enough to meet on equal terms the technical challenges of contemporary building. If these challenges are met, he is then confronted by the third part of his task—the achievement of a true integration of his art with the surrounding architecture.

Whereas the Petroleum Club mural received understanding and encouragement from the architect and decorator, as well as the client, the problem of true integration was of paramount importance and a difficult but stimulating experience.

One thing I found in doing this mural is that when an artist sincerely works to attain his own particular creative objective, others are quick to sense it. Consequently the chances of acceptance turn out to be far greater than they would be had the artist felt it necessary to hold back and compromise. Please yourself and you will please others. Try to please others, and you accomplish exactly nothing. Such seems to have been the case with both this and the Baptist mural.

ROBERT PREUSSER

In late 1948, as a member of the jury for the All-Texas Annual Painting Exhibition, I first saw the work of Robert Preusser. For that event we of the jury voted to him our top award in honor of the painting *Hydroscopic Realm;* the decision was unanimous. Since then, due to that opportunity for a state-wide survey and other later ones, I came to regard Preusser as one of Texas's most significant younger artists. On meeting him in his home city of Houston and seeing a collection of his work at the Houston Museum of Fine Arts, where he was teaching, I found a mature, complex, yet extremely subtle expression and a conscious philosophy of art; this artist knew where he was going and why—and was definitely on his way. Asked to explain his philosophy he complied thus:

> My constant aim in painting is that of making evident an emotional expression and bringing it into a revealed tangible form through a combined intellectual and intuitive approach. The medium and tools are used experimentally and the forms evolved abstractly. The visual elements in themselves become the subject-matter and are intended to create a dynamic rhythm consistent with the two-dimensional picture plane.
>
> By such an approach to painting—that of a combined use of the intellectual and intuitive faculties of both the artist and his audience—I believe the act of visual participation can become a much greater experience than is possible in painting which consists of static literary facts, and in which

nothing is left for the imagination. Abstract art allows—in fact demands—the observer to relate his own experiences to the visual effects created. It is for this kind of visual participation that my paintings are intended.

This creed of a young artist—Mr. Preusser was born in Houston in 1919—is so thoroughly in harmony with the one animating these pages that no additional comment is necessary. Two questions, however, spring to mind in relation to it. Does the work indicate he has assimilated the creed and applied it from inner conviction, rather than having merely echoed a modern cliché? And how did he arrive at the creed at a time when many thousands of art students are still being mistrained via academic standards, or blundering into confusions nourished by a similar goal of "emotional expression"?

The answer to the first question is an unqualified yes; he has assimilated the creed. The Preusser paintings are thoroughly designed creations. Their arrangements of colors, planes, spaces, textures, and forms are complex, subtle, highly sensitive, and entirely his own creations. They are not "echoes of Paris," though his healthy indebtedness to Paris is obvious. He has definitely assimilated the basic values of the Modern Rebirth and bent them to his own expressive needs. His brush responds to both his "intellect and intuition." He proves that abstract painting can be in the international idiom and still be personal. He too has responded to the deeper realities which compel so many serious artists to turn to the abstract as against the obvious surface truths.

There is no self-conscious regionalism in these works; the artist is not expressing directly the Texas of his birth and residence; his "message" is for all men and into it one can even read cosmic implications. It demonstrates a kind of internationalism much needed today to facilitate mutual understandings between the nations of this earth; it is an example of the universal language art is supposed to be.

The paintings shown in Figs. 140 and 141 will serve to illustrate the above claims. Their titles, *Twentieth Century Baroque* and *Directional Multiplicity,* are mainly but identification labels; the sensations they offer go far beyond these implied limits. *Harmonic Angles* or *Ejaculatory Sensations* would serve as well for Fig. 141, as might also *Organic Tissues* for Fig. 140.

The sensation offered by the latter is smooth and flowing; that embodied by Fig. 141 is dynamic excitement. In the latter, note the counterplay of the thin lines versus the wide spaces as one accented feature. Such interpretations can go on and on; meanings are open for all to read. A scientist, it is conceivable, might so read into the ragged textures of *Twentieth Century Baroque,* the diseased tissues of the body politic and into *Directional Multiplicity* the meanderings of international political intrigue. (Scientists might well profit, by the way, from such a widening of their search for truth.) Thus can the proffered deeper realities be interpreted without limit by the fertile imagination of any world citizen. Beyond such imaginings, however, lies the other significant contribution of abstract art—controlled visual sensation. And, it is interesting to note, Preusser's sensations delve into three dimensions without losing their aesthetic controls.

The answer to the second question is simple. His early influence was from an art teacher in his native Houston—Mrs. McNeil Davidson—who started him in the creative direction. This was followed by two years at the Institute of Design in Chicago where Moholy-Nagy and Gyorgy Kepes confirmed and amplified the direction. Hence the fundamentals were deeply ingrained, without the usual conflicts implicit in academic training; to him designed creation was the normal way.

Robert Preusser is aware of his directions and of the social values involved. He knows that intellectual activity must be balanced by the emotional outlet of creative art "to avoid reducing man to a machine." He knows that the art of the picture should be carried over into the things which make environment. "The painter," he says, "or any other worker directly connected with the arts, should be more of an integrated person with the society in which he lives. His scope should be broadened and applied to the design of implements which are used daily—automobile, furniture, textile, jewelry, and so forth." To which this author says a heartfelt, if not pious, Amen.

I was listening to Aaron Copeland's *Rodeo* as I wrote these interpretive lines and it seemed that the surprises in the Copeland "Theme and Variations" furnished an excellent parallel to the surprises in the variations of the Preusser theme.

Fig. 140. *Twentieth Century Baroque,*
by ROBERT PREUSSER.

Fig. 142. *Prismatic Refractions*
by ROBERT PREUSSER, 1953.

Fig. 141. *Directional Multiplicity,*
by ROBERT PREUSSER.

Since 1950 when the above was written, this artist has continued on his dynamic way—as painter, educator, and participator in many community art events. The record, in fact, is incredible, breathtaking. He teaches at the University of Houston and the Museum of Fine Arts, where he is also Associate Curator of Education. Then he is a member of the Board of Directors of Contemporary Arts Association, Four Arts Theater, Allied Arts Association, a member of the Accessions Committee of the Museum and Contemporary Arts, member of the Advisory Committee for Regional Scholastic Art Awards, and a member of the Steering Committee of the Community Council Development Project. "All this activity," says Preusser, "verifies my philosophy that a contemporary painter is more completely in the swim of things when he reaches out into society in more than one channel. Also it is true that teaching and museum work come closest to being the most agreeable compromise necessary to making a living in the non-profitable profession of painting." An artist who thus extends his influence by personal contacts in many directions that widen the understanding of all art, is serving his community beyond the possibility of appraisal.

All of this dynamic activity, fortunate to relate, plus the added chore of designing and building a new home, has not stopped the equally, or more, important flow of Preusser paintings. In witness whereof I present two, from a choice of some thirteen, new works.

Prismatic Refractions (Fig. 142) illustrates a design theme that has increasingly attracted this artist in 1952 and 1953—the playing of sticklike lines in front of planes—the lines so arranged and related as to give the feeling of constant motion. The colors here are somewhat grayed primaries, much alike over the entire work, except that the upper area above the light peaks is more dark and neutral, thus fading back as a foil.

I feel [says Preusser] the creative artist is in a constant search for REALITY. To be sure, he relies on intuition as much as observation, in his searching. And here I think it is interesting to note that a great deal of the "reality" of abstract painting is not verified as reality until after it has been done.

You will note that in my recent works I have, in a few instances, referred more directly to objective content than usual. This may be a new facet to my development—only time will tell how often such emphasis will recur.

My basic interest and concern remain the same. I, quite frankly, do not believe there can ever be a completely "non-objective" picture because every artist's mark on the canvas results from some kind of experience that has emotional or intellectual significance. In this sense abstraction is a quality measured by degree. This is not objecting to the use of the term "non-objective" I use it often myself); for it has its use in the tremendous problem confronted by artist and critic in communicating with the general public. S. I. Hayakawa says in his Introduction to *Language of Vision* by Gyorgy Kepes: "Whatever may be the language one happens to inherit, it is at once a tool and a trap." This is certainly true of the term "non-objective."

These are pungent and socially useful comments by the artist himself. They indicate that Robert Preusser knows where he is going and is well on his way.

ALEXANDER CALDER

Alexander Calder, in his Mobiles, has exploited one aspect of that seemingly limitless sensitivity in man named *design,* to limits beyond which the ordinary imagination, or even that of the mature artist, rarely sees. The one aspect is *balance.* In some cases Calder appears to lift balance off the earth and give it complex wings of delicate metal which allow it a slow-motion fluttering in air, responsive to every breath of movement in that invisible element. These are the mobiles in which support is from above by a near-invisible wire. When support is from below and necessarily more stable, it is still as delicate as is physically possible. The tie to earth is acknowledged but the wings and balance are equally subtle. The idea is to minimize, not abandon, support and to dramatize floating balance.

The design of these mobiles is functional in that balance is established from a single point of suspension between a large plane and many smaller ones with endless variations of position, grouping, directional angle, shape, size, and even color. Movement, which stays within the limits established by the demands of this balance, is still fluid enough to give the spectator ever-changing relationships of parts. And because movement is slow and can pause, there is time to apprehend and enjoy the sensations of these relationships. Actual static sculpture gives forth the

A

Fig. 143. *Mobile,*
by ALEXANDER CALDER.

same sensations when the observer moves slowly about it; each work is a hundred "pictures" in one. In the mobiles, the elements we actually see in sculpture—the surface planes—are extracted and perform for us with modulations we could hardly achieve if we did the moving. It is a liberated new dimension derived from sculpture which this artist presents to the alert observer.

I think that at that time [1930] and practically ever since, the underlying sense of form in my work has been the system of the Universe, or part thereof. That is a rather large model to work from.

What I mean is that the idea of detached bodies floating in space, of different sizes and densities, perhaps of different colors and temperatures, and surrounded and interlarded with wisps of gaseous condition, and some at rest, while others move in peculiar manners, seems to me the ideal source of form. I would have them deployed, some nearer together and some at immense distances. I would have great disparity among all the qualities of these bodies, and their motions as well.

ALEXANDER CALDER   231

No more need be said. Words are here more superfluous than usual. Much better it is to observe the Calder Mobiles in delicate action. Fig. 143 suggests the means to that action about as well as a photograph can. The point of suspension is at A.

At the International Biennale Exhibition in Venice in the summer of 1952, Alexander Calder was awarded the first prize for a foreign sculptor. The jury was international in membership.

PART IV - REALISM-SURREALISM

The term "realism" is used as defining the work of the following artists in the sense explained in Part I under the heading, Definition of Terms. It implies the opposite of "naturalism."

Since Surrealism has ceased to exist as a formal movement, the term is here employed as a convenient title under which to group artists who still individually follow its general philosophy.

I-THE REALISTS

IVAN LE LORRAINE ALBRIGHT

As a preface to these comments, I should like to place in the record my appraisal of and quotations from Ivan Albright as set down in my book *Experiencing American Pictures,* in 1943. My belief that this artist is an outstanding modern master and that his painting *Wherefore Now Ariseth the Illusion of a Third Dimension* (1932) is the greatest work of art in still-life painted in our day, remains unchanged; it has in fact been fortified by events. One of these events was the honor of a double page spread of this work in *Life* magazine of March 17, 1944. Under this largest of all possible magazine reproduction, and it was in color, an adequate caption said, "Except for *The Door* with the funeral wreath, this painting is considered not only Albright's greatest masterpiece of still-life but perhaps the best that has ever been done in this country." Two years later, as a member of the Jury of Awards of the Pepsi-Cola Exhibition of 1946, I was unable to convince my confrères (consisting of three artists and one museum director) of the validity of this appraisal as it affected the selections for top prizes. The voting placed it below fifth place as one of the fifteen $500 awards. (The first award was $2500, to Paul Burlin.)

That Which I Should Have Done I Did Not Do (or, in shorthand, *The Door*)

Fig. 144. *That Which I Should Have Done I Did Not Do*, by IVAN LE LORRAINE ALBRIGHT, 1931–1941.

Fig. 145. Detail from Fig. 144.

is a dramatized metamorphosis of an object, or two objects, into another masterpiece of contemporary painting. Started in 1931, completed in 1941, it re-creates a door bought from a second-hand-dealer for $2.50 and a wax flower funeral wreath costing $5.00, into a pictorial concept with epochal implications. These implications are obvious enough not to need amplification in words. Neither should the art in this great work need verbal interpretation. It is sufficient to note the carefully considered subtle distortions which add character to fact, the amazing enrichment of textured surface and the arbitrary color—an all-pervading gray-green, from which the only contrasting notes are the soft reds of the flowers in the wreath, the echo thereof in the one flower dropped to the floor and the hand near the door-knob. For this hand, so the story goes, a young girl posed every Sunday for two years. The meticulous carried to the nth degree. Yet never did this painstaking technical mastery dominate the artist or the work. The art remained throughout in full control.

Another event which turned a well-earned spotlight on Ivan and brother Malvin (who signs his work Zsissly because he wants his name to end alphabetical listings) was the commission from Hollywood in 1944 to paint several portraits of Dorian Gray to be used in the motion picture of that name. The brothers collaborated on that venture with uncanny effectiveness, dramatizing the theme of Oscar Wilde's story, of the decay of a portrait instead of the man, its subject, in a way that could be done in no other medium and by no other artists. Not the least significance of this event was the recognition by Big Business that artists have a place in the sun, are actually useful—like bricklayers and advertising executives—and are worthy of their hire. The hire in this case was plenty— rumor says it was $75,000—which, if true, makes artists almost as important as bank presidents. Value was delivered, since the resulting portraits certainly exploited the theme of moral and physical decay. And the paintings strutted and fretted their hour upon the stage as chief actors in a drama that was seen by the millions—the kind of audience artists should have for their creations in this mass-production era.

The next important event on the Albright calendar was the completion in 1946 of the canvas *The Temptation of St. Anthony,* painted for the

Bel Ami International Competition, for the purpose of selecting another theme-painting for a motion picture. Max Ernst beat Ivan to the tape in this race but the latter produced a masterpiece which is fantasy run riot —a rhythmic and detailed rioting which may never have been surpassed in its exploitation of theme and detail in twentieth-century art. Poor Anthony writhes in a degree of agony that is anything but sweet; the female bodies and breasts are all there at their worst, with rotting flesh in places mocking the fleeting and obviously vulgar charms, while death-heads and animals from underground and overground, and the fishes and devils of the sea, look on in jeering sympathy. Even the rocks, shells, and plants of the earth echo the riot and the jeers. Textures also run riot and add to the excitement, from the ragged burlap drapes of the Saint— the sack-cloth, if not the ashes—to the smooth flesh of the bodies, the hair of humans and fur of animals, and the grit and crinkle of rock, foliage, and heaven-knows-what. It is a truly amazing work.

Then came a respite—a mere two years on a painting, just to keep hand and brush in form—*The Wild Burtch* of 1950 to 1951. Again the meticulous, the amazing, and all the other adjectives. Except that here is less "social significance" and more amplified still life with the multitude of details under full control; note the unity of the whole—the receding walls which do not interfere with the main motifs, the dramatized spurs in the little window—which become the pictorial focal point for roving eyes.

> Traveling around the world [says Albright] wouldn't move me any more than sitting right here in my studio. Actually one place is just as good as another. It's the meaning that you bring to your painting that's important. Nature herself can go only as far as your mind can bring it.

The latest Albright opus is another masterpiece, on which planning began in 1942, concentrated work was resumed in 1948, after the interruption of the Hollywood commission, and to the fame of which sonnets will doubtless be penned in dedication ceremonies celebrating its completion in 1955. An exhaustive report on this painting, its planning, philosophy, methods, materials, and technical minutiae, written by Marilyn Robb, appeared in *Art News* of August, 1950. It is an incredible story

Fig. 146. *The Picture of Dorian Gray,*
by IVAN LE LORRAINE ALBRIGHT, 1944.
Painted in 1944 for the M.G.M. motion
picture of that title, in collaboration with
his brother, Zsissly.

Fig. 147. *The Wild Burtch,*
by IVAN LE LORRAINE ALBRIGHT, 1950--1951.

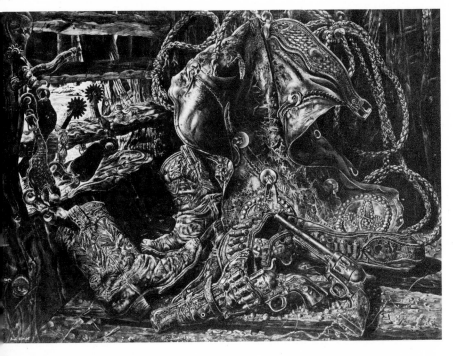

about ten years of work and thought on a single painting; illustrations are ample; the report should be read by all. Again decay, ruin, and death are the themes. So complex, however, are the developments built around these themes, it would be an injustice to attempt any condensed explanation and I have no space for the full statement. This work is already making history and its completion bids fair to be top art news of its decade.

Color in the Albright paintings is always muted into subordinance to forms, textures, and tonality. It enhances these favorite qualities; in fact, it sometimes seems to rescue them almost casually from preferred monochromatic or duochromatic effects. Never is color sensuous or luscious with this artist; that role he has shifted to textures which he has dramatized as has no other painter of the century. The smooth versus the rough. The refined surface played against the coarse. But with infinite variations, with nuances, which are the more striking because so few contemporary artists have discovered the potentialities of textures, let alone exploited them. Albright does exploit textures and gains a paradoxical effect. Textures are a feature of surface and the painter who represents surface with skill is normally a naturalist. Here is a painter performing a super-representation of surface with consummate skill, yet he attains a realism that can almost be called the opposite of naturalism. His exploited surface seems to reveal character down, in, and through.

It *is* a paradox. It is a tour de force validated by an uncanny insight and a profound purpose. That purpose would seem to be the dramatization of the real—the tangible reality—to its ultimate limit, a purpose which has been eminently achieved. The fact that color plays a minor role in gaining this end is an interesting sidelight on the event. "You can never get color alone," says Albright. "Colors are to me but the form within. I never think of color separately."

Several years back the redoubtable Ivan stated his creed thus:

All of which is merely a suggestion that, in evaluating American art, we blow out the chaff of illustration, eliminate the political process and discover that America still has painters who do not need to resort to the fanfare of bugles and drums.

Has this artist "blown out the chaff of illustration"? One has to pause a moment and consider. *Dorian Gray* is illustration carried to the extreme limit. So is *The Temptation of St. Anthony* the illustration of a theme. But both are more than the mere illustrative function of recording the obvious, the tangible. They dramatize, as well as illustrate, intangibles as well as tangibles. They are super-illustration in actual fact. I would revise the Ivan statement to say it is well *to blow the chaff out of illustration,* as he has done. As to political processes, certainly he has avoided them. Fanfare of bugles and drums? Is high drama a resort to such fanfare? It causes it, no doubt of that. But we certainly need something to get excited about in this drab and dreary life of vicarious experiences, and if an artist's work can hand us that great gift and cause us to beat the drums, all honor to it.

Albright's painting is designed super-realism, with textures and details developed to such an extreme the eye cannot absorb them but cries for rest-areas as balancing contrasts. With this exception, the marriage of design with subject seems near-perfect in these complex epic works. At times the Albright philosophy is cynically concerned with death and decay. At others, as in *The Door,* it exploits character of subject to the ultimate limit, distilling its own high beauty from the commonplace. Both eminently achieved goals command respect.

WILLIAM ZORACH

William Zorach is a classicist in the art of our time. He is a direct descendent from, and inheritor of, the great periods of Egypt, Greece, the Orient, and the Modern Revival, to which he has been an important contributor. He is carrying on his great inheritance. Of these influences, the Greek is most evident.

Born in Russia, Zorach came to America as a young child. He progressed through the usual academic art instruction of the early years of the century (and survived it), went to Paris in 1910, first exhibited paintings in the Salon d'Automne of 1911 which were influenced by the ferment of the "New Art," returned to New York in 1912, exhibited cubist-type paintings in the Armory Show of 1913, turned to sculpture in 1922

Fig. 148. *Mother and Child*, by WILLIAM ZORACH,
1927--1930.

Fig. 149. *Adam*, by WILLIAM ZORACH, 1948.

and has been producing, teaching, and at times writing to date. To his students Zorach frequently addresses this warning:

> Never under any circumstances do anything that you think will sell or please the public—but once you have done something to your satisfaction, to the best of your ability—sell it.
>
> If the student has that which it takes to become an artist he should become an idealist and keep in mind always what he has set himself to do, using his talents to the best of his ability and never allowing any experience to sidetrack him from his purpose. He should treasure his talent, allow nothing to degrade it and do nothing to nullify or stultify the senses. He should live art, think art, sleep art, talk art and write art.

Such advice highlights the integrity of the man and his uncompromising resistance to commercial influences in a world fundamentally antagonistic to the genuine artist. Zorach himself does not compromise.

To ascribe the Zorach sculptures to the classic tradition is to concentrate all the accepted and enduring virtues into a single word. Masterful technique, universalization of subject and forthright expression of its essential character, realization and expression of form as form and its adequate functional design that merges into subject, are among these virtues. All the works here shown demonstrate these classic qualities plus a sufficient personal flair to brand them as Zorach creations whether or not a signature is seen. Vision and realization may slip at times, as I think they did in the recent work *New Horizon*, exhibited at the Metropolitan's American Sculpture showing in 1951 (where Zorach was an influential member of the jury that made many controversial decisions). The slipping in this case was mainly in the concept; body parts were distorted by compression which offended on this count without any compensating gain. Also inspiration seemed lacking; it was a pedestrian work.

In the head of Fig. 149, however, the older personal interpretative power gained momentum, I think, and the results are supreme achievements of sculptural art. In contrast, the earlier works seem much more impersonal. Their generalizations of themes and other classic virtues suggest a like generalization of artist's approach. "Suggest," please note; I do not say achieve or prove. The Zorach impact is still amply discernible.

Fig. 150. *Kneeling Figure,*
by WILLIAM ZORACH, 1947.

Fig. 151. *The Future Generation,*
by WILLIAM ZORACH, 1950.

Fig. 150, one of the later works, also is more personal. Here is the rhythmic grace of womanly form extracted somehow from the actual living body and pilloried (if I may use that word) for all to see. Forms shed some reality and take on the elusive feel of spirit. The inner transcends the outer truth. It is as if the many years of dealing with actual form had mellowed the Zorach chisel, had given it the insight to release intangibles from the stone. Here, as in the portrait heads, the artist adds his own gifts to the classic tradition.

HENRY LEE McFEE

The following is a statement of his creed by artist Henry L. McFee, whose death in March, 1953, is a distinct loss to American art.

I think I have always been interested in pictures. Drawing and painting were a lively and vital interest to me all through my youth, and since those days they have taken more and more of my time and energy. I have liked above all things pictures and the enthralling puzzle of their power to hold and move me. . . .

I have studied Renoir, Cézanne, Picasso, and Braque, and I daresay have been influenced by them. Corot and Delacroix have been an important interest in my art life, as have the early Italian painters of the Renaissance, and El Greco. All these have helped me see what plastic painting could be. They are the men who have stirred me and made me realize what power great painting has, and what depth of understanding of life there can be in it.

I came to know that it was not the well realized objects that made the picture compelling, but rather the significant way the canvas was put together. I sensed a life of the forms that was not always the result of vision but rather a clearer understanding of the motif.

When we think of the motif, that particular piece or section of the visual world that we have under consideration, we must realize that the spaces are as important as the objects, and remember that we have the problem of making of that which is before us a living plastic unit of design. If we can organize our efforts and get beneath the surface—find out what is really significant to us—we have a chance of making the picture live. I once had the experience of suddenly perceiving in my garden with its familiar background of trees and sky the overpowering design that explained the whole. It was as if the very spirit of the motif projected itself.

Sometimes we can sense at once what will be the dominant organic rhythm of the emotional form of the complex material before us. At other times it is by experimenting and analyzing that we arrive at the certainty of what is right. This certainty we must have. The painter may be interested in the architectonic qualities alone or he may desire to realize as well something of the richness, fullness and glory of the visual world. The essential thing is that the completed picture shall be a living unit of design, strong in tactile values and plastic in every sense.

These words are taken from a monograph on McFee, published by Scripps College of Claremont, California, in 1950, which is one of the soundest and most revealing presentations, not only of a man and his work but of the basic philosophy of art which is the Modern Movement, that I have read. The introductory article by Arthur Millier is informed and lucidly expressed in its explanation both of the artist and the movement which gave him his direction and motive power. Then the words of the artist, from which the above are taken, complete the elucidation. This book should be recognized as a basic text on Modern Art and required reading for all art students and art lovers.[1]

What do these pregnant words mean?

The issue (of their understanding) is probably the most crucial one facing the contemporary international art word. If there could be a basic training course for all residents, lay and professional, of that world, confusion would be a minor cultural issue instead of the major one it now is. Feeble talents would at least work within the Grand Tradition; major talents would not, in many cases, waste themselves; significant work would be much more widely understood, valued, and supported; the millenium would be within range of the general public comprehension rather than hovering on its horizon. Can milleniums never in our "en-

[1] My own searchings and discoveries have so closely paralleled those of McFee, except that my professional medium was etching, that I could jointly sign the references to "a life of forms," "spaces as important as the objects," "organized efforts," "making the picture live," "organic rhythm of emotional form," "architectonic qualities," and "a living unity of design, strong in tactile values and plastic in every sense."

I even had an experience similar to his of "suddenly perceiving in my garden the overpowering design that explained the whole." Only for me it was a mountain landscape near Taos, New Mexico, and the date was about 1917—some four years after the profound and welcome shock of New York's 1913 Armory Show.

Fig. 152. *Landscape with Houses,*
by HENRY L. McFEE, 1919.

Fig. 153. *Still Life with a Green Jar,*
by HENRY L. McFEE, 1945.

Fig. 154. *Broken Pot with Blue Vase,*
by HENRY L. McFEE, 1950.

lightened age" materialize? There have been a few golden ages in the past when basic values were understood. The Modern Movement represents such an age existing in our time. If it can be understood it will survive. Henry McFee was an important member of the relatively small group of artists who have contributed significantly to that survival.

Landscape with Houses (Fig. 152) is one of McFee's earliest paintings, produced in 1919, which shows his initial searchings for "a life of forms" and a "living plastic unity of design." The search for enduring values, here imperfectly but significantly realized, was continuous thereafter, with ever increasing insight and gaining maturity of realization. Fig. 153 illustrates the maturity as of 1945. Note the interplay of the folds of cloth, the contrasting forms of interacting objects—from the spheres of fruit to the different rotundity of pots, to the opposed types of star-like and crinkly leaves, to vertical versus horizontal planes, to the subdued against brilliant colors and tones. The color is of course the binding element that penetrates and relates all motifs in addition to the interweaving of forms and movements. Fig. 154 of 1950 is more complex in its solution of all these matters; the broken round forms are one means to such an end. Another means is the repetition of the same motif, of cloth folds on front of table, with form variations within each, all of these contrasted to the surface-designed textile at left and its echo at right. Again there are the two types of plant forms—the soft leaves versus the sharply pointed ones with their highly complex movements. The "organic rhythm of emotional form" is adequately realized.

Did McFee gain all the objectives that he saw and stated as his goal? In the main, it seems, he did. But words like "the *significant* way the canvas is put together," and, "the *life* of forms," have implications without horizon whose limits cannot be grasped by eye or mind. His solutions were always concrete and fully realized. Does this suggest the flesh rather than the spirit of the specific things which are his subjects? Can an artist express the spirit rather than the flesh of tables, apples, pitchers, and plants? Cézanne has shown that he can. Spirit is more intangible than flesh both in life and painting, and demands, therefore, some degree of the intangible for its adequate expression. There is a point here worthy of consideration both by the artist and his audience.

GEORGE BIDDLE

George Biddle is a realist. He extracts realities from the life of his time and builds them into modern design. He digs deep into the character of his varied subjects, whether they be individuals, as in his portraits, or events, as in his war pictures or the "Carnival in Rio" series, or dramatic expressions of idea or story, as in his murals. His work stirs the imagination, both ideologically and plastically, in all these fields; it is an interpretation of the spirit as well as the body of the theme portrayed. He has tried, especially in his more recent work, "to evoke a mood," as he puts it, "through color and design and the mechanism of paint—a mood which is the life we live in." I think he has succeeded in this aim.

The Biddle portraits should place their author in the front rank of our officially approved and highly rewarded portrait painters; commissions should pour in on him from presidents of this and that and from society matrons and debutantes. It is an ironic sidelight on the state of our culture that there is no such flood. In fact, in a recent New York exhibition of his portrait paintings, only one among thirty-three canvases was a commission—and that was from a friend. Our upper classes, it seems, prefer the sweetness of skillfully recorded surface charms to the light of inner and outer realities, as they announce by their predominant choice of naturalistic portrait painters. The choice may be canny in many cases —for personality reasons—but it hardly wins them or the nation cultural credit. Biddle gets character in his portraits, as did the old European masters; it is essential truth he is concerned with. His designed realism is the opposite of chaotic, or even composed, naturalism.

In the murals, the Idea emerges with terrific impact. So compelling are idea and story that they harden the plastic expression into a metallic crispness of concrete finality; there are no overtones of subtle gradations, no nuances, no mellowness. This has been true of his murals from the days of the Arts Projects and his Treasury Department commission for the

Fig. 155. *Portrait of Kuniyoshi*, by GEORGE BIDDLE, 1938.

Fig. 156. *My Neighbor, Al*, by GEORGE BIDDLE, 1939.

Department of Justice Building in Washington to the latest, in 1945, for the Supreme Court Building in Mexico City. Here he had an unparalleled opportunity—in the size and importance of the wall space, and in a unique experiment of combining a mural with a sculptural relief into a unified whole. Helene Sardeau (his wife) was the sculptress and the collaboration seems to have proved fertile. Certainly it made history in wall decoration and attained harmony in concept and execution in two related media. Both artists worked with the same deep concern with subject—*Cannibalism of War*—and both built subject into designed realism. Fig. 157 shows one of the most successful panels of the series.

In 1943 and 1944, Biddle did an inspired series of war paintings (later published in book form) expressive of the ironic and tragic sidelights of war. One about the Italian campaign, for instance, shows Averso Francesco, age 24, in his coffin and this was the caption:

> All day he dug gun emplacements under guard. On Halloween they shot him. . . . Burial is not always sordid at the front. In the villages the casket is sometimes of vermillion and gold. White shrouds clothe the loved one. Cries of the mourners, flowers and church ritual will ease their sorrow. And the featureless thing within? He was shot in reprisal because he loved his country. Not with cruelty but with the logic of a logical warrior race.

Back to easel painting in recent years, Biddle has grown markedly in subtlety, mellowness, and a balanced expressive power. The series done in Brazil in 1947 and called "Carnival in Rio" eloquently illustrates this gain. Not all artists are able to keep the curve of art power in their work always on the upgrade; the parabolic rise and decline is often inevitable. Biddle's latest creations mark the top of his curve to date; there has been no recession—and there is no sign of one to come.

> In the "Carnival" series [says Biddle] the mood could be of frenzy or madness; an effort to sublimate in a moment of Dionysiac exaltation the chaos and insanity of a drab world. In the circus pictures there is, as always, the suggestion of sadness and tears behind the mask of gaiety, color and laughter. Negro Spirituals, as much as anything in our inheritance, dwell on the awareness of guilt, expiation, salvation and the need of faith. There are those in the world we live in preoccupied with the same problems.

Fig. 158, one of the best of the "Carnival" series, effectively imple-

Fig. 157. *The Cannibalism of War*, by GEORGE BIDDLE, 1945.
One panel of the mural, from the Supreme Court Building of Mexico City.

Fig. 158. *Two Negroes*, by GEORGE BIDDLE, 1947. From the "Carnival in Rio" series.

Fig. 159. *Not Even He May Rest,* by GEORGE BIDDLE, 1952.

ments these words. Here certainly is the mood or spirit portrayed without distraction of any kind; this *is* the "frenzy or madness" of the dance. Character is highly dramatized. The whole of the picture works to its one thematic end.

Biddle's color tends throughout practically all of his painting to a gray harmony with muted notes emerging therefrom. This long-time trait, by the way, has been the one characteristic which has tended to counteract with its restraint the harshness of form in the early work and in the murals. It still contributes its quiet charm, and is greatly enhanced in the paintings of recent years by a corresponding gain in mellowness of form and a more fluid play of textures with their softening sensations. His design as a whole always is functional, in that it takes its character from subject.

Never does it escape and play pure visual music. Design, to this realist, is a means, not an end. In this materialistic (in the untainted sense of dealing with tangibles) art philosophy he is in good company, however, for the long list of realists of European history held to the same belief and provided the tradition which the Biddles of today are carrying on. He does honor design, notwithstanding, and employs it consistently with feeling as well as intellect motivating his brush. That is the important matter which, next to his ardent drive to extract meaning from life, places him well within our modern revival.

President Truman appointed George Biddle a member of the United States Fine Arts Commission, where he can serve effectively to coordinate Government and art. It was a significant appointment and a fortunate one—provided this erudite artist represents all of his distinguished fellow-workers instead of one ideological group.

JOSÉ de CREEFT

In teaching my students [says José de Creeft] I try to impart the joy which comes of rejecting (with only seeming egoism) the unhappy world outside us in order to concentrate on the things that last—like the work of the old masters. If we study our materials—the stone and wood that nature offers us—if we love our tools and so come to master them, we always find that these apparently humble things contain the secret of all the mysteries and of all achievement. By contemplating the substance of which our world is made, by carving directly into it, the artist reaches his true role as a creator.

Time is needed. There are things on which I have labored for over ten years and which are not yet finished. But my happiness in the work, and the happiness I see in the faces of my students as they throw off old enslavements, both assure me that the ancient art of sculpture is still capable of giving endlessly to its practitioner and to its public.

A far too modest statement, this. I object—on one point. The materials and tools contain the secret of all the mysteries and all achievement, says de Creeft. How about the artist? Does he earn no share in the credit for "containing" some of the mystery and the achievement? Of course he does. To rule him out is ridiculously unfair. The laborer must be worthy

Fig. 160. *Maternity*, by JOSÉ DE CREEFT, 1923.
First prize, $5,000, Artists for Victory Exhibition
at the Metropolitan Museum of Art in 1942.

Fig. 161. *Portrait of Lorraine*, by JOSÉ DE CREEFT, 1949.

Fig. 162. *Nebulae*, by JOSÉ DE CREEFT, 1950.

of his tools. I claim, for instance, that Mr. José de Creeft deserves a considerable amount of credit for belaboring his materials by means of his tools. If some of the mystery had not resided also in him, his belaboring would not have won the respect of his fellow artists and citizens to a degree that compelled his inclusion in this book. By contemplating the substance of which our world is made and carving directly into it, Mr. de Creeft may have *begun* his "true role as a creator." But he never "reached" it until some of the mysteries *contained in him* flowed through his tools into the materials.[1]

Now, having won that argument, I can think of other things. What other things? What other thoughts does this Spanish-born sculptor, trained in the ateliers of Barcelona, Madrid, and Paris, and a resident among us since 1930, inspire?

He inspires the thought that he is as honest as he is modest. Direct carving is an honest approach to sculpture—as has been amply demonstrated by a long procession of carvers in wood and stone, from the primitives through the Egyptians, the Greeks, Michaelangelo, the African Negroes, and many, but not all, of the sculptors of today. Also, his main concern, it seems, is with the universal theme. His *Maternity* of Fig. 160 is the generic portrait of all motherhood, as *Nebulae,* of Fig. 162, appears to be that of all young womanhood. He can change to the specific subject, as in the portrait of his wife, *Lorraine,* but here, I assume without his authorization, he is really combining the two, by extracting the individual from the universal. The head of *Lorraine,* for instance, might also be that of an Egyptian Princess. The arbitrary treatment of the hair heightens the feeling of this duality, as the semi-emergence from the rough, untamed rock in many of his works suggests release from the eternal mysteries of the universe. Only a broad mind would dig out these realities from the conglomerate of life and only a rugged, forthright character would want to preserve in the work the duality of beauty extracted from chaos.

[1] Later, Mr. de Creeft admitted this amendment to his previously published statement and revised it to read, "———and so come to master them (the tools), we, as artists, will be able to pour forth through these apparently humble things, some of the contents of our mind and spirits."

A rugged honesty, then, is probably the best way to characterize the contribution of José de Creeft to his "materials." In addition to them, however, he adds the timeless fundamental of sculptural form.

MARION GREENWOOD

Marion Greenwood is another on the small list of artists who should be compelled, by an insistent demand, to make portrait painting her chief métier, and would be, if that section of our aristocracy which dispenses portrait commissions could take its aesthetics straight, rather than diluted to the facsimile of the hand-made color photo. As in the case of George Biddle, the outstanding virtue of the Greenwood portraits is an incisive characterization, a catching of the inner spirit as well as essential outer trappings of her subjects; the only deterrent, therefore, from commissioning her canny brush should be fear of inner revelations. Important people who do not so fear, who want posterity to know them as thoroughly as possible through the medium of the painted portrait, should command an artist like Marion Greenwood to serve society and themselves in this way. Both paint and bronze endure for an embarrassing length of time.

In her long list of uncommissioned portrayals of human life, artist Greenwood has been attracted to ethnic groups whose inner character shines through externals with easy availability, without the masks of respectability and sophistication. She has painted the life and people of Mexico. She has portrayed Negroes. Recently she has given us "a vital and poignant record of Chinese life." She has studied and traveled in North Africa, Europe, Mexico, Asia, and China. She has painted murals for the Mexican Government during a four-year visit to that aesthetically vital country at the height of its renaissance. Returning here in 1936, she continued her mural work on our Government art program. The portrayals of life then reverted to the single picture of the individual subject, including citizens of the U.S.A. The assumption is justified, this record indicates, that Marion Greenwood knows the human drama of her time.

The uncanny power of this artist to capture and dramatize the inner, as well as the outer, nature of her subjects, either singly or in groups, is

Fig. 163. *Mississippi Girl,*
by MARION GREENWOOD, 1944.
Second Prize, Carnegie Institute, 1944.

Fig. 164. *Dancers Resting,*
by MARION GREENWOOD, 1946.

typified by the paintings shown herewith. *Mississippi Girl,* of Fig. 163, is the portrait par excellence. Painted in 1943, before the China adventure, it concentrates into one canvas everything the portrait should be, everything it has been in the great periods of Occidental art. It is realism, not naturalism; the reality is excavated from beneath surface fact. Every item is controlled, reorganized, dramatized. Nothing is copied as is. Character is an open book for all to read. Color is orchestrated with a high note of orange in the handkerchief and the delicately grayed blues and whites of the careless dress, playing against the dark colorful browns of skin and the dulled blues and greens of background and chair. The high note of orange is echoed in the reds of skirt ruffles but these brighter colors are so restrained that they do not detract from the human color of the girl from the South. The merits of this portrait were justly acknowledged by a Second Prize at the Carnegie National Exhibition of 1944.

In *Dancers Resting* of 1946 (Fig. 164), there is the same penetrating characterization and the same power of designed creation. But added is the sensitively expressed interplay of bodies, movements, colors in these four resting girls as they relax between performances. Here is a moment of human life captured, purified, and preserved inviolate for all to see. It is a record, yes, but a dramatized record—so much more than the color photo or the skilled handmade copy of a scene can give. These girls are not posing models. They are living dancers resting. The difference can easily be overlooked but it is of epochal importance. It makes the difference between craft and art.

The *Rice Line* of 1947 (Fig. 165) is less masterful in organization, perhaps, but the characterization, the revelation of the poignant suffering of these tragic people, is expressed so eloquently in every look, gesture, line, and movement, and in the grayed color harmony, that the impact of the scene will penetrate any but the most callous mind. It is this expressive power in character delineation which is probably the richest contribution of this talented artist. Only the enrichment, be it well noted, is two-veined; it flows from the dramatic form as well as the content. Design, intuitive and conscious, is in full control. It marshals all its facts into effective array. It sings its visual songs of harmonic color and space.

Fig. 165. *The Rice Line,*
by MARION GREENWOOD, 1947.

Fig. 166. *Eastern Memory,*
by MARION GREENWOOD, 1950.

It delights as its subject informs. And the whole provides that balanced ration which is the province of art at its fluent best.

"I paint human beings first," says Marion Greenwood, "what race they are is secondary. Whether it be my little Jewish tailor next door, or the Italian grocery boy, or a beautiful woman in a night club, or a Bowery bum, or a Chinese coolie, it is always the human thing that counts."

Miss Greenwood is modest. Other things also count. And she is a master of those other things. Because of the fortunate blending of the two "things," her work, I venture to prophesy, will live.

ORONZIO MALDARELLI

Oronzio Maldarelli is one of our significant modern classicists. He builds into his sculptures a just balance between content and form, both masterfully realized, and thereby earns immediate recognition as an artist who is carrying on the Grand Tradition. His content is for the most part feminine form. His "form" is functional, in that it combines with the real. It is not overstressed for its own aesthetic merits via distortion or semi-abstraction. It is because the enduring art of many different cultures throughout the long course of history has maintained such a just balance that it is called classic.

Coming to this country from his native Italy as a child in 1900, Maldarelli has lived through, watched, and participated in the growth of the Modern Movement as it developed both abroad and here. His early work was mainly abstract, with interest centered on form design—as all early explorings should ideally be in order to learn the complexities of the organization of parts. But in the mid-1930's he began to be dissatisfied with the segregation of form from content, and an exhibition of his abstractions at the Midtown Galleries in New York in 1935 seems to have marked the turning point in his career. Thereafter he did not have a solo exhibition until 1948, at the same gallery, where the change to designed reality was thoroughly manifest. In the meantime he had been receiving honors and many important commissions, including ones from St. Patrick's Cathedral, the New York City Housing Authority, Columbia University, New York World's Fair Irish and French Buildings, the U. S.

Treasury Department and, more recently, two ships of the American Export Lines. For many years past he has been head of the Department of Sculpture in Columbia University's School of Painting and Sculpture —where, incidentally, he carries out his own work, believing that students should work with their "master," just as they did during the European Renaissance.

Maldarelli's knowledge of form-organization is not limited to a single form such as a human figure. It leaps intervening space to integrate two or more forms into a unified whole—a unification which can and does include that most difficult of problems, the controlled relationships of forms in movement. An early work which illustrated this was a group of birds in flight. An outstanding recent one is the *Spirit of Youth* of Fig. 168. Here the running movements all interweave, playing with and against each other in complex rhythms and counterpoint, which, to be fully realized, must be studied carefully from a score or a hundred revolving points of view. Design, in other words, penetrates into and throughout the total work.

Gemini #1, of Fig. 167, illustrates the same unification in two subjects seen in repose. Again, all forms interrelate.

Woman is the almost invariable Maldarelli subject. One critic has commented that this artist's women are enthroned upon a pedestal where he, like the medieval bard, caresses the beauty of feminine form with respect and understanding. Her sex is ever recognized, but more as an ethereal adornment than as a corporeal promise. If all men shared artist Maldarelli's attitude toward womanhood, knighthood would still be in flower.

The Maldarelli migration from the abstract to the real may well foretell a like swing of the art pendulum in the not-too-distant future from the present widespread popularity of abstraction, back to a content with tangible meaning. Art as well as nature has a way of balancing its motivating forces through the decades and centuries. If such an event transpires, this sculptor will be one of those who today is pioneering a "new" direction.

Commenting, in early 1953, on the current popularity of the abstract

Fig. 167. *Gemini #1*, by ORONZIO MALDARELLI, 1943.

Fig. 168. *Spirit of Youth*, by ORONZIO MALDARELLI, 1947.

(both designed and chaotic), Maldarelli said he saw this as a dehumanizing trend, a swing away from life, a loss of the subconscious outpouring that comes from the heart. "Many young sculptors," he observed, "are engaging in mental gymnastics. They are carrying the abstract too far—so far that forms become sterile." In this category he included the riot of constructions that lose their design controls. Asked if "constructions" belong under the sculpture title, he said he would prefer to see them listed separately as a category of their own. For himself, he concluded, he wanted the life and warmth that comes from the human figure as the source of design.

DORIS ROSENTHAL

Doris Rosenthal owns a mature talent for characterization. The subject which she has elected to characterize is Mexico and its people. Since 1932 she has made many trips to our southern neighbor, sometimes staying two years at a time. On these trips she makes hundreds of sketches and studies, then brings them back to her Connecticut home and works them into mature paintings. This process announces itself as creation rather than naturalism and the announcement is correct. The Rosenthal paintings are designed realism.

Incisive characterization is the dominant quality in all these works. The essence of the nature of her Indian children studying so seriously in school, or of Indian women primping or carrying burdens or taking a siesta in hammocks, is distilled and purified by selective elimination of all extraneous matters. It is the outer realities she is dealing with but the process of purification seems to release inner realities as well. You feel as if you were meeting her people face to face; you can hear their Mexican chatter, know what they are saying, even the nature of their thinking—it would seem. Clothing (usually) does not conceal body forms; it reveals them; you see and can sense the sturdy bodies of a sturdy people. When an artist forswears the cluttering details of surface and uses penetrating vision to get at and express essentials, as this one has, significant results are normal.

Fig. 169. *Girl and Bananas*, by DORIS ROSENTHAL, 1940.

Fig. 170. *La Criatura*, by DORIS ROSENTHAL, 1941.

Fig. 171. *Don Pasquale*,
by DORIS ROSENTHAL, 1944.

The Rosenthal design is functional, as with so many realists, but it escapes at times from the sober confines of function and gambols happily about the painting on its own. It does this delightfully, for instance, in *La Criatura,* of Fig. 170, where the bars of basket and the criss-cross motif of its sides play a delicate counter-note to the sturdy forms of the baby, and the smaller repeats of those forms in the fat bananas with their subtle variant of the dots. The frills of grayed white around the infant's head echo this light motif differently but keep the mood. And there in the center, holding the pictorial stage with complete assurance, is the sleeping child—serious and real. The design gets more serious, incidentally, in the billowing form arrangements of pillow and body, and in the subdued color harmony. Rosenthal likes grayed harmonies, with the dominant note frequently running into rich red and orange browns.

Fig. 171 tells its story with the utmost pictorial economy. The concentration on the teaching and learning tasks is complete, both on the part of the serious actors in the little drama and on that of the picture as a picture. There is no waste motion or thing to distract. Characterization is uncannily shrewd; the grouping is compact but varied; note how the one note of distortion, in the door, adds a touch of liberation from the dominantly real. And all forms, the round versus the straight, emerge with clarified power.

The *Girl and Bananas* of Fig. 169 is a folk-portrait in which character and swirling forms and colors again merge into a work of art.

> I strive to say with conviction and simplicity [says Doris Rosenthal] my reaction to the incident which has caught my attention. I think the language in which art functions is of secondary importance to the main question, Is it or isn't it ART? I like people who live close to Mother Nature—people who are not merely clothes-horses—people whose language is art and who live it daily.
>
> Last summer [1951] I spent in the Caribbean area, hoping to find Negroes as creative and expressive as the Indians of Mexico. Instead, I found the English, French, Dutch and Americans had given these people law courts and sanitary toilets and drained them of creative expression. But when I arrived in Haiti, I found a superb creative folk with music, dance, literature, painting, crafts—and voodoo—a rich, creative, self-respecting folk.

Doris Rosenthal's painting is honest, useful, and rewarding. She has carved out a sizable niche for herself in contemporary art's mansion and fills it with distinction.

KARL FORTESS

I was six at the time of the Armory Show. I have therefore always taken as a matter of course the break with tradition caused by that fermenting experience. It must however, be recalled that the art of today is the sum of all of art's yesterdays.

I cannot identify myself with what is the vogue in so much of our contemporary painting. This kind of art only strengthens in me the conviction that I am closer to Courbet than to Kandinsky. I believe that painting is a positive statement. My experience has made clear that the history of painting is the story of man. I therefore fail to see the necessity of inventing a new method of saying nothing.

I accept the category of myself as a romantic painter who uses the elements of realism and surrealism to establish his mood. I paint the things I see and feel strongly about, and try to evoke in myself and in others some of the poetry that exists in life.

KARL FORTESS

Fortess dares to be himself. He believes that painting should be a positive statement conveying meaning. He would have his paintings establish his mood—as a basis for communication—and then proceed to communicate the things he sees and feels strongly about, including the poetry that he *reads into* life. Because he does want to get across tangible meanings, he cannot get interested in new methods of "saying nothing." If he is charging all abstract art with that negation, he can, of course, be called to account; some abstractions convey plenty; some nothing. He should specify which is what. (To this he later commented, "Shall be glad to.")

Aside from this positive philosophy, Fortess, to hear him explain it, seems to work from an intuitive search for the significant meaning.

I have been painting for twenty years [he says]. In the beginning I used to finish a painting in two days and then feel embarassed by it a few months later. Now I work as long as necessary—and am not so quickly embarassed. I want to clarify what I say. I need to paint to find the way I want to say the thing that is particularly me. I don't think in terms of titles; they come as afterthoughts. I work intuitively and try to be objective later. Yet, even later, I don't analyse the paintings. The process with them is unconscious, at least it is primarily that. Feeling, or the mood, I suppose you could say, is the actual bridge.

The paintings bear out this statement of a deeply felt philosophy. And it *is* deeply felt; one immediately senses that fact from talking to the man and studying his work. If the drive of profound feeling authenticates art, this work is authentic. There is meaning in it that goes beyond the stark, created symbolism of reality. There is drama. There is rich, arbitrary color. All parts are designed; this is plastic painting.

The *Entrance* of Fig. 172 demonstrates all these qualities. The memory of the life that was and is gone. The lonely, pondering figure—perhaps the exile returned to what was home. The dead tree, the unused poles. The door with its boards nailed at just the right angles, the roof fragment, the dramatic sky as the backdrop for the human drama. Color heightens that drama, coming to a focus in the red door and the echo of softened, red-orange buildings in distance.

The *Big Tree* of Fig. 173 forcefully dramatizes the death of the giant. It is all there—the sturdy stump, the prostrate severed trunk, the whitening skeleton limbs, the background of dark living foliage, the light fluid sky, again the unused telephone poles reared by man and ironically enduring after man's brutal passing. All woven into the perfect, felt "form." Content and form. The recipe of the ages. Here it again functions.

And the *Group of Trees* of Fig. 174; here the drama is of the life of the woods, the diversities within repeats of the same motif, the interplay of verticals, the lights and darks controlled as foils where foils are needed. The textures differentiating neighboring trunks.

This is significant painting. It is eminently needed today for its enduring qualities—and to counteract the copious flood of those works which have "invented a new way of saying nothing." The pendulum of popularity has now swung far toward the abstract, and will doubtless swing still further. But pendulums have a way of reversing their trends. They

Fig. 172. *Entrance,* by KARL FORTESS, 1945--1950.

g. 173. *Big Tree,* by KARL FORTESS, 1950--1951.

Fig. 174. *Group of Trees,* by KARL FORTESS, 1951.

come back to the regions from which they started. Dramaticized realism will hold its significance through all such meanderings.

CONCETTA SCARAVAGLIONE

Sculptress Concetta Scaravaglione is one of those artists who, from time to time, is capable of achieving a masterpiece. Her *Icarus,* done in Rome during 1949 and 1950 while she was on a three-year Prix de Rome Scholarship, is, in my opinion, just that. Shown for the first time in this country at the Metropolitan Museum's National Sculpture Exhibit of 1951, it commanded immediate respect, I might say homage, as an outstanding creation of sculptural art, not only in that controversial showing, but on the national stage for that year, or several years.

The theme—of a body falling through space—is admirably realized. The body is universalized sufficiently to remove it from the category of an actual, individual human form and to stress the generalized theme. This is a human body—it can easily stand for all human bodies—falling. Even sex characteristics are submerged and forgotten.

> I tried to get away from the conventional, explained Miss Scaravaglione, in her big ground-floor Greenwich Village studio, among many other universalized creations. I played with space relationships. I wanted to get the spiral effect—like that of a leaf falling. I worked hard on *Icarus.* This was the main project for nearly a year—to get the feeling of coming down through space.

The interplay of body parts is as deeply felt and sensitively carried through to a completely realized unification as is the expression of theme. This is design of moving form—a synthesis of all elements, a living work of art. It lives because the artist has endowed it with the life of her own integrated concept.Obviously it is an inspired work. These are the qualities, I believe, which earn the title "masterpiece." (See Fig. 176.)

Incidentally, this masterwork was overlooked by the jury of awards. Near it stood one brutally clumsy prize winner and another uninspired but capably simplified pair of busts—of *Two Men*—which received top award. Another honored piece, *Animal Form* by Rhys Caparn, which won second prize, was perhaps equally sensitive in its control of univer-

Fig. 175. CONCETTA SCARAVAGLIONE
and her earlier works.

Fig. 176. *Icarus*, by CONCETTA SCARAVAGLIONE,
1949--1950. Produced in Rome on a
Prix de Rome Scholarship.

salized form but of much less grandeur of concept and total design. However, these are the opinions of but one critic and there were three critics on the jury.

Fig. 175 shows artist Scaravaglione at work among her other sculptures. All, it will be noted, have the massive, universalized, impersonal form of classic art. Eminently, all belong within the classic tradition which our leader-moderns are carrying on. But the *Icarus,* it seems, reaches above and beyond them to win the more rarified title.

II-THE SURREALISTS

MAX ERNST

Among the surrealists, Max Ernst's stature is measured by the vast amount and range of his work, by a copious list of writings by and about him, and by the spread and growth of his fame among the intelligentsia of two continents. Some of that fame has seeped down to the general public, but in every case publicity has been won on merit, not on the newsworthiness of tactical maneuverings. The winning in 1946 of the $3000 award for the best painting portraying the *Temptation of Saint Anthony* for the Loew-Lewin motion picture production of *Bel Ami, or the History of a Scoundrel,* was news, for instance, and was amply reported. In this painting and many others, like the *Eye of Silence* of 1944, the drama in the works themselves is so powerful that it attracts the crowd wherever it is shown. In this contest, by the way, Ernst won in competition with his wife, Dorothea Tanning, with Dali, Albright, Berman, and others. Which illustrates, as a headline in *Art Digest* put it, "THE IMPORTANCE OF BEING ERNST."

That importance rests so solidly on the quality of his paintings during more than a third of a century since his first exhibition in Berlin in 1913, that other events, such as the copious reactions of the brass hats of sur-

Fig. 177. *Vox Angelica*, by MAX ERNST, 1943.

realism and the intelligentsia of Europe and America, the move to the United States, and the like, take secondary place. The work, in other words, is more important than the fame.

Before me are photographs of ten Ernst paintings produced in the years from 1936 to 1951. Each is strikingly different from the others—in theme, treatment, and design. Two themes are epochal—*Eye of Silence* and *Time and Duration.* Three are human drama—*Dream and Revolution, Vox Angelica,* and *The Temptation of Saint Anthony*—with universal implications. Three, according to their titles, are intimate and personal—*Cocktail Drinker, Double Wedding at Beverley Hills* (presumably his own), and *A Beautiful Day.* These three titles, however, are highly misleading. Ernst, apparently, cannot confine himself to the intimate, the personal, or the obvious. None are obvious, obviously. And all reverberate with symbols of universal meaning. The two later works, both of 1951, illustrate Ernst's departure from the official ranks of surrealism into the wide open spaces of a shifted balance of powers—where the abstract and its design gain precedence over fantasy and the meaningful symbol. Ernst declines making any verbal comment on this shift of balance but the evidence in the paintings themselves announces it as being from the domain of intellect into that of a purified aesthetics.

One remarkable aspect of such a group as this is the diversity on every count. The symbolism is not limited to meaning of subject data; it permeates to the bone of mood, style, color, space, texture, movement, and to the design which binds all the disparate elements into a unified whole. Take any one or two of these elements, segregate them from the whole, and the designed control is uncanny in its visually dramatic power. The *Eye of Silence,* for instance, boils with an extreme busyness of textured detail; whereas *A Beautiful Day* is at the opposite pole of almost empty and textureless rectangular spaces relieved only by a circle, a couple of triangles, and a few delicate lines. Then *Vox Angelica,* of Fig. 177, is a synthesis of all-rectangles, small and tightly packed into their big main rectangle, each aglow with an amazing divergency of textures and symbols. In *Cocktail Drinker* (Fig. 178) it is movement that emerges as the supreme sensation—powerful, curving movement, broken into by the extreme contrast of soft foliage textures played against harsh and sharp angular forms. Subject symbols here are few—two hands, a mask, a draughtsman's curve—and are submerged in the dominants of texture-form-movement. The richness of this diversity marks the range and depth of the mind behind the brush. If these paintings are based on hallucinatory powers, then Ernst has certainly used his hallucinations creatively. As certainly as he expressed the "essence of the spirit of the essence of his subjects." And his "fragments of the labyrinth" surely have discovered new affinities. André Breton is right when he says, "Ernst has discovered in his art the possibility of living, of living free, and this perhaps is the root of his profound humanity."

With Ernst, design or form has rarely been dominant. Normally it has merged into subject or concept. Neither has it been consistently plastic; at times a sky color in a painting will be as remote visually as its counter-

Fig. 178. *Cocktail Drinker*, by MAX ERNST, 1946.

Fig. 179. *The Temptation of Saint Anthony*, by MAX ERNST, 1946. For the Loew-Lewin Production, Bel Ami, or the History of a Scoundrel winner of $3,000 First Prize.

part in nature; it forgets to acknowledge and decorate the picture plane. At other times all colors perform this double function. Nor does design ever seethe with unbridled emotion; the check-rein of intellect keeps control; a just balance is preserved.

A balance between diverse and powerful forces can be thought of, in fact, as an outstanding characteristic of the paintings of this artist-explorer of the universe. His spirit is unbridled but never its expression. Ernst, like Chirico before him, has amply proved that surrealist painting can and must be the product of "artistic quality," the "plastic point of view," and "aesthetic interest." His work has stood the rugged test of appraisal from these sometimes disbarred points of view.

The fact that the artist, in his recent work, of which Fig. 180 is typical, has eloquently validated the plastic point of view and aesthetic interest, is significant. It is significant because it runs parallel with a tendency of the times among our strong artists. In *The Weatherman*, a masterfully controlled interplay of colors, spaces, and movements delights the eye with its harmonic relationships, undistracted by the concerns of intellect. In *Dancers Under a Starry Sky*, intellect barely has time to announce the entrance of the three female dancers before the program of the same harmonic interplay is in full swing. We observers can relax and drink in the sustaining aesthetic nourishment to the limit of our sensory capacity.

I shall not trespass on the sacred preserve—sacred to each individual, be he layman or expert—of Meaning in the Ernst paintings. The experts have spoken voluminously.[1] Each explorer can and should be his own interpreter. The findings will then be right for him—more right, without much doubt, than the verbal cocktails brewed by certain members of the "intelligentsia" to prove they also can create fantasy—in words. Enrico Donati and Ernst have inspired many examples of this pungent brew.

How long will Max Ernst, the inveterate innovator, steer a course parallel to that of many of his fellow artists—the course of design-dominant aesthetics? The answer is anybody's guess; probably the artist himself does not at the moment know. My own guess is, not long. He has

[1] See the book *Beyond Painting*, by Max Ernst and His Friends (New York: Wittenborn, Schultz, Inc., 1948).

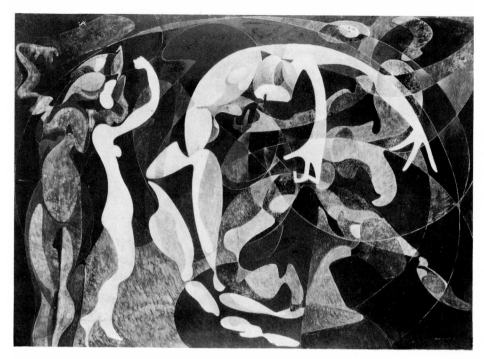

Fig. 180. *Dancers Under the Starry Sky*, by MAX ERNST, 1951.

drunk too deeply of the heady wine of symbolic meaning to get along placidly without its stimulus. The degree of fantasy therein is less important than the symbolism itself. Surrealism may have run its course as a group movement but not as a field of operations for artists. Its name may change, along with the proportion of the fantastic; Ernst may even do some rechristening on his own responsibility. But that he will return to the balanced ration of meaning and form is a fairly safe prognostication.

KURT SELIGMANN

Born in Switzerland in 1900, Kurt Seligmann studied in Basle, Geneva, Florence, and Paris where he was associated with the surrealist group for some five years. He came to New York in 1939.

The Seligmann fantasy keeps more contact with reality than does that of Tanguy, in that it deals mainly with recognizable human figures or

278   KURT SELIGMANN

parts thereof, gathering them into chummy, costume-ballish dancing or marching groups. The slight liberties he takes with his women and men —of reducing them to their skeletal foundations and then dressing them in fantastic, baroque swirls and curls—from which will emerge a man's head metamorphosed into a bird or block—do not offend; in fact they have a convincing inevitability. One can accept them at once and in spirit join the dance or march. Perhaps we have already joined such marches and dances—to death or frivolity or war—and the artist is merely telling us we have done so. Seligmann turns these events into pageantry and sets them on a stage that extends to infinity; but the ground is solid and the sky is a sky, at least in some cases. The color in which these unreal forms are built is rich and subtle in its varied hues and values, yet powerful in its total impact. Design is in full control—of every color, space, form, and movement—with emphasis on movement. Bodies and drapes interrelate, interweave with and against each other with uncanny precision. Form and content supplement each other in just and lordly balance.

As with Tanguy the change of scene from Europe to the States has had no apparent effect on Seligmann's philosophy of life or its end product, his paintings. He has imported his art intact and our specific scene has been absorbed into the world picture. A relatively minor item, this, which is noted only because of the necessity of some arbitrary limitation to any survey of any panorama. Seligmann has now become a part of our panorama in the fact of his physical sojourn among us and he honors us by his presence.

Asked why he used the frills and furbelows so consistently over a long period of time, Seligmann replied:

> Because people seem to live mainly in vestments they have donned. I use them because the individual is hidden under all his assumed attributes. I am fascinated by all these trimmings; there is something in them that is ambiguous for me. To cover up their own unconscious antagonism to the truth and beauty and to the conflict and abyss between real life and the desired life is human. I try to reach the person through dramatizing the contrasts of the irreconcilables. Who is behind all these rich garments? I try to reach him also through form and color. I am not moralizing. I am

not prophesying the future. I am earthbound. It is much easier to paint these things, by the way, than to put them into words. That is your job. The onlooker should himself read the meanings; my task is only to present the situation. I do this with the thrill of the frivolous. But it also has its beauty—the beauty of color and plastic shapes and form.

Seligmann is still a surrealist, although that movement has ceased to exist as a unified group. "All the surrealists," he says, "are different, except for their praise of the irrational. And the irrational earns its praise; never forget that. Columbus was irrational when he set out into the unknown. The irrational and the imagination it releases are the great promoters of invention, and the arts, and of all man's creations."

"How about this cult of the professional beginners," I asked, "those who have discarded both content and form and call themselves the 'avantgarde' of modern art? Their double negation is irrational, in the historical view. Are they surrealistic thereby?"

"Some of them have taken over from surrealism all that I have discarded. I do not believe in pure automatism. It is a beginning only. It must be sustained by a creative will and a discipline. Automatism is a nefarious influence on the younger generation. It is dadaism all over again—and that was a consciously destructive element. Surrealism is a positive force. It constructs—in unfamiliar terms."

The paintings here shown illustrate this philosophy. The earliest, done in Paris in 1931, reveals the simple beginnings of the later complexity. In the more recent, the frivolous curlicues can no longer offend, as they may do at first glance, when one knows the reasons behind them. They have content and distinguished form. Their time coverage—from 1941 to 1950 —shows the consistency of both. It is interesting to note that the earliest is the more abstract; the *environment* of a chateau is detached and played into intriguing color-shape-textures of swirling cloth-like forms. Riotous but tamed imagination. Of course this is irrational—but what of it? Esthetique, if I may coin a word, is in full command. This painting is to be enjoyed for its sensory embellishments of the motif, among which brilliant color and striking textures are the most rewarding, quite regardless of whatever the meaning may be. Intensity and brilliance of color

Fig. 181. *One-eyed Creature,*
by KURT SELIGMANN, 1931.

Fig. 182. *Environment of the Chateau Argol,*
by KURT SELIGMANN, 1941.

Fig. 183. *The Age of Reason,*
by KURT SELIGMANN, 1950.

played against mutings of grays and at times interpolations of blacks and whites is always vibrant in these works and the most satisfying of their variegated rewards. (See Fig. 182.)

Fig. 183 is called *The Age of Reason;* all that has been said delightfully applies.

Kurt Seligmann is making a unique contribution to contemporary art.

YVES TANGUY

The fantasies of Yves Tanguy in grayed whites and vaporous blues need to be seen rather than talked about. They are all fantasy; they have no rational significance; they exist in an unreal space that is not landscape yet suggests an ethereal earth and sky. Objects are mainly pearl-like, rippled surface, fantastic forms gathered in the foreground of cosmic emptiness. Some seem to rest on what might be sand or a smooth cloud; others float in ethereal atmosphere. Titles give the observer no help so far as tangible meaning goes; they are but convenient labels. The Tanguy style and content has not changed since 1924 when he began painting in Paris as a member of the group of surrealists for which Breton was spokesman, and the Hitler-inspired change of scene to New York in 1939 has in no way affected them. His is a transplanted European art which has not taken root in our soil. There is no indulgence of the plastic excitements in his work; design is solely a grouping of subject forms and a constant reiteration of one type of color scheme with minor variations. This endless repetition of the same types—in subject, color, and empty space —results in a monotony from which there is no relief; there is the feeling that when you see one Tanguy painting you have seen all. The artist has built his own stage and presents thereon his own play. That play has had an exceedingly long run—a quarter of a century to be exact; the virtues which have kept it before the footlights of public attention for so impressive a time must be sought for on their own specific terms.

Breton, the expert on remote searchings of the human mind, has found the deeper values which others might well miss.

Tanguy's painting [he says] has as yet confided nothing but its charm— later it will reveal its secret. . . . I am convinced that the elements of the

Fig. 184. *Herédité des Caractères Acquis,*
by YVES TANGUY, 1936.

Fig. 185. *Elle Viendra,* by YVES TANGUY, 1950.

paintings which defy interpretation will become clearly understood in relation to the future development of the mind. These elements are the words of a language we have not yet heard, but a language we shall soon learn and speak and which will be the best adapted to our new relationships. . . . We are not in the abstract with these formations, but in the very heart of the concrete. . . . His starting point is not the insensitive bark of the tree, but its heart, from which sap-wood rings spring forth. . . . The inner landscape changes every minute—it does not consist of simple, independent, easily recognizable objects, but of indistinct reachings which fade into each other. We are behind the scenes of life.[2]

Pierre Matisse, Tanguy's friend and dealer, commented on the above remarks somewhat as follows: "Some artists don't need radical change. For Picasso, change was in his nature. But not for Tanguy. He stays within vast spaces—the vast spaces seen from a plane—but his materials change. He does not think in terms of symbols; his approach is purely irrational; it is impossible to have meanings. But the irrational has a structure for him, has a definite reality beyond reality."

KAY SAGE

Surrealism in this country, one might say facetiously, is becoming a family enterprise; at least two justly famous families are doing yeoman's service in keeping it in good health and productive vigor. And in each case the performers within the family keep intact their individual integrity; no one partner dominates the other in their dual roles.

Kay Sage is the wife of Yves Tanguy—but no one would know it from her work. For her fantasy ties to and manipulates real forms. The fantasy, in other words, lies not in the concept of the unreal (as with husband Tanguy), but in what she does with the real—to the perturbation of engineers and delight of all free souls who feel the often compelling need of escaping from the logic of the materialistic life. Materialism demands that its man-made forms be nice and functional and do what they are supposed to do, all correct and proper. Not so the dream-functionalism of Kay Sage. It takes liberties. It does what it is not supposed to do—

[2] From the book on *Yves Tanguy,* by André Breton (New York: Pierre Matisse Editions, 1946).

Fig. 186. *Small Portrait,* by KAY SAGE, 1950.

Fig. 187. *Unusual Thursday,* by KAY SAGE, 1951.

in some, but not all, instances. For this artist plays with opposites. She contrasts a proper bridge or a functional square block with a controlled tangle of non-functional props and beams, as in *Unusual Thursday* of Fig. 187. No sense of guilt is observable in this mixing of the drinks, this kicking over the traces of logic, this commonsenselessly performing no function at all; she obviously enjoys the doing. And we enjoy the looking at what she has done.

The Sage love of opposites goes further. It likes to contrast the soft textures and rounded forms of drapes and ribbons with the hard surfaces and sharp angles of stones and beams. Also the counter-play of movements—the long straights of bridge and horizon with the interacting short straights and curves of foreground. And it enjoys the contrast of bold versus delicate, of soft, near-flat grays with brighter, more active colors, of darks in opposition to lights, of empty versus crowded space. If contrasts and their surprises contribute to drama, as they obviously do, then here are dramatic paintings both in content and form.

All of these dramatized virtues come to a head, or are concentrated into a head, in *Small Portrait* of Fig. 186. Again it is the fantastic manipulation of real forms which are out of context so far as the actual forms of a head are concerned, but pressed into a fabricated context of their own that, amazingly enough, does say *Head*. Is this a "portrait"? Perhaps so. There are other attributes of a head and of the particular person who owns it, as we all know, than the familiar outside forms. So why not explore down into such attributes and feature them as a portrait? Commissions may be slow to materialize in such a case, but this artist, it is reasonable to assume, is not interested in commissions. She is interested in deeper matters—and achieves them. Among the deeper matters is adventure—adventure of the spirit, an adventurous questing for the non-obvious. We spectators hunger for adventure, especially of the spirit. Here we can drink deeply of that stimulating fare.

The paintings of Kay Sage are original in concept and realization, technically mature and thoroughly designed. They make a valuable contribution to the important surrealist tradition.

286   KAY SAGE

OTHER SURREALISTS

Lack of space unfortunately forbids the inclusion of at least three other distinguished exponents of the unreal in painting. One is Enrico Donati, whose paintings, to quote from a French review, have "concretized all the chromatic symphonies which are half perceived in dreams." Another is Dorothea Tanning, wife of Max Ernst, whose highly original and technically mature fantasies deserve ample honors.[3] Then there is, of course, Salvador Dali.

In the case of Dali, I have an additional alibi for his omission. Thanks to the shock-value of his amazing fabrications—and his talent for exhibitionism—he is probably the most famous artist recently operating within the United States and therefore is already well known to a wide public. Since a brief survey would not do justice to his dynamism, we shall allow the spirit rather than the body of his work to animate, via the magic of his name, this book.

Many other artists, let me again make clear, who are making a valid contribution to the art of our time, have been omitted from the book due to lack of space—without any derogatory implications as to the value of their work. A review of this kind, as has been said, should be a continuing process.

[3] Jimmy Ernst, son of Max, has also won his spurs as a resourceful, and disciplined, abstractionist in his own right.

PART V - CONCLUSION

Is This a Renaissance?

> *Never do dead forms rise from the grave*
> *save when living forms have summoned them.*
> —ANDRE MALRAUX

What is a renaissance? A rebirth. A resurgence. A flood-tide of creative energy pouring forth from an aroused spirit in man. But a flood-tide which is under certain controls—the controls which hammer content into form. Rebirth implies resurrection and a continuation of that which is resurrected. Creation as a language of the spirit has been an integral part of man's equipment since cave dwellers first began to carve and paint meaningful symbols. It is still a part of his equipment. In the past hundred years or more it has been submerged by heavy overlays of the practical and literal attitudes of mind and their resulting physical activities. But this creative spirit is too vital a power to stay submerged; it must burst all obstructions when the time is right and again assert its age-old authority. It is this bursting forth, of which Cézanne was one of the vital outlets, that has flowed with increasing volume up to today. The evidence says it will continue its flow; the ebb tide, if it must come, has not yet begun, except in one much publicized area.

Does the evidence of the paintings shown herein substantiate this claim for a resurgence of art in our time in this country that is now in full flood? My belief and argument say that it does.

The evidence is on view for all to perceive and study. The responsibility is on each "lover of the arts" to make his own decision and it is the total of these decisions that will write the verdict that becomes a page in history. But the decisions that write history must be informed decisions. Democracy in aesthetics has its limitations and, when the majority decision is based on mis-information, it must be contested. An aristocracy of the mind and the sensitivities is imperatively needed here and the most important service of a book like this should be to increase its effectiveness and range.

We have had among men a sufficient number of other aristocracies— of birth, rank, power, wealth, and religion; we now again must extend the authority of the aristocracy of the spirit which is related to, but different from, religion. Man's religious spirit, that is to say, can find an authentic outlet in the arts as well as in worship of a deity named God to whom we give credit for creating the universe and all the mysteries of life within it. The spirit of creation in man is one of the manifestations of the Divine Power and man should be granted by men full recognition for this gift from the Divine as it manifests itself in his creations. Hence it is logical to search out and recognize and reward all such manifestations that may occur in our time and place.

Such manifestations of the language of the spirit can be of infinite variety. They can be simple and crude but authentic. They can be complex and mature and supported by a thorough understanding of our vast inheritance from the past and also authentic. They can be a tour de force and barren, or corrupted by base motives and negligible, or blundering and confused and so confusing. Artists can be spiritual leaders, pioneers exploring unknown domains, rollicking entertainers, sensualists or sensitivists, philosophers, visual musicians, tragedians, mystics, or thinkers.

It is tempting to separate the corrupt motivation from all others and say it is divorced from spirit, that mind only can be corrupted; also that confusion and ignorance can be assigned to lazy intellect—that they do not necessarily tarnish spirit. Whether spirit can thus be kept clean or not I do not know. If one believes in the inherent nobility of the human spirit, this classification helps. The point is that the language of spirit needs to be heard and the fact that it can speak on many levels of maturity and achievement extends its potential audience. We should be severe in separating the genuine from the false, but tolerant of the many dialects in which artists speak.

Many hundreds of artists among us today are serving as authentic outlets for the resurgence of spirit, as are those amateur artists who have not allowed themselves to be deflected into the impasse of skilled copying and those children who have not been spoiled by the imposition of materialistic adult standards. Through some of these outlets the flood flows in abundant volume, through others in meandering rivulets, and in some as tiny trickles. But it does flow; that is the important matter. Ignorance and confusion are but mud-banks in the stream which will be washed away in time. If they could be dredged out in a year—what a grand release there would be. Every individual can be such an outlet—child, amateur, professional artist, citizen. Why are they not? That also is a question that needs answering.

> In the matter of mental flexibility [says Harry A. Overstreet], as in other matters, the individual is in large measure a cultural product. If, by some concourse of influences, he becomes sensitive to the consequences of rigidity, he may, to be sure, work out for himself a limited independence of the cultural pattern. If his independence is cast in a small mold, and if it has more of negativity than of creativeness in it, he may be simply the misfit or the eccentric. If his independence is cast in larger mold and is charged with insightful creativity, he may become one of the landmark figures of human history. He may help other people to rediscover in themselves possibilities that have lain dormant because there was no cultural invitation to release them.[1]

But back to the artists whose work is significant; it is with them we are chiefly concerned. And to the question as to whether or not they have assimilated and integrated their two main inheritances—the ancient one that reached its zenith in the European Renaissance and the contemporary one that has flowered in the Modern Movement. Have we answered that question?

No, we have not answered it—adequately. Partially, in some places, perhaps. The question is too broad and deep for quick and easy answers.

[1] From *The Great Enterprise,* (New York: W. W. Norton & Company, 1952).

Research, study, deliberation are needed—in the special case of each performer—more than can be given in this condensed survey. The glib decision is worse than no decision. Weighing of the parts takes time and time is well spent on ultimate judgments. The judgments we have been making in these pages are preliminary ones, tentative ones—a gathering of the evidence. Additional evidence will help and must be gathered. History is in no hurry. The years and decades flow serenely, or raucously, by; opinions build up, layer by layer, into cumulative verdicts; we play our part and constructively aid history if our opinions find their place in that fabric. It is my hope that the data and arguments here presented will facilitate this process.

In a closer study of the artists here considered, particularly the direct quotations from each, several points should be noted. One is a remarkably wide agreement on basic issues. Many, for instance, proclaim their concern with spirit rather than matter and have turned to various degrees of abstraction as a means to that end. "The art consciousness," says Max Weber, "is the possessing of the spirit of things rather than the matter of things." Said Max Beckmann, "I am seeking for the bridge which leads from the visible to the invisible." Some, perhaps all, name the *realities* as one of their goals; Xavier Gonzalez speaks for his fellows when he writes, "The naturalism of form will be transformed into the realism of painting, even if our newly acquired realism has no apparent likeness to our preconceived concept of nature." Seymour Fogel confirms this when he states about his complete abstractions, "My paintings are not abstract. They are what I see."

Russell Cowles, in restating his philosophy in 1953 as it bears on recent events, has this to say:

> After several years' thought about non-objective art, I have decided definitely that it is not my meat. Art to me is an expression in concrete form of the dramatic (dynamic) tension that exists between the external world and the subjective world of the artist's consciousness. I don't deny that the artist's mental world, including his subconscious, his emotions, ideas, dreams, intuitions, etc., is a part of "Reality" and hence a legitimate theme for the arts. But I think the artist's inner world always has *some* kind of a relation

to the external world, and the artist's eternal problem is to create a form that expresses this relation.

The French critic, Henri Focillon, has said: "The function of form is to give definition to the psychological landscape. In so far as the so-called 'avant garde' painters have really *defined* their psychological landscape, and not merely 'expressed' it in a vague, mystical way, they have created new form and their products must be accepted as art. But to me the trouble appears to be with what we mean by 'define.' Definition is a very concrete thing or process, and as an act it involves, not just getting into the artist's inner world, but also getting outside it—seeing it from without as well as from within. I would even say that this inner world can only be defined in terms of what is *not* itself. The recent tendency to call some modern works 'Action' painting and to imply that the 'act,' which necessarily takes place in the external or 'real' world, should satisfy my strictures as stated above, seems to me to beg the question. The cry of a frightened child is also an act, as is the making of an undesigned, photographic copy of an apple. But they are not art. The only act or action that is significant is the creation of Form that expresses and defines whatever it is that the artist wants to say—whether the Something that he wants to say pertains mainly to the inner or outer world."

These are eloquent words of authorities with insight based on long experience. They are worth pondering. They adequately sum up the philosophy herein presented in respect to "artists" who gain "psychological release" at the cost of rampant confusion.

Agreement on the imperative necessity of the organizational controls of *design* or *form* or the *plastique of painting* would be amazing as evidence of unity among the diversity of our leading artists—if that very vision had not been a main requirement for inclusion in this list of outstanding exponents of the modern renaissance in American art. Again, Gonzalez speaks for all when he condenses this vital argument to ,"Painting is the geometry of feeling."

In one of his daily music reviews in *The New York Times,* Olin Downes speaks of the performance of Beethoven's *Missa Solemnis* by the Philharmonic Symphony in these words:

It cannot be heard with any awareness on the listener's part without his being stirred by its nobility and pathos, *the immense power of the tonal struc-*

ture, the immense feeling of the music and its poignant humanity. . . . We can love the genuine feeling, consciousness of the inherent quality of the music, and the *quality of its magnificent architecture—the relations of each of its tremendous parts to the incommensurable whole.* (Italics are mine.)

There is a critical affinity, it seems, between the musical and visual arts. *Art is not chaos.*

At the First Annual Festival of the Creative Arts at Brandeis University, the head of the school's Creative Arts Center and director of the Festival, set the tone for the occasion in these words:

> This is a moment of inquiry for the whole world: A moment when civilization looks at itself appraisingly, seeking a key to the future. In this spirit we shall examine the creative arts, examine them by performance, by asking questions, by the answers we receive. We cannot pretend to wisdom; but through performance we can provoke thought and free discussion; through discussion we can learn; and through learning we can rediscover our culture and ourselves.
>
> —Leonard Bernstein

If these few statements of opinion do fairly represent the many, this fact, plus the evidence of the work itself, gives sufficient proof that we *are* in the midst of a history-making renaissance and have artists who are carrying on its age-old standards as the genuine advance guard of today.

INDEX

Set in Intertype Baskerville
Format by John Rynerson
Lithographed by The Murray Printing Company
Published by HARPER & BROTHERS, *New York*